THE WORK AND FAMILY REVOLUTION

HOW COMPANIES CAN KEEP EMPLOYEES HAPPY AND BUSINESS PROFITABLE

Barbara Schwarz Vanderkolk
and Ardis Armstrong Young, Ed.D.

Facts On File
New York • Oxford

The Work and Family Revolution: How Companies Can Keep Employees Happy and Business Profitable

Copyright © 1991 by Barbara Schwarz Vanderkolk and Ardis Armstrong Young, Ed.D.

Facts On File, Inc.
460 Park Avenue South
New York NY 10016
USA

Facts On File Limited
Collins Street
Oxford OX4 1XJ
United Kingdom

Library of Congress Cataloging-in-Publication Data
Vanderkolk, Barbara Schwarz.
The Work and Family Revolution: How Companies Can Keep Employees Happy and Business Profitable / by Barbara Schwarz Vanderkolk and Ardis Armstrong Young.
p. cm.
Includes bibliographical references and index.
ISBN 0–8160–2364–6
1. Employer-supported day care—United States. 2. Employee fringe benefits—United States. 3. Parental leave—United States. 4. Hours of labor, Flexible—United States. 5. Work and family—United States. I. Young, Ardis Armstrong. II. Title.
HF5549.5.D39V36   1991
313.25—dc20   91-10785

A British CIP catalogue record for this book is available from the British Library.

Facts On File books are available at special discounts when purchased in bulk quantities for businesses, associations, institutions or sales promotions. Please call our Special Sales Department in New York at 212/683-2244 (dial 800/322–8755 except in NY, AK or HI) or in Oxford at 865/728399.

Text design by Donna Sinisgalli
Jacket design by Donna Sinisgalli
Composition by Facts On File, Inc.
Manufactured by the Maple-Vail Book Manufacturing Group
Printed in the United States of America

10 9 8 7 6 5 4 3 2 1

*To our families, who were both the support
and inspiration for this book.*

TABLE OF CONTENTS

Acknowledgments vii

Introduction ix

**1. A Work and Family
   Revolution   1**

Dealing with New Realities 1
Transfer to New Values 4
A New Definition of Success 7
Why Companies Care 9
Obsolete Corporate Cultures Can't
   Respond 10
Other Countries Have Solutions 13
Creating a Healthy
   Interdependence 14

2. What Families Need   17

Everyone Needs a Wife 18
The Work/Family Split 19
Creating Balance 21
Meeting Basic Needs 23
   A Living Wage 23
   Preschool Child Care 23
   After-School Child Care 27
   *Sick Child and/or Overnight
      Dependent Care 28*
   Eldercare 28
   Health Insurance 30
   Family Leave and Job Security 31
   Flexible Work Schedules 32
   Flexible Workplaces 38
   Special Problem Help 38
Inappropriate Corporate
   Responses 40

**3. Not for Women Only—
   But . . .   42**

If the Shoe Fits 42
A Woman's Place 43
Round-the-Clock Workers 45
Money Talks 46

Media Mind-Shapers 50
Special Challenges for Women of
   Color 51

4. What Business Needs   54

Profitability 54
A Good Image 55
Recruitment Advantages 57
Productivity 59
Low Absenteeism 60
Retention of Employees 62
Benefits of Family Friendliness 63
On-the-Job Training 66
Increasing Worker Participation 68
The Unique Dilemma of the Small
   Firm 71
Employee Benefits in the Year
   2000 73

**5. What Businesses Are
   Trying—Models for
   the '90s   75**

A Long History of Work/Family
   Sensitivity—Merck & Company,
   Inc. 76
A Comprehensive Family-
   Friendly Package — Time
   Warner, Inc. 78
Thriving on Alternative Work
   Schedules—Levi Strauss &
   Company 80
Extended Personal Leave—
   Creating Child- and Eldercare
   Resources—International
   Business Machines
   Corporation 82
Job Training—Security Pacific Bank
   of Washington 84
Flexible Hours—Microsoft
   Corporation 86

A Child-Care Center On Site—
    Carver Corporation 88
Emergency Child Care—Ernst and
    Young 89
Parent Support Programs— AEtna
    Life and Casualty Company 91
Overnight, Sick Dependent Care,
    and Other Innovations—
    Hewitt Associates 93
Preventative Education
    Approach—3M Corporation 97
The Ultimate Work/Family
    Package—Johnson & Johnson
    98
Intergenerational Day Care—
    Stride-Rite and St. Francis 101
Leaders in Work/Family Also
    Most Profitable 104
Results of Family-Friendly
    Programs 105
Results of Workplace Flexibility
    106
Calculating the Advantages 108
The Edge Provided by
    Work/Family Programs 109
Firms Without Work/Family
    Programs 110

6. How a Firm Can Become Family-Friendly 112

Influences for Change 112
Corporate Decision Making and
    Family-Friendly Policies 115
Taking the First Steps 116
Formulating a Task Force 116
Surveys and Pilot Projects as Tools
    for Change 117
Changing the Culture 119
Overcoming Resistance to
    Change 120
Developing a Family-Friendly
    Mindset 121

What Qualities Make
    Family-Friendly Firms? 124
Steps to Attaining a Solution to
    Your Firm's Work/Family
    Needs 124
Program Options 125
Debunking Myths 143
Creating Your Own Plan of
    Action 148
Survey Examples 149
Employee Questionnaire 152

7. How Government Can Help 154

The Present Reality 154
Pitfalls of a De Facto Policy 156
What Other Countries Are Doing
    158
State Governments Are
    Responding 162
Partnerships at the Local Level Are
    Effective 165
Do Tax Incentives Really Help? 167
Encouraging May Be the Best
    Strategy 169

8. Advice for the Next Decade 172

Take Care of Basic Needs 173
Be Flexible 176
Think Female 178
Reframe Policies to Reflect New
    Values 183
Welcome Diversity 188
Redefine Leadership 190
Form Partnerships 192
Reward Right Action 193
First and Last: Supporting the New
    American Family Is Good
    Business 194

References 197
Index 207

ACKNOWLEDGMENTS

The authors are very indebted to and thankful for the fine technical skills of Dian Cole, Mary Crowder, Paul Alexander, Tracey Nielsen, and Arri Parker. Dian and Arri saw us through the final revisions and typing challenges with a great deal of grace, enthusiasm, and patience.

Those businesspeople and professionals who shared the stories of their organizations' efforts to become family-friendly, gave us the motivation to "spread the word." They are Tom Bryan, Seattle Times; Alan Gibbs, New Jersey commissioner of human services; John Lipman, KIRO TV-Seattle; Judy Runstad of Foster, Pepper, Shefelman; David Williams, of the University of Washington; Wayne Weed, U.S. West; Karol Rose, Time Warner, Inc.; Rosemarie Meschi and Rick Fox, Ernst and Young; John Getzelman and Sydney Brown, Security Pacific Bank of Washington; John Prumatico, Microsoft Corporation; Michael Carey and John Brown, Johnson & Johnson; Jenny Crowe-Innes, Levi Strauss & Company; Dr. Stanley S. Bergen, Jr., University of Medicine and Dentistry of New Jersey; Lynn Cederholm, Carver Corporation; Linda Foster, Hewitt Associates; Ellen Galinsky and Carol Hernandez, Families and Work Institute; Tema Nesoff, YWCA Seattle–King County; Arlene Johnson, The Conference Board; and Nancy Kolben, Child Care, Inc.

Family members, managers, and employees who represented their concerns and ideas so well that the first several chapters almost wrote themselves were: Marcia Fujimoto Louie and Martin Louie, Susan and David Johnson, Ann Cardwell, Lue Rachelle Brim- Donahoe, Helen Marieskind, Glen Pascal, Martha Darling, Margaret Elwood, Russ Taylor, David Zeigen, Holly Miller, Wendy Bonvechio, Rusty Walker, Elaine Kraft, Lee Somerstein, Jeri Rowe, Irene Hopkins, Charlotte Raynor, Aaron Brown, Kelby Fletcher, Janet Boguch, Margaret McKeown, Peter Cowhey, Jerry Farley, Blair Butterworth, Carol Smith, Rudy Moz and Jane Middleton-Moz, Linda and Stan Pomarantz, Bill and Penny True, Leonor and Jay Fuller, Donalee and Fred Rutledge, Sharon and Seth Armstrong, Phoebe Anthony, Nancy Crisci, Kristie and Allen Strasen, Debbie Healy, Liz and Frank Mendizabal, Sharyn and Tom Parker, Barbara Pedersen, Sally and Ron Penley, Tom Fields, Dr. Barbara Mackoff, Stuart Dim, Cheryl Tice, Marianne Rees, Kim Osterhoudt, David Lister, Claudia Dowling, Victor Ericson, Bill Neukom, Florian and Florence Chauveau, Nina Ummel, Claudine Paris, Maryel Duzan, Julie and Louis Turpin, and many, many others!

Finally we express our sincere appreciation to Deirdre Mullane, Kate Kelly, and Neal Maillet, our editors at Facts On File, without whose generous professional expertise this work would not have been possible.

Most of all, we are grateful to our own families, clients, employees and employers—past and present—for providing us with the experiences that made this book a work from the heart.

INTRODUCTION

The next decade will foster a new relationship between work, workers, and their families. The major issues facing business, nonprofit organizations, and government illustrate the changes taking place as nearly all adults, male and female, are entering the work force. They are needed on the job, but they are also needed at home by their families. How to provide the caregiving that meets all of society's human needs is the challenge for workers and employers in the '90s.

Recent publications as diverse as Inc., Business Week, and Family Circle have devoted cover stories to the timely topic of families and work. The concerns are clear—but solutions seem complex and distant. Private-sector businesses, large and small, are the pioneers in this arena. *The Work and Family Revolution* is a book about those businesses, and their visionary leaders, who are changing the workplace to meet the needs of families. In the process, they have found that business is better and the future is more secure.

In the past decade, there have been significant shifts in family composition and structure. Much of this change has been a result of more women in the paid work force. Other causes include delaying marriage and child-rearing until an education is obtained; the "graying" of America; adult children returning to live with parents; and increases in teenage- and single-parenting. According to the Bureau of Labor Statistics:

- 63% of married couple families reported both spouses working in 1988, an increase of 20% from 1975
- Working couples with children have increased by 61% to 13.4 million people from 1972 to 1989
- Nearly all parents of young children will work outside the home in the '90s; there are now some 8 million women in the labor force with children under age six
- Older family members are living longer, requiring personal and medical attention as they age
- The pool of trained, able workers is shrinking. Most new job candidates will be women and minorities of both sexes

- The new economic reality means companies must strive "to do more with less"
- Family stress has been identified as a major concern in this country, resulting in a multitude of legislative initiatives and the phenomenon of corporate fast-trackers "dropping out" to keep their families together
- Employee turnover, absenteeism, and increased medical costs related to family needs have taken a toll on the bottom-line productivity of businesses
- Traditional caregivers—those who took care of babies and sick children, elderly parents, and disabled spouses—are now, or will be, fully occupied in the work force

These changes will profoundly affect the nature of the work force. Into the '90s, business will experience increased pressure to attract and retain able workers. Continued consumer demands for quality goods and services will exacerbate this need. International competition will fuel the drive for cost-saving and productivity-improvement programs by American industry. At the same time, the human needs of workers and their families must be met. In addition to the basics— food, clothing, and shelter—quality child- and eldercare have become essentials.

Families and business are interdependent. Families supply the human resources that enable businesses to function. Today's parents are raising the next generation of workers. Businesses supply the goods and the incomes families need to function and succeed. Thus, family problems and business problems are economically and socially interdependent.

Business is now being called upon to acknowledge this fact and respond in new ways. Our research focused on how business is reacting to make it easier to both work and parent. While we knew that some firms were experimenting with flextime or hiring child-care consultants, we didn't realize the diversity of the initiatives. We were surprised to discover the number of firms both large and small embracing work/family programs, and the extent to which these innovations were benefiting both employer and employee.

In this book, CEOs and managers explain why and how they have developed benefits such as child-care and eldercare programs, flexible work schedules, job-sharing, relocation packages, new management options, telecommuting, and leave policies for employees. These business leaders explain how pro-family policies are profitable.

While a great deal of empirical data is not yet available, anecdotal results reveal that an investment in human resources yields positive economic results for the firm. Decreases in turnover, absenteeism, lateness, and increases in employee loyalty and productivity are yielding tangible bottom-line benefits for both small and large businesses.

We started by interviewing a cross section of workers with family concerns. Most were parents of young children or teenagers; others were taking on responsibilities for aging parents. Written surveys were sent to a sample of workers in dual-career marriages, single parents, and workers in executive, professional, technical, and support positions throughout the country. Focus groups of working parents and business leaders augmented the surveys and research. Names throughout the book are those of these people who graciously consented to share their thoughts and concerns. These interviews with workers, both male and female, reveal a new "dedication to family" that is dramatically influencing the career choices they make.

We also include a chapter on governmental initiatives that indicates that family pressures are also being addressed through the legislative and legal systems. There is clearly a need for business and government to work together. We offer some suggestions to enhance this synergy.

In *The Work and Family Revolution*, the authors pull from their own experiences and from in-depth research on the subject of families and work. Barbara Vanderkolk is a longtime management consultant and lecturer, based in Princeton, New Jersey, mother of a young son, and partner in a dual-career marriage. Ardis Young, a former corporate manager, now an academic administrator in Pullman, Washington, is a single parent whose two grown daughters are trying to delicately balance job and family.

This book was developed out of our concern that work policies that benefit families are often viewed as compassionate but nonessential "social policy" for American business. We discovered nothing could be further from the truth. While family-supportive policies may initially have resulted from "social conscience," they have proven to be extremely important to every business's bottom line. In reality they are pragmatic business tools as critical to future profitability as replacement of aged equipment or computerization of payroll functions.

The authors' goal in *The Work and Family Revolution* is to provide businesspeople at all levels with the ideas they need to strengthen the support they provide for their employees' families, and at the same time, do it profitably. More than a dozen company owners and managers summarize how they arrived at their decisions, what tangible benefits they provide to their employees, and the result for their businesses. Specifically, several company presidents explain that these benefits make their firms both more entrepreneurial and more humanistic. We believe that this can only result in a better business climate, a healthier society, and a stronger economy.

1

A WORK AND FAMILY
REVOLUTION

This country is experiencing a family and work revolution. A new interdependent network is being created. Where families have always been dependent on the products of work—such as wages—a new phenomenon is occurring. Employers are now aware that they are equally dependent on the strengths good families give workers.

How has such a radical change in this relationship come about? Peter Drucker, in his 1989 book *The New Realities*, lists some of the factors in our present socioeconomic paradigm that point up the inevitability of this new relationship. They partially answer this question. The rest of the answer may be found in new attitudes toward the place of work in one's life and a recently synthesized, radically different, definition of success adhered to by the baby boom generation.

DEALING WITH NEW REALITIES

Drucker's list of new realities includes:

- A shortage of skilled workers
- Increased needs for high productivity in the face of formidable global competition
- Women forming the major part of the labor pool, accounting for 63% of net labor-force growth
- More minorities, including new immigrants entering the work force
- More nontraditional families such as two-career, single, or gay parents

1

- Tragic social problems running rampant: teenage pregnancy, poverty, and homelessness
- Serious health problems becoming national concerns, such as AIDS, addictions, and lack of insurance
- More elderly living well past their eighties
- Government's inability to solve society's problems

The shortage of skilled workers has been well documented by industry analysts and national research reports such as *Workforce 2000: Work and Workers for the 21st Century* (issued by the Hudson Institute and the U.S. Department of Labor in 1987). It sends chills down the spines of company leaders because it will have profound effects on American businesses well into the next century. According to the Bureau of Labor Statistics, between now and the year 2000 the labor force will grow at the shockingly low rate of about 1% per year. This is half the rate it has been growing in the last two decades. This dearth of new workers is a result of a significantly lower birth rate. In 1990, the Census Bureau projects that the number of 18-year-olds will drop by 8% and will not reach the levels of 1989 until 2003. By 1995, in many parts of the U.S. only five new workers will enter the labor force for every six jobs created.

As a result, companies will be forced to dig deeper to find workers, reaching out to inner-city minority youth, immigrants, older and part-time workers, and women with young children. A recent Purdue University study concludes that by 2000 the median worker age will rise to 35 years and 85% of new workers will be less technically trained women and minorities of both sexes. These unskilled and undereducated workers are frequent victims of poverty and will require company-provided training in basic reading, math, and technical skills. A key fact one must face in projecting job growth is the requirement in these positions for workers with more than entry-level skills and with the ability to think logically, exercise self-control, and take action. Many managers believe that these skills are not being taught well enough in American public schools.

The productivity race in the United States has just begun. A great deal of competition has already been levied by other nations, and the entrance of China, a united Germany, and a capitalist USSR into the world market holds unknown threats to U.S. market share. Seventy percent of America's manufacturing industries and most of its business services, from publishing to consulting, are now exposed to foreign competition. There is no doubt that increased productivity is an important goal for most U.S. firms.

Since World War II, the number of working women has increased 200%. The reality of women constituting the largest part of the labor pool during the '90s also has many complex implications. Most of them are explored in this book, but perhaps the two greatest impacts this reality creates are the almost complete loss of society's caregivers to the paid labor force and the increased power women can command because they will form a new "critical mass" within the labor force. That means their concerns are likely to be taken very seriously by management.

As immigrants and ethnic minorities, both male and female, enter the labor pool in record numbers (estimated at 29% of new workers), two challenges to U.S. business become evident: Management will need to learn about the life culture of these new workers and adjust some policies to accommodate them. Most cultures outside the U.S. have much greater respect for the family unit, and meeting the needs of those within it. Secondly, with 22% of entrants into the labor force being new immigrants, the need for education and training at the worksite is obvious. This may include courses, internships or apprenticeships on topics as diverse as English as a second language, to understanding U.S. income tax laws, or using the latest technological equipment. Not only must firms devise ways to assist these new workers, they should promote to all workers the value of cultural diversity and the varied experience these vital new workers bring to the workplace.

The traditional family is now far from the norm. Only 7% of U.S. households now consist simply of a mom, dad, two children, with mother working at home on family business. The rest of the country is made up of single-parent families, blended families, dual-career couples, or homosexual parents. Considering that most institutions, such as churches, schools, public agencies, and businesses, are still operating under the assumption that the traditional family is the standard, there are many incongruities between need and policy.

What these dramatic changes reinforce is that child care, and increasingly eldercare, are not "women's issues" or "luxuries" in a benefits package, but business necessities. Women, as primary caregivers in our society, are now working outside the home because they have to, and business needs them. We can no longer afford to deprive ourselves of the skills, effort, and talents of more than one-half of the population merely because they are female. Nor can we as a society or as businesspeople afford to let the children and elders slip through the cracks when their traditional female caregivers join the sphere of paid employment.

Throughout the industrial age, social problems and personal health problems were neatly separated from the world of business, its goals and programs. For many years alcoholism was the only "personal" problem addressed by business. Programs were reluctantly established for alcoholic employees, and stigmatized the employee who was, generally, *forced* into the program. Today, health problems of depression and addiction, as well as family problems such as teenage pregnancy, spouse and child abuse, are so prevalent that they have a recognized negative impact on worker productivity. One of the managers interviewed in the process of writing this book lamented the fact that he had screened 15 prospective employees for a $30,000 per year job that required the use of heavy equipment, but not one of them passed the drug test. For these reasons, business has a stake in the wellness of its employees and their families.

There was also a time, previously, when a 60-year-old employee would receive his gold watch and go home to die—while his wife lived a little longer in the house of one of her children, "helping out" with her grandchildren. This is now rare. Older people are living longer. Few have families who can take them in; even fewer have the resources to hire help or receive modified nursing care. The question of how to live well into old age, being productive and yet needing some additional care, is a family concern that is now greatly influencing the decisions made on employee benefits in business and industry.

Chapter 7 explores the reality of diminished government help in solving society's problems, but a comment in that regard is also needed here. Roosevelt's post-depression job programs made the first remedial connection between poverty and government- generated jobs. Soon federal government job programs blossomed to an unbelievable number and by the early '70s were often an unworkable size. Then came the Reagan years. Few employment or vocational training programs withstood the budget cuts of that administration or the will of Congress as it sought to maintain military expenditures. Social service and health programs also went by the board during this period. The current need caused by escalating social problems and demands for trained workers has yet to be acknowledged by federal lawmakers in a way that will bring about effective solutions.

TRANSFER TO NEW VALUES

In addition to the new socioeconomic realities Drucker brings to our attention, it is evident that people of working age in the United States today hold decidedly different values regarding the place of job or career in their lives than do those people just now reaching retirement age. Dr. Bradley Googins, director of the Center on Work and Family at Boston University, has said that the concept of the "organization man" has been replaced by "the organization family." His reference to William H. Whyte's 1956 book, *The Organization Man*, reminds us that in the '50s and '60s the popular culture painted a picture of the rising young male executive's devotion to the corporation being rewarded with increased pay, promotion, and responsibility. In 1956, Whyte described the relationship between these employees and the organization: "The ones I'm talking about *belong* to it as well. They are the ones of our middle class who have left home, spiritually as well as physically, to take the vows of organization life, and it is they who are the mind and soul of our great self-perpetuating organizations . . . it is the common problems of *collective* work that dominate their attentions." In exchange for these vows, they received protection, promises of security, and a high standard of living.

These workers did not, according to Whyte, have any "great sense of plight." They believed they saw an ultimate harmony between themselves and the organization. In other words, these workers saw themselves as belonging to their companies and indeed saw this not as a sacrifice, but as desirable and harmonious. Contrast this word "harmony" with the feelings today's workers who are also parents express when their child falls ill on a workday. Conflict, guilt, and resentment are most often heard. Parents without corporate policies on family leave feel a sense of anxiety and dread—a push/pull between concern for the child and concern for their job. What will the boss say if I'm gone today? What will coworkers think? Am I jeopardizing my promotion—my job itself? These are the conflicts today's workers face.

Of course, Whyte saw no conflict between "*man* and society." He advocated creating an equilibrium in which the needs of society and the individual are one and the same. Those *men* by and large all had stay-at-home wives who took care of the house, children, food shopping/preparation, school committees, and community-service obligations of the family. On the surface it was easy for Whyte's male worker to pledge loyalty to the corporation, working long hours, and devoting little time, attention, or energy to his family, because his wife took care of everything else. The only thing he had to do was be the loyal company worker and bring home his ever-increasing paycheck. But at what cost? Some of us have fathers who were those "organization men." We watched them gain weight, compromise their health, or go through divorces. We heard them express regret at the lost childhoods of their offspring and the burdens they inadvertently placed on their spouses. These "organization wives," often relegated to lives of suburban isolation punctuated by endless carpooling, housecleaning, cookie baking, and corporate entertaining, also emerged full of regret and resentment. It was possible in those years of relatively high salaries, low housing costs, and low divorce rates for families to live comfortably on one income. All of that changed, however, with the rise in service jobs, most of which were minimum-wage, replacing more lucrative manufacturing positions; the increase in the divorce rate due to women's expanding consciousness and growing economic independence; and skyrocketing housing costs fueled by the real estate boom of the early to mid-'80s.

The '60s and '70s saw a time of disdain for the organization and a questioning of corporate America's values on everything from race and sex equity to environmental practices. In some instances this escalated in worker demonstrations and labor unrest over plant closings, as the country moved from a product- to service-based economy. In the '80s this disdain escalated to treachery with incidents of workers sabotaging production lines or goofing off while top brass ripped off the company through insider trading deals. It is only in the last few years that the clash between the workers' and the company's values has begun to be resolved. It has occurred in part because of the burgeoning labor shortage and because of the dramatic increase in the number of women (many of them mothers) in the work force. A key motivator has also been women and men who came of age in the '60s with a different mindset about work and parenting.

Their values are not only a product of their resentment of their fathers' work habits, but also influences of the counterculture, the civil rights and women's movements, and protests against the Vietnam War. The counterculture stressed a questioning of authority, the rights of the individual, self-improvement, new health habits, and the pursuit of relaxation. At the same time, the civil rights movement challenged the validity of institutions, when these very institutions treated people differentially based on their skin color, sex, or religious preference. Vietnam taught many to distrust authority and value peace. Growing up in the swirl of these debates caused many to look inward, to doubt the old order, and to reject much that had come before. Thus, it seemed like an anachronism to many born after 1945 to pledge one's time, life, and soul to one's employer, particularly if that organization didn't address and reflect this worker's values. This new perspective emphasized choice, individual freedom, responsibility to one's children, shared household tasks, parity between spouses, continual self-growth, environmental protection, and the promotion of equality among all people.

A NEW DEFINITION OF SUCCESS

At first blush the values of "the organization man" seem to be diametrically opposed to those of the workers in the '90s. The '90s are emerging as a time when the needs of the individual and his/her family are often taking precedence over work and the needs of the organization. Success has been redefined. Refusals to work overtime, to accept a transfer, or to vie for a promotion if it means longer hours are becoming the norm for many people who came of age in the '60s and '70s.

Given a choice of two career paths—one with flexible full-time work hours and more family time but slower career advancement, the other with inflexible work hours but faster career advancement—78% of the *men and women* surveyed chose the slower, family-oriented track. "I have no desire to work like my father did," said one 40-year-old manager. "We never saw him during our growing-up years. He was always either at work or playing golf with his corporate buddies. He called it part of the job. I want my children to know who I am and I want a role in their development." His words rekindle not-so-fond memories for those whose fathers were "organizational men." Another woman with a busy consulting practice said, "My own father counsels me to take it easy. He reminds me that the only thing all his work gave him was a case of ulcers and regret that he didn't spend more time with us kids while we were small." A lawyer in her late 30s added, "I made clear to my husband that if we were going to start a family, we both had to make a commitment to cut back our billable hours and 'be there' for our child. I told him I had no intention of being a single parent, like I felt my mom was for all those years my dad traveled the world for his company."

These baby boomers were raised by "organization men" and grew up feeling a loss, the lack of an active father in their lives. While this could have also been true of mothers who fulfilled the expectations of the corporation, few women in the '50s and '60s worked outside the home; and if they did, were likely to be single or childless. Many parents of the '90s will define themselves a success if they have time to spend with their children and play an active role in nurturing them into adulthood.

Our interviews with workers regarding their family worries reinforce this new definition of what constitutes personal success. It begins with an unwillingness to live by the old rules of the American workplace. Virtually everyone admitted to a shift in priorities after becoming a parent or becoming responsible for their parents. Janet Boguch, a West Coast artist, development consultant, and parent of a preschooler, explained that "family has become more of a priority than before. I am still ambitious but more patient and more realistic about achieving goals." Several other parents indicated that they believed they were more productive since their children were born. "My home responsibilities have forced me to become more efficient during the hours I'm at work. I don't bring work home anymore, and I still feel that I'm three times more efficient than most of the other people I work with because I utilize my time better," said one East Coast health technician. "I don't take time for long lunches, unnecessary committees or after-work receptions," explained Margaret McKeown, a partner attorney with a large Seattle law firm. "Having a child puts work in perspective, and makes certain job pressures and crises seem less critical."

When the Roper Organization, a noted survey firm, asked 2,000 people in 1990 to define the most important aspect of success, the top choice was "being a good wife and mother, or husband and father." Four years earlier the top choice was "being true to yourself." This change in attitudes is also recognized by best-selling authors John Naisbitt and Patricia Aburdene in *Megatrends 2000*: "The tendency—often attributed to women—to want to balance the top priorities of career and family (along with other personal interests) is generational—not gender-specific."

Yankelovich Clancy Shulman, a research firm, noted a shift in worker wants in its annual survey of *American Values and Lifestyles*. "Both women and men are beginning to reassess trade-offs between work and family," says Barbara Caplan, the vice president of the firm. "We're finding that having it all and doing it all is neither desirable nor practical." While she sees women deeply committed to work, "the issue here is options," Ms. Caplan explains. "And while men don't want to be Mr. Moms, they're rethinking how much of their family lives, friends, and leisure they are willing to give up." In a 1986 *Fortune* magazine survey of 400 men and women with children under 12, surprisingly fathers were almost as likely as mothers to say that their job interferes with family life. These same men were also somewhat more likely to claim that they would sacrifice career opportunities if that would cost them time away from their families.

"Dropping out" of the corporate fast track or metropolitan pressure cooker is an action that puts this new definition of success on a very practical plane—and thousands of families are opting to do it. The Turpin family is an example: Louis, an architect at a prestigious firm, and one of the youngest to become a full partner, recently resigned his position and sold his Manhattan apartment. After the birth of their second daughter, his wife, Julie, realized that the demands of her job as a buyer for a major department store chain were less important than the needs of her children. They both fell in love with life in a small community upstate. Louis is now developing his own business there, while Julie is busy lining up a job where she too can use her skills and still have time to watch her children grow. To do this, in her words, "is truly to succeed!"

When the new realities of the '90s workplace come together with the changing values and definitions of success that were the norm a few years ago, it becomes obvious that this country is in the midst of a work and family revolution. Family workers are making reasonable demands. They have a right to exchange their talents, skills, and labor for a life-style that will allow them to nurture and support their families, and to join in the pursuit of happiness.

But what about business? Why should business care? Does it have to make all the accommodations—become the new welfare program in this country? What sort of return on investment can business expect if it chooses to bend to these demands? What will happen if it doesn't?

WHY COMPANIES CARE

Companies are increasingly motivated to recognize the work/family revolution and come to grips with its implications. This motivation comes from two major pressures: the labor shortage and the costs the company has to absorb when workers cannot carry out both their home and work responsibilities.

In mid-1990 the Hudson Institute, an Indianapolis research group, and Towers Perrin, a New York benefits consulting group, released a study to follow up on the influential 1987 *Workforce 2000: Work and Workers for the 21st Century* report. The earlier study drew much attention because it projected massive demographic changes in the work force. The 1990 study documents the work force changes currently occurring and the ways corporate America is dealing with them.

Most businesses are coping poorly. Pressing shortages of technical workers are reported at 70% of the surveyed companies. Skilled craft workers and professionals in general are in short supply; and 55% of the firms queried reported trouble finding secretaries and clerks. While all industries are affected to some extent, shortages are expected to be most severe in consumer products, health care, and industrial firms.

Many working parents we interviewed talked of the stress involved in balancing work and home and the anxiety resulting from inadequate child care or lack of respite care for a disabled elderly relative. Medical Management Planning, Inc., a California firm, estimates that 50% of worker stress comes from sources outside the work environment. These stresses don't just exact a toll from the workers, they cost the company as well. The external manifestations of stress, such as lower efficiency and productivity, as well as increased absenteeism, turnover, and higher health risks, induce these unnecessary costs. In the health-care environment, for example, hospitals have been warned that worker stress costs hospitals approximately $1,003 per employee annually, based on conservative estimates by the American Hospital Association. This could mean costs as high as $1.4 million a year for a large 400–500 bed hospital.

And, the cost of losing a worker and retraining a successor is estimated by one major pharmaceutical firm to cost one and a half times the employee's salary, while another estimates more conservatively at least one-half the cost of annual salary and benefits. In either case, the costs are high enough that these figures alone have motivated many firms to begin work/family programs.

OBSOLETE CORPORATE CULTURES CAN'T RESPOND

The Hudson Institute study also found that managers are not responding quickly enough to these new realities. The report cites a lack of " 'leading edge' recruitment and training strategies, as well as a scarcity of progressive support structures for all women and minority male workers such as daycare centers and mentor programs." Fewer than one-quarter of firms surveyed are rehiring retirees or recruiting the elderly, disabled, or other nontraditional workers. Companies have also been slow to invest in training for the workers they do hire. Two-thirds of the surveyed firms spend less than $2,000 for training first-year workers, which may partially account for the high turnover rates. Half of the firms in the survey reported 28% annual turnover rates for new employees. This is a staggering figure and one that negatively impacts these companies' bottom lines. One-fourth of all firms in the survey reported that their corporate cultures were not open to diversity. Twenty-nine percent said discrimination was a problem, and 15% reported "overt harassment of minorities." Forty-two percent of the firms in the study engage in "explicit minority recruiting" but only 12% train minorities for supervisory positions and just 10% have mentor programs. For all women, white or minority, the picture is not much brighter. Management training for women exists at only 32% of firms and only 8% have created mentor programs for women. Less than one-third of these firms reported offering maternity leave and only 15% have near-site child care available.

These issues clearly bode poorly for America, where white males are projected to dwindle to a single digit percentage of new entrants to the work force by the year 2000. This is due both to a slower birth rate and significant numbers of retirements. Robert D. Kennedy, chairman and CEO of Union Carbide Corporation, wrote in the *Wall Street Journal* that, "Business survival depends on how well managers read trends and anticipate the problems they create. Yet many companies are ignoring the powerful signals of trouble ahead in their most critical competitive resource—the work force." He goes on to explain that more than 95% of the current crop of senior executives are white males, out of sync with the future workplace when 85% of work force entrants will be minorities, women, and new immigrants. "Such statistics send an unmistakable, urgent signal to business: We all have to do a better job of recruiting and developing diverse managerial talent or we will run out of the people we need to run our companies," he concludes.

Some firms however, have launched innovative programs aimed at recruiting and mentoring women, and minorities of both sexes. Du Pont has developed a mission statement that commits in part to "making changes in the workplace and fostering changes in the community that are sensitive to the changing family unit and the increasingly diverse work force." They are being rewarded with just that—an increasingly diverse work force and a new crop of potential executives. Changes in corporate mission statements must also be accompanied by training and mentoring programs to assure access by women and minority men to positions at every level in the organization. These programs must be undertaken not only out of a spirit of fairness, but less altruistically, out of sheer concern for profitability. Inescapably, minority men and women of all races will be leaders in tomorrow's workplace.

When the labor force consisted of white males as the breadwinners with wives to stay at home and tend all family needs, "traditional" personnel practices worked. Women provided the support system that enabled male wage earners to be productive working outside the home for at least 40 hours every week. This is now the exception rather than the rule. Most of American business is still run on the assumption that all families have two parents with a stay-at-home wife and no dependent elders.

Fran S. Rodgers and Charles Rodgers of Massachusetts-based Work/Family Directions remind us that we act like the 40-hour work week is sacrosanct, and that we confuse effort with results by equating hours of work with productivity. The price we are paying for this confusion is quite high. Our children are growing up neglected and without basic skills. Industries are short the workers they need to be productive, and the U.S. is falling behind other nations with lower infant mortality rates, higher literacy figures, and comprehensive work/family legislation. Fran Rodgers explains that it's not only companies that are currently experiencing labor shortages that need to move into comprehensive work and family plans. "The ones that are smart are worried whether it's affecting them now or not. . . . Costs that used to be unthinkable aren't unthinkable anymore when you can't find people to work."

Those of us who are concerned about the future of both the family and the U.S. economy must join together to lobby for the policy changes and funding needed to improve delivery of education and job training, increase the minimum wage to a living wage, assure health care, and enhance access to quality child care and eldercare. A collective of voices from business, labor, and education raised in unison would augment the initiatives taken by the individual firms highlighted in this book.

Money is still, however, the reason many firms may not be moving towards adopting a work/family program. Many fear that the costs of initiating family-friendly benefits are too high. It is costly to establish a child-care center. It does cost money to change a company's benefits program. Family-friendly programs all require a significant investment. Perhaps the greater fear, however, should be *what will it cost us if we don't do it?* As we will see, these expenditures are *offset by the results:* loyal, motivated workers who are absent less and are more productive on the job.

Another very real hesitation of some managers is the potential for resentment and loss of privacy that may result from questions about a worker's personal life. Queries about elderly parents or young children are very personal concerns. Yet the workers we interviewed didn't judge employer's questions in these areas as an intrusion, rather they viewed them as legitimate and thoughtful, if put in the context of potential employee benefit plans.

Finally, a reason some firms haven't become family-friendly is through sheer ignorance. They simply haven't noted the demographic changes in the nature of the work force and the increasing number of single-parent or dual-career families. Perhaps their workers haven't told them of their inevitable struggles to balance work and home. Or perhaps the employers know of this turmoil but haven't responded to it. Some managers may be guilty of sexism and believe that women with children or aged parents belong at home. Some of these same executives may ignore the prevalence of single parenthood because they personally don't believe in divorce or unwed parenting. Businesses are going to need to clear these old cobwebs out of their heads, because the society has changed and whether we approve of these changes or not, they're real, they're here to stay, and they have profoundly changed the worlds of work and home forever.

OTHER COUNTRIES HAVE SOLUTIONS

More than 100 nations have comprehensive, well-thought-out parental leave policies. These countries have governments that have recognized the integral link between family well-being and their nation's economic success. Most European countries have national policies related to:

- Mandated paid and unpaid leaves of various lengths in connection with childbirth
- Direct cash allowance paid to families to help defray the costs of raising children
- Free universal health care
- Public child care for young children

It is important to note that in these countries there is little need for out-of-home infant care, due to the generous leaves allowed for birth or adoption of a child. Universal access to health care combined with greater flexibility in hours of work combine to help families deal with the special needs of children and elders while maintaining high work outputs. In addition, in the U.S., women's participation in the work force is as high as it is due to stronger, equal employment laws than most European nations. But the U.S. has lagged far behind in its lack of comprehensive child-care or eldercare policy. Thus, as a country we are wasting two vital corporate resources: women and their children who must be the next generation of workers. U.S. business cannot afford to run its companies in less than the most cost-effective manner. A growing number of tax incentives, combined with productivity increases, make even the more costly options such as providing onsite child-care or eldercare centers most cost-effective in the long run.

Arthur Strohmer, executive director of human resources, staffing and development of Merck & Co., Inc., speaking at a conference on Women and Work, urged his audience to avoid talking about expanded benefits programs as "women's issues." "We find our most vocal requesters of child care are males," he said. "We in corporate America see a significant shift in people's needs and people's views of their priorities." He also noted that the slate of expected employee benefits will broaden as changing demographics, a shrinking labor pool, and dual-career couples require adaptations in the workplace.

Once America's government and businesses start viewing these family-friendly benefits as investments rather than costs, the U.S. competitive advantage in the world marketplace will improve.

CREATING A HEALTHY INTERDEPENDENCE

Curiously, some similarities can be found between Whyte's Organization Man and the values held in the '90s. Today's workers want their employers to accommodate their family responsibilities. In exchange for this recognition, they are willing to be loyal and productive, much like the traditional "organization man." In this way companies that do change to accommodate family can expect the best from their employees. Increases in productivity and morale, decreases in turnover, absenteeism, and tardiness are some of the results being documented by firms adopting family-friendly ways of doing business, or as Whyte put it, "organizations can rid themselves of their tyrants and create a harmonious atmosphere in which the group will bring out the best in everyone." The difference is not in desired outcomes then, but in approach.

While Whyte counseled workers to sublimate their egos, defer to the needs of the group, and fulfill the instinctive need to belong, today's managers promote on-the-job training, sensitivity to the needs of the individual and family, flexibility, and a greater degree of self-determination.

Perhaps the '90s will be known as the decade when these attitudes came full circle. In the '50s the worker merged into the organization, in the '60s workers disdained and challenged the organization, in the '70s the workers and the organization were in conflict, in the '80s rank and file workers and managers took advantage of the organization, and in the '90s the organization and workers' needs merged, resulting in the whole being greater than the sum of its parts.

Employees are now recognized as having needs apart from the organization. Some firms have risen to this challenge and in so doing have created companies that are healthier and more successful than their predecessors. The challenge for managers in the '90s is to create a new set of rewards that may involve pay, promotion, and responsibility but will also include family-friendly benefits. Such managers will learn to reward performance without requiring a slavish devotion to the company, demanding that the worker forsake the needs of the family in order to meet corporate expectations that Whyte noted more than three decades ago.

The primary question managers of companies, business owners, and directors of nonprofit or governmental entities must answer today is what is their overriding philosophy with regard to work/family programs? Are these an accommodation, a nice gesture, a gift to employees, or are they seen as an integral business strategy? Hewitt, Johnson and Johnson, IBM, and others take the latter approach, in essence saying, "This is a partnership. We give flexibility and in return we want flexibility on the employee's part to go the extra mile, act on a desire for excellence, or implement quality in their work." At Eastman Kodak, for example, the belief that a flexible approach can be implemented everywhere in the company is so strong that they put the burden of proof on their managers: Managers must prove that an employee's request for a flexible work arrangement won't work. Other firms are trying to cut back on the extensive travel, relocation, and long hours that can exclude many women with families from the ranks of top management.

These changes in attitudes, resulting in new benefits, promotions, and pay, are essential to keeping and recruiting the best workers in firms across America. As one young public relations executive and mother of two told us, "I left a well-known manufacturing firm where I never felt accepted as a woman to join a smaller company where I believe my chances both for promotion and work/family flexibility are greater." This is a tale doomed to repeat itself unless American companies commit to changing both their formal and informal ways of doing business.

To make the kinds of modifications required by businesses to stay competitive in the '90s will require both leadership and character. After the '80s many workers are filled with cynicism, fear, and mistrust of that era's corporate takeovers, leveraged buyouts, downsizing, and insider-trading scandals. They may initially be wary of an organization's efforts to create work/family initiatives. That is why it is of critical importance for management to communicate their goals clearly and to involve their employees in the creation of policies, objectives, and programs that will help these employees balance their work and family needs.

These improvements will also require a change in the corporate culture of many organizations. AT&T's Burke Stinson argued, "We hope by the end of the century we'll see an end to this whole idea that being a family person doesn't mean you aren't a company person," as he noted that AT&T recently embarked on a program to replace rigid personnel policies with a more flexible approach. "For years people who wanted to take Thursday afternoon off to see their son's soccer game, or who came in late Monday morning because their child had a doctor's appointment, invented an excuse," Stinson explained in a Newhouse News Service interview. "Now the company's emphasis on flexibility encourages employees to take time off and tell the truth about it," he says. "There is no need to lie and sneak out."

While this flexibility enhances the dignity of work, lowering anxiety and stress, many employees may still be fearful about asking for time off or that there may be insecure managers who "will give employees a rough time." To overcome these obstacles, some employers are instituting training in new ways to look at family and work issues, to better understand the needs of a more diverse work force, or to impart knowledge about changes in corporate culture or policy. IBM has recently trained more than 25,000 managers in the importance of work/family issues, and Johnson & Johnson is in the process of educating its entire domestic work force in its new work/family policies. Microsoft has instituted e-mail information exchanges and the Seattle Times Newspaper Company encourages brown bag seminars for employees at all levels to learn more about meeting family and work obligations. These formal and informal methods are being tried at large and small firms that seek to attract new workers, retain good employees, and nurture the best performance.

2

WHAT FAMILIES NEED

Wendy Bonvechio, a sales director with a large hotel chain, is married to a police detective. They have two adopted preschoolers. "According to corporate policy, I was not permitted maternity leave so I had to take a 'leave of absence' from my job when my child arrived. I was not paid for any time off." Because both Wendy and her husband, Russell Walker, have jobs that often require unexpected overtime, Wendy believes her work productivity suffers when she is thrown into a panic trying to find evening child care. She believes that our current society is insensitive to the needs of families and children. "I resent having to choose between my family and my job."

David Zeigen, a widower, quit his job as executive director of a large nonprofit agency to take care of his teenage son and eight-year-old daughter. "Kids at age fifteen really need parent care. Too often we think of child care for infants and preschoolers, but the intensity of current pressures regarding drugs, alcohol, sex, and violence convinced me that I needed to spend more time with my kids than my job would allow." According to plan, David went back to work in a position with shorter hours and more flexibility.

Louise and John Stern, both employed at a major electronics firm, are facing other familiar dilemmas. Louise's mother has recently become bedridden and she and her sisters are trying to find quality institutional care. John is an only child, who fears for his own mother's health as she cares for his aging father, whose Alzheimer's affliction grows worse. Their 30-year-old son is between jobs and he and his family are living with them temporarily. John has used all his leave time, but needs more to assist his mother. The company has no unpaid family leave policy. The stress for everyone in the family continues to escalate.

David Johnson, an agency director and therapist in private practice in Seattle, claims that business, labor, and families need to have the courage

17

to admit their interdependence. How do we bravely build new families as parents and workers?

EVERYONE NEEDS A WIFE

Every family needs an old-fashioned "wife"—the traditional nanny, baker of brownies, applier of bandages, caregiver for the elderly, and nurturer of young children, as these are the activities that foster the development of a sound society. This isn't possible, however, in an economy that requires all the able-bodied to be out making a living—a living that rarely includes enough to pay a full-time housekeeper or caregiver. So, the nurturing needs of families and society must now be met in new ways.

Workers—both male and female—are searching for the key to balancing job and family. Interviews with company-loyal employees reveal a new dedication to family that is dramatically influencing the career choices they make. Their employers, concerned about losing top performers and attracting talented workers in the future, are looking for ways to respond through a variety of "family-friendly" programs. Families need child care and eldercare, flexible work schedules, adequate health care coverage, leave policies that make caregiving possible, job security, a living wage, help with special personal problems, and additional salary allowances for special work conditions such as relocation.

In the past, many of these job-related needs were considered "women's issues" and of secondary importance. Recently, however, both male and female workers have begun to speak up for their families. Men who came of age in the '60s and '70s have values beyond the workplace and now routinely turn down transfers or promotions if they conflict with the needs of family. A number of fathers in various executive positions who were interviewed all reported an increasing unwillingness to uproot their families during school-age years in exchange for a promotion. One Northwest executive requested outside consultant assistance and reduced hours to spend more time with his two young children after their mother's death. Men are increasingly active parenting partners with expectations for paternity leave and responsibilities for their child's schooling and day-to-day care. Wyatt Co., a Chicago compensation and benefit consulting firm, recently offered a part-time path to its employees with the option of returning to full time. A new father of twins was one of the first employees to jump at the offer.

At the same time, female baby boomers seek jobs with opportunities for advancement, as well as flexibility to recognize that it is likely that they will want to parent, as well as manage, compute, teach, or assemble. Now both parents feel the need to be "super mom" or "super dad" at home and highly effective, achieving, upwardly mobile employees at work. Dual careers and dual family/work roles frequently lead to stress, which, with its byproducts of physical and mental problems, can result in lowered work productivity. In this age of two wage-earner families, the nature of corporate careers must change for everyone.

THE WORK/FAMILY SPLIT

When and how did our roles at work and in the family become so distinct that in many instances they are viewed as being in competition? If we think about the nature of work as it has evolved through the ages, the dichotomy we are now experiencing is a relatively new phenomenon. For centuries, families worked together to grow or hunt food, build shelter, create clothing, fashion implements, and tend the young. Mothers', fathers', and children's days were woven around survival and reliance on each other. Only in times of war were families separated when men went off to battle.

Even as skill specializations occurred with the rise of craftsmen and merchants in the late Middle Ages, work was still centered near home. The potter and blacksmith worked out of sheds next to the house, and the baker's family often shared a hearth with his shop. At the end of the last century when the farmer left to take his goods to market he was often gone for extended periods, but many days he returned home at midday for lunch and time with his family. Following that practice, many community schools sent children home for lunch.

It wasn't until the dawn of the industrial age, a mere hundred years ago, that a distinct and apparently permanent split occurred between family and work. Industrialization required that large numbers of bodies work rigid hours with specialized equipment at locations near transportation and other services. Suddenly, many men and some women were away from home from dawn until well past dusk. Huge factories gobbled up urban land, destroyed housing, and belched smoke and fumes. With the rise of the labor union movement, the work day was shortened but quickly grew again with commuting time. Suburban roads swelled with escaping factory workers, because families began moving away from these dehumanizing plants as soon as they could afford to. Home became a refuge, clearly separate from either working on or supervising "the line." The only deviation from this grim picture occurred briefly during World War II when women's labor was needed outside the home as well as within it. However the work/family supports that blossomed at this time, such as child care centers, vanished just as quickly at the war's end. A vast majority of women were again relegated to their domestic duties.

From approximately 1950 to 1970, the suburbs became a sort of female and child middle-class ghetto for many white families. Men left with lunch pails or briefcases in early morning hours to join the commuter rush, not to return home again until late afternoon or early evening. Unlike generations past, children only saw mothers work in the home. Fathers' child-rearing and home caretaking time was severely curtailed. Many children never saw where father worked, let alone participated in helping him accomplish that work—and fathers seldom saw their children.

In the last 20 years, as large numbers of child-bearing-age women of all ethnic backgrounds entered the world of paid work, the split between work and family became complete. By the end of this decade, 80% of all mothers will have a career during some portion of their child-rearing years. Many infants are now in child-care centers all day, while school-age children either receive no before-and-after-school care or are also tended in institutional settings. Mother and father both go off to work environments divorced from their identity as parents.

This alienation often occurs immediately after giving birth. Workers are expected to return to work after the briefest of maternity leaves—six or eight weeks. Yet child development experts warn that the crucial infant-parent bond is still fragile at this early point. Further, few employers take into account the importance to both mother and child of continuing breast-feeding and offer no work-site or work-hour accommodations.

A precedent-setting international United Nations Conference on children in late 1990 included as a goal the promotion of breast-feeding for infants throughout the world. Yet little is being done right here in the U.S. to facilitate this important disease-prevention, maternal-bonding practice for millions of working mothers. One immunologist-turned-therapist told us that she sees breast-feeding, not only in the traditional notion of protecting the child against serious illness, but also nurturing a critical bond and providing greater emotional stability. Some medical experts now recommend extending nursing well into the second year of a child's life. Many employers ignore employee's responsibilities to their families, or overemphasize them, using family responsibilities as an excuse to deny promotions.

It doesn't have to be that way, however. A living wage, dependent care, health insurance, some flexibility in hours and places of work, job security, and help with special family problems can ease the schizophrenia plaguing family workers in the '90s. Women and men don't stop being parents when they open the office door or factory gate, nor do they hang up their responsibilities to their elderly parents and their communities. Many businesses, government agencies, and policymakers are starting to understand the changing needs of American society's largest institution—the family.

CREATING BALANCE

Balancing work and family is a tough job. Ellen Galinsky, former director of work and family studies at Bank Street College of Education in New York, claims that three out of five employees say it is difficult to meet family needs while trying to focus on a career. When that many people are having problems, it is not only an individual matter, it is a public concern.

Parents struggle because their commitments to work often sabotage commitments to their children. Most parents find that their time and energy are stretched to the maximum. However, they seem determined to find ways to satisfy needs of career and family. Employers with vision are able to understand that children with good substitute care grow up to be the kind of workers the entire society wants. Parents who have some assistance in providing that good care are more focused, productive, and loyal workers. As R. Gordon McGovern, president and CEO of Campbell Soup Company puts it, "When you make a company a better place to work, you attract better people."

Marcia Fujimoto Louie, a lawyer in private practice, said that after becoming a mother, she redefined what success means to her. "I still hope I can be a partner in a large law firm, but I know I cannot do it all." Charlotte Raynor, a reporter for an NBC affiliate and new mother of an infant daughter, revealed: "I still enjoy my work, but it's no longer the most creative and rewarding endeavor in my life. Somehow, being a successful mother has made me more confident professionally and less self-conscious. I think this frees me to experiment in my work and find fresh approaches."

Dr. Bradley Googins, of the Boston University Center on Work and Family, reminds us that "We know that, in a purely economic sense alone, it takes two people [working today] to do what one could do in previous generations." In 1987, Googins and a colleague conducted a study of more than 1,500 employees of two large firms to see how well workers were balancing their work and family lives. What they discovered confirms the stresses voiced by the parents we interviewed:

- absenteeism among married and single female parents is higher by about four days per year than female non-parents and all males
- almost one-quarter of all parents surveyed worry about their child most of the time or all of the time that they are at work
- a surprisingly large number of parents bring their children to work, particularly on school holidays or snow days (as they can't find or can't afford backup care)
- incidence of depression is strongly linked to job-family stress
- child-care benefits were mentioned most often in recommendations of policies to make employees' lives better

Googins summarizes the results in this way, "The key is recognition. The corporation must say, in effect, 'We recognize that (work-family) stress is an issue for you and for us. We cannot solve the problems any more than you can. But what we can do is try and work together.' " He advises that the "critical first step is the cultural breakthrough of recognizing the problems and owning them together with the employees."

In 1987, a representative sample of 600 adults with or without preschool children in U.S. households with incomes of $25,000 or more revealed that:

- 73% of adults believe child-care accommodations by employers are enhancements to everyday work life
- 84% favor employers offering flexible work hours
- 80% want employers to offer child-care referral services
- 70% want employers to offer on-site child care
- 58% want employers to subsidize child care
- 71% percent of women and a surprising 73% of men admit to taking time off from work to attend child-care related matters

Unanimously, the scores of working family members interviewed thought it was time for American business to help them meet their family obligations. Above all, they need a living wage, then they need help with child care and eldercare. They need health insurance, and unpaid leave time that doesn't threaten their job security. Family workers often need flexible work schedules or alternate workplaces; and, when the company insists that a worker move, families need relocation assistance. Sadly, many more families today also need help in crisis situations. Addictions, depressions, uncontrollable teenagers, violence against spouses or children, and severe financial problems all take their toll on worker productivity.

MEETING BASIC NEEDS

A Living Wage

Americans still carry the legacy of the pioneers in their need to be self-sufficient. Self-sufficiency in modern society is almost totally dependent on being able to earn a living wage. Ironically, the plague of poverty, though not new to this age, appears to be settled in among those groups of people most likely to be needed to fill jobs in the '90s—women and minorities. A major motivator for individuals in these groups, then, is likely to be a salary that brings them above subsistence level.

The necessity of a living wage is so basic it is almost overlooked when thinking through family needs. Because the average income of a family goes up $150.00 per week when two members work, and that amount could keep them slightly above the inflation rate, the number of two-earner families rose by 625,000 in 1989. Almost 80% of women have incomes of less than $17,500 a year, compared with 49% of men. "Adequate salary" is cited by workers as their number-one goal. A study by the Economic Policy Institute indicates real wages for the average American worker have declined by almost 10% over the past decade and since 1979 an additional 5.8 million of these people are living at poverty levels, defined in 1989 as $12,675 per year for a family of four.

Although the national minimum wage was recently increased to $4.25/hour, working full time at minimum salary still leaves the worker at the national poverty level. The same worker, when trying to support a family on this salary, soon realizes the absurdity of it, and gives his/her responsibilities over to the welfare system to correct. This forced choice results in an ever-increasing burden on taxpayers, schools, and social service agencies.

Preschool Child Care

The most talked about family need is for quality care for young children. Television programs and articles in newspapers, magazines, and trade publications keep the public aware that finding quality day care can be

WHAT DO WORKING PARENTS WANT?

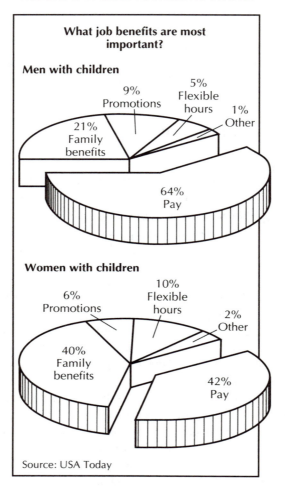

What job benefits are most important?

Men with children

9% Promotions
5% Flexible hours
1% Other
21% Family benefits
64% Pay

Women with children

6% Promotions
10% Flexible hours
2% Other
40% Family benefits
42% Pay

Source: USA Today

a crisis for working parents. Employer-supported child care is the fast-est-growing segment of child care in America. This is a direct result of recognizing that businesses lose $3 billion annually as a result of child-care related absences, according to the Child Care Action Campaign, an organization that works to establish a national system of quality, afford-able child care using public and private resources. These costs are in part due to increased turnover and absences of parents of preschoolers.

The Conference Board, a business-supported research organization, did survey of companies and found that child-care services are offered by only 4,400 of the nation's 44,000 companies with 100 or more employees. That is only 10%—a very small percentage of the work world. Of these, 2,000 offer a dependent care option in a flexible benefits plan; 1,077 sponsor on-site child-care centers; 1,000 offer resource and referral services; 50 offer family child-care support, after school, or sick child- care services; and 50 offer vouchers or discounts for child care. Even though some larger companies are offering help, many of the parents who most need child-care assistance do not work for the larger companies. The special circumstances of small firms and some of their unique experiments are explored later in this book.

Most parents think that they are the best caretakers of their children, but feel caught in a social and economic environment that requires two incomes. They are also afraid of leaving their children in situations where abuse or molestation may occur. While many highly publicized incidents make it clear that moral, balanced, trained child-care workers are essential, they can't be guaranteed without adequate screening measures.

The child-care problems most workers face involve high costs and concern about quality, accessibility, and availability. More specifically, parents worry about convenience to home and work, appropriate ratios of caregivers to children, adequate numbers of openings, and appropriateness of the type of caregiving setting, including safety, cleanliness, and quality/variety of activities for children. Indeed, according to a recent Harris poll, 85% of respondents believe the federal government should establish minimum standards to ensure child care of acceptable quality. What then should be our ideal to strive for in creating a child-care program that meets the needs of parents and children? This is the question to be asked, rather than, "Why do we need child care?"

Elaine Kraft, a community relations director for the Adolph Coors Company, explained how child-care arrangements affected her work life: "When we lost our first nanny, our entire energy was focused on finding appropriate and acceptable day care that was financially affordable. I spend most of my work time quietly and frantically on the phone." Elaine further added that she changed jobs to be more available to her children's needs. It is important to her that she have the ability to work at home if necessary should her children become ill, or should she wish to attend one of their school activities. "My job is flexible and the emphasis in the final interview for this position was that regardless of the evenings, weekends, or early mornings I would have to work, my family comes first." She accepted the position because she said Coors told her that they believed in this kind of flexibility, because in their view, "A happy employee is a better one."

Kristie Strasen, an international textile consultant based in New York City, laments the lack of quality child care for working parents. She believes that more emphasis must be put on the training and education of child-care workers so that those in the field are given the respect they deserve. The mother of a five-year-old and a toddler, Kristie is a former teacher who remarked that, "America's failure to recognize the importance of quality day care and subsequent education will put us in the back seat in the global village." When queried about how being a parent had impacted her work, Kristie explained that the energy she used to make arrangements for her daughter's care during the day had to be subtracted from the energy needed to work after hours.

The need for quality child care is growing among all economic classes. Two out of three mothers with children under 13 will be working outside the home by the end of this decade. It is predicted that through the '90s more than half of America's labor force will be female and an estimated 30 million infants and children will be in need of child-care services. Many of these children come from low-income, single-parent families where the mother is head of the family. Public assistance to "learn and earn" is a welfare reform trend. Right now, 3.7 million mothers on welfare have 3.1 million children under six years old. As labor needs become greater, this population of women will be in demand in the work force full time, adding to the need for employee-assisted care.

"The child day-care program at my company is a big plus for the corporation and to its employees," said one single parent. "It is such a relief to be able to go to work knowing my child is right on the grounds if she needs me, just footsteps away. And I enjoy that she's learning and working in a structured environment all day. That is what makes me regret that I have to take her out of the day care this summer for financial reasons. It would be nice if the company could pick up more than 10%; maybe a schedule based on salaries," she suggested. Another parent expressed gratitude at her employer's subsidy of the off-site day-care center's fees, "Our employer provides excellent fringe benefits in rates for all employees. I could not provide care for him anywhere for the amount I pay daily."

Both rank and file employees and managers we interviewed believe that providing child care, especially on- or near-site enhances the work environment by tearing down the artificial barriers that separate home and work issues. Demolishing, or at least diminishing, this dichotomy eases employee stress. Among the model firms providing on-site or near-site programs are: America West Airlines (24-hour child-care center in Tempe, Arizona); Fel-Pro (employee's day-care center in Skokie, Illinois); Wang Laboratories (child-care center in Massachusetts); Cigna Corporation (Kinder Care Center); Campbell Soup Company; and Disney World, as well as those companies highlighted in Chapter 5.

After-School Child Care

School-age children pose another type of worry for parents. Estimates project that there are more than 18 million children in this country between the ages of six and 14. Typically called "latchkey children," these are boys and girls who are too old for group day care, but not mature enough to be entirely on their own after school. Some community groups such as the Boys or Girls Clubs, YWCA and YMCA, along with other community-sponsored after-school programs, provide care and activities for "latchkey" kids. There are not enough of these programs, however, to meet the needs of all the families for after-school care assistance.

This age child may pose an even greater threat than infants to parental work productivity. Parents of pre- and young teens know that this group is the one most vulnerable to pressures to become involved with drugs, gangs, vandalism, and sexual activity. It's amazing how all the switchboards at most workplaces light up between 3:30 P.M. and 4:30 P.M. every day as parents feel the need to check up on the after-school whereabouts of their children—or children are in need of the reassuring voice of a parent upon entering an empty house.

As of May 1984, only 125 out of 15,000 U.S. school districts offered before- and after-hours child-care programs. Now business is joining in. Soft Sheen, an 800-employee black-owned firm is one of those that provides care for children up to age 16 on Saturdays and Sundays. They discovered that absenteeism on weekend shifts dropped sharply when this benefit was available to their workers' children.

The Houston Committee on Private Sector Initiatives coordinates funding from 30 companies to enable nonprofit agencies to offer after-school services in schools, churches, and storefronts. Other companies like Fel-Pro, Wang, and 3M have created summer day camps on company-owned or nearby community property.

Parents with higher incomes most often have access to child care and may not be as concerned with cost, but they join with parents of lower- and middle-income levels in concerns about quality and accessibility of care. And, all parents face a dilemma if their children are ill.

Sick Child and/or Overnight Dependent Care

Sick children account for a large percentage of absenteeism on the job. Medical experts estimate that a young child experiences an average of six to seven viral infections per year. In some communities, hospitals are attempting to solve this problem. Harbor Hospital Center in Baltimore set up a Sick Child Day Care Program. Nearly 350 children, six weeks to 16 years of age, used the center during its first week of operations, while over 800 people have preregistered to use its services if necessary during the year. Innovations such as this are fairly new and seen as expensive (although they are in fact proving to be cost saving) and therefore are not yet accessible to many working parents, whatever their income.

While there clearly are stresses related to child-care availability, dentist or doctor appointments, and sick children, another not so obvious area of conflict relates to jobs requiring travel and overtime, or night shifts. Service-sector workers most often have night or shift jobs, with salaries that can rarely pay for at-home child care. According to Dr. Harriett Presser, sociologist at the University of Maryland, more than one in six mothers, and one in five fathers, work night or rotating shifts. The expectation is that the number will increase in the '90s. It is also estimated that currently 33% of women and 66% of men hold jobs that require overnight travel. This travel, as well as overtime, can result in more time away from family, more household chores for the stay-at-home spouse, guilt, fatigue for both partners, child-care scheduling problems, and resentment from children. Again, this can result in diminished effectiveness off and on the job, handicapping the employer, employee, and society at large.

Eldercare

Eldercare is a natural consequence of the graying of America. The over-85 age group is the country's fastest growing population. By the year 2025, the proportion of people over 85 will increase from 1% to 5% of the total population. Better nutrition and medical care and healthier life-styles have increased life spans for millions of older Americans. Increased longevity means more and more older Americans will require some form of care in their later years. According to the National Council on Aging, nearly 6.6 million people over age 65 need some type of physical assistance, and they project that this figure will grow to 9 million by the year 2000. Adequate care services and facilities, however, are lagging far behind need, due to this relatively new phenomenon of living past 65 years. Few working families are able to provide home care for sick and/or elderly parents. The result is increased stress or tardiness and absenteeism for workers. The American Association of Retired Persons estimates that 38% of employed people who provide eldercare have lost time from work as a result of their eldercare responsibilities, providing an average of 10 hours a week of care. "Thus, many employees are 'working' a job and a half when taking caregiving and employment responsibilities into account," said the AARP study.

In addition to adult day care, workers caring for elderly parents often need counseling and referral services on nutrition and health services, transportation help, homemaker and chore services, support groups, telephone reassurance, and legal advice. Increasing numbers of community and voluntary agencies, as well as entrepreneurial businesses, are springing up to address these needs, but workers with elderly dependents may need help in sorting out all of these options and services. About 300 companies now offer benefits for care of the elderly, compared with a handful in the mid-'80s. IBM is one of those firms that launched an eldercare referral service in 1988 that was used by 10,000 people during its first year.

The term "The Sandwich Generation" describes yet another dilemma for working families. Many parents of children who require care are also the children of elderly parents needing medical attention or day-care services. Middle-aged couples are often squeezed from both ends, financially and physically, trying to provide loving care to two very different generations—while working full time. This stage often requires outside help for workers, so they can continue to perform at optimum levels at work.

Testifying before the U.S. House of Representatives Select Committee on Children, Youth, and Families, James E. McEuen from Bethesda, Maryland, described the series of stressful events that affected his family emotionally and financially. He testified, "In 1986, we learned of my mother-in-law's cancer. We were trying to give care and solace to her and my father-in-law. . . when my father died. He collapsed trying to help my mother up from the bathroom floor where she had fallen. I was home sick that day; before I could go to the hospital, I had to pick up my son at day care and then my wife at work downtown so she could stay with him. My father was dead by the time I reached the hospital. . . . On the day of his funeral, we learned that my wife was pregnant." McEuen still has responsibility for attending to his ill mother in a nursing home and for making childcare arrangements for his two children. He emphasized the need for information and referral services so families would know where to turn for support and reliable caregiving.

Health Insurance

Thirty-seven million people in this country have no health insurance. Benefits that include quality health and hospital coverage are becoming more important to prospective employees than high salaries. A new hire in a university computer program relates, "When I graduated in computer science, I turned down three really good jobs because their insurance plans didn't cover dental or eye care, and were very skimpy on basic health needs. The job I took paid a little less, but I feel secure that if I have any health problems, I'll be okay financially." Buying health insurance as an individual can increase the costs by 75% over belonging to a group plan. Almost 80% of employees who went out on strike last year complained about health benefits. Young people and others employed in essential, but low-paying jobs, find themselves in no-win situations regarding health care. If they take the risk of not having insurance, one illness can put them years behind financially. If they pay the hefty premiums monthly, they don't have enough to cover food and housing costs. Labor unions have been especially vigilant about health benefits; Richard Trumka, a president of United Mine Workers, said, "People will no longer tolerate the fact that they work 40 hours or more a week and don't have health care—that their children don't have health care."

The near future will bring collective resentment from workers who are scared and angry about the escalation of health care expenditures and restrictions on access and how this affects their lives. According to Jim Green, labor historian at the University of Massachusetts, "We are going to see a lot of social unrest as people start to realize that there has been a real decline in their quality of life." Much of that quality is dependent on good health care.

Americans value good health today more than ever, so it is ironic that the U.S. and South Africa are the only developed nations in the world where health care is not a right of citizenship. Despite a new concern with fitness, as demonstrated by increasing sales of designer tennis shoes and gym wear and America's continued standing as number one in GNP, it is nothing short of amazing that we rank seventh in life expectancy. In the United States, infant mortality, which is one of the indicators used to judge the overall health of a country, is a deplorable 17th among developed countries.

Health care policies must include prenatal care and well-baby checkups, as well as routine immunizations against childhood diseases. The Marriott Corporation, a giant in the hospitality industry, launched a program called Healthy Expectations. It gives employees additional benefits for seeking out prenatal care. Marriott and other companies have discovered that for every $1 they spend on prenatal care, $3.39 is saved in neonatal intensive care costs. This becomes a cost-management strategy, as long- range health-care costs to employers are reduced when up-front health-care services are provided to pregnant workers, new mothers, and their children.

Among the more successful family-friendly innovations attempting to provide adequate health care while controlling costs, is the concept of flexible benefit plans. In 1990 the number of firms nationwide adopting flexible benefit plans grew by about 20% to over 1,200, according to a recent study by Hewitt Associates, an employee-benefits consulting firm. These are programs that allow employees to select from a variety of health insurance plans and other benefits, including vacation days and dedicated accounts for dependent care needs. These plans reduce costs for employees by eliminating benefits employees don't need (an employee who already has hospitalization coverage via a spouse then chooses to get only dental or vision coverage). Just as important, they can steer employees towards lower-cost alternatives by requiring co-payments. They benefit employees by providing some tax savings through care spending accounts that earmark dependent care funds in a separate account, thus reducing the taxable earnings of the employee.

These new programs are no longer just in the provence of large firms; new advances in personal computer programs and prefabricated plans now make them accessible to small firms as well. Examples of large and small firms offering flexible benefit plans include Educational Testing Service, Comerica, American Can, Steelcase, and Procter & Gamble.

American families need health care. They are looking to their employers to provide it.

Family Leave and Job Security
The birth or adoption of a new child requires time for parents to bond to the child and adjust schedules and life-styles that will accommodate a new family member. Significant blocks of time are also needed to deal with an illness or chronic problem in a family. These are not "frill" activities, but essential to the well-being of the individual or family, and ultimately their ability to produce and function constructively in society. Most work policies have not allowed family members to deal adequately with these situations, in some cases requiring several months' absence, without losing their jobs. Only 44% of U.S. companies offer *unpaid* maternity leave and just 5% provide *paid* maternity leave.

Beverly Wilkinson reported at a congressional hearing that she had worked for a firm in Atlanta as a secretary right up until the day her son was born. She then took five weeks of unpaid maternity leave and two weeks of vacation. The day before she was due to return to work, she received a phone call from her supervisor explaining that her job had been eliminated. "I was stunned," said Wilkinson. "I felt betrayed. I had invested five years of my life in that company."

The question of priorities or what is most important—the maintenance of the family in society or the efficiency with which business is run—has garnered a great deal of legislative attention. Many state legislatures are leaning in favor of family maintenance. Washington state has enacted a law that requires all employers with over 100 workers to provide unpaid leave to both male and female workers upon the birth, adoption, or terminal illness of the worker's child. Full-time employees with at least one year of service can take three months of family leave during any two-year period. Vermont law is requiring at least 12 weeks of unpaid maternity leave for female workers. A bill is now in the California legislature to require employers to grant up to four months of family care leave under needy circumstances.

Women, whose job security has been most threatened by lack of extended maternity leave, find paternity leave to be a double blessing. It is a sign that society is finally declaring the father's rights and responsibility as a new parent, by allowing males the same leave privilege.

Flexible Work Schedules
As long ago as 1974, the U.S. government adopted the policy of flextime whereby employees could choose their starting hours and ending hours while still working a full eight-hour day. Often the employees chose such hours as 7:00 A.M. to 4:00 P.M., 8:00 A.M. to 5:00 P.M., or 9:00 A.M. to 6:00 P.M. This action was based on a survey of federal employees who cited flexible hours as important in dealing with work and family problems.

Flexible hours at work, or "flextime" is both a need and solution for managing family life in a complex society. Taking care of one's financial affairs, volunteering for school or community functions, or making doctor appointments can seldom all be done after work or on weekends. Yet, these activities are vital to a fully functioning family, school, and community. Flextime is a way to meet family emergencies with less stress. When a spouse works swing or night shift, flextime benefits allow their working partner opportunities to spend time together and communicate more frequently—both being essential to lasting relationships.

According to New Ways To Work, a San Francisco–based clearing house on workplace changes, new scheduling options include:

- Flextime: a schedule that allows differences in starting/quitting times around a core working schedule, such as 9 A.M. to 3 P.M. or 10 A.M. to 4 P.M.
- Compressed Work Week: a full week's work completed in fewer than five days
- Regular Part-time Work: less than full-time work that includes job security and often benefits
- Job-sharing: two people voluntarily sharing one job with prerated salary and benefits
- V-time: voluntary time, allowing workers to reduce their hours and compensation temporarily
- Leaves of absence: paid or unpaid time away from the job without loss of employment rights

Flexible work hours were desired by virtually all working parents interviewed, from entry-level health technicians to senior executives. Frequently mentioned were permanent part-time work, job-sharing, flextime, half-day vacations, and 4/40 work weeks. The Bureau of Labor Statistics noted that in 1989, 61% of the firms surveyed offered work practices aimed at helping parents care for their children, such as flexible work schedules, voluntary part time, and flexible leave. In a survey conducted by John P. Fernandez of AT&T in 1986, summarized in his book, *Child Care and Corporate Productivity*, workers agreed that employers should offer employees the option of:

- Choosing to work part time
- Selecting various forms of job-sharing
- Selecting flexible hours
- Selecting half-day vacations

Parents aren't the only ones favoring more flexibility, a 1989 Louis Harris and Associates poll revealed that 89% of the public believes that companies should be encouraged to adopt flexible and part-time work schedules.

The Conference Board surveyed 521 of the nation's biggest companies in 1989, and found that 93% offer at least one kind of flexible work scheduling. Employers are reporting good results. Eighty-four percent say the greatest advantage is improved employee attitude and morale; 79% say greater accommodations for working parents, and 65% say increased worker job satisfaction.

In addition to flextime, *job-sharing,* where two or more employees work one full-time job, is an option that has been tried with some success. Because it requires the employer to rethink scheduling benefit plans and methods of supervision, however, it is not used as frequently as would be helpful. *Personnel,* a magazine published by the American Management Association, recently reported that less than 1% of the work force is engaged in job-sharing. There are now, however, some reported successes in job-sharing, particularly at nonmanagement levels. Nancy Lewis and Debbie Kelly, seasoned employees at Snohomish County Public Utility District in Everett, Washington, are both mothers of young children. Neither wanted to quit work when their children were born but both believed that a 40-hour work week would be too stressful and deprive them of needed time with their infants during this critical developmental stage. They now share one job as

---

THE 4/40

Driven initially not by family needs but rather by environmental concerns, a number of employers are adopting four-day, 10-hour-a-day work weeks. Seeking ways to reduce paralyzing traffic congestion and air pollution, 6% to 8% of Southern California employers with 500 or more workers have switched to a four-day work week, compared with 2% to 3% nationwide. Firms as diverse as aerospace companies to food processor manufacturers and automakers are trying the shortened work week to comply with the South Coast Air Quality Management District's new edict that aims to cut regional traffic by 25%, thus removing 200 tons of carbon monoxide emissions daily.

Besides aiding the environment, the good news for employers is a better workplace. California State University at Long Beach conducted a study that revealed improved employee morale, increased productivity, reduced absenteeism, and enhanced opportunities for new worker recruitment.

Workplace analysts predict that the 4/40 work week will become increasingly popular in the next decade, particularly in urban areas suffering from high levels of traffic congestion.

administrative assistant to the director of rates and analysis for the utility, Coe Hutchison. Coe describes with enthusiasm the results of the job-share, "I think it has worked tremendously well. I get two highly motivated productive employees who both give me their best in terms of time and energy." As the father of young children himself, Coe is sensitive to family needs and has been a vocal advocate for more job-sharing opportunities at the utility.

While still fairly uncommon in the world of upper management, Dianna Bowler and Alisa Michaels Metzner are vice presidents at Bank America in San Francisco. After each gave birth to a daughter, they received approval to share one management job and salary, while working in strategic planning and analysis for the bank. As reported in the October 3, 1988 issue of *Time* magazine, they split the work week in half with one working seven hours daily on Monday, Tuesday, Wednesday, with the other one working seven hours Wednesday, Thursday, and Friday. The overlap day allows them to coordinate their work. Bowler describes it as "the best of both worlds" in terms of personal and professional rewards.

Despite the fact that only 3–10% of American companies have some job-sharers, it "is a trend that we are going to see more of," predicted Stephanie Decker, the internal staffing manager of Hewlett-Packard. Her firm, as well as American Express, Levi Strauss, U.S. West, and Time Warner, Inc., are some of the more well-known firms taking advantage of job-sharing. Steelcase, a furniture manufacturer in Grand Rapids, Michigan, has been a pioneer in job-sharing at the management level. Patricia Konwinski and Martha O'Brien share a job as recruiters for the company's marketing division. After two years they term it a success and have been promoted as a team. "Job-sharing has brought sanity back into our lives," said Ms. Konwinski, who has sons ages one and four. "I have time for myself, to do my errands, and unharried time for my son," said Ms. O'Brien, whose child is three years old. "We see job-sharing as an opportunity to retain employees who are highly valued and motivated," said Peter Jeff, the senior public relations representative for the firm. Steelcase has two other teams of women sharing management-level jobs and 70 other employees, including one man, who share clerical and assembly line jobs.

Part-time work is another option for flexible scheduling. The federal government has been the leader in this area as a result of the passage in 1978 of the Federal Employees Part-Time Career Employment Act, which encouraged government agencies to create part-time positions. The advantages to employees are similar to those of job-sharing. For employees, both approaches provide an opportunity to attract a pool of talented people, especially women who do not wish a full-time position. It also results in retention of valuable employees, who after giving birth, don't want to resume full-time employment or who are having serious child-care problems or who have special-needs children. Thus, companies avoid the costs of recruiting and having replacements for workers who might otherwise leave the company entirely. Leonor Fuller, a lawyer with the City Attorney's office in Seattle, chose a part-time work week after the birth of her first son. The city retains her talent and experience while she is able to nurture her infant and keep her legal skills current.

Because of the appeal of part-time work to women in particular, firms are better able to meet their goals for equal employment opportunities. However, there is often not enough power in part-time work to demand adequate salaries or benefits from employers. Part-time work thus accommodates the *time* needs of some family members, but often excludes them from the *security* offered by adequate pay, health, and retirement insurance plans. Since most part-timers are women, they are very vulnerable during periods of illness and at the time of retirement. So are their children.

To deny all benefits to part-time employees may negate the potential benefit of this option, since it may discourage workers from trying it. Conversely it may be too expensive for firms to offer full benefits. Such issues warrant careful study and some firms such as Microsoft Corporation have decided to prorate their benefits package based on number of hours worked. Security Pacific Bank chose to offer full benefits to anyone working more than 20 hours a week, stating that today it's an employee-, not employer-driven job market.

A recurrent theme of parents interviewed, both male and female, was a strong desire for *"part-time plus" work*. Martha Darling, a manager with the Boeing Company, explained that she didn't mean half-time or job-sharing—she didn't think that would be feasible given her professional level of responsibilities, rather she wished for perhaps four-fifth's time. More flexibility to come late or leave early, depending on her son's school activities, is a continuing need. "Providing this option communicates a level of trust to employees which is sure to pay off in loyalty to the firm," she stated.

Many executives reject the concept of part-time workers, automatically assuming that it means *half-time* or 20 hours or less per week. Interestingly, recent surveys of workers, particularly those in managerial, professional, or technical positions, revealed that what is sought is a 30 hour or four-day work week. The workaholic generation who spent the last decade career-obsessed is now concerned with putting family life back on track. They are balking at grueling hours, frequent overnight travel, and marathon meetings. They seek an equilibrium between work and family life, even if it costs them promotions and pay.

In fact, the executive recruiting firm of Robert Half International unveiled the results of a recent survey reporting that more than half of 500 men polled said they'd be willing to cut their salaries as much as 25% to have more family or personal time; about 45% said they would be likely to turn down a promotion if it meant spending less time with their families. As active partners in the parenting challenge, men would like more flexibility to participate in school events, minister to a sick child, or deal with the emotional crises that happen to kids from twos to teens. Glen Pascal, a Seattle business writer and consultant, hypothesized about the benefit of a two-third's-time work day. "I crave to do domestic things," he said, explaining that he knew how much work it takes to keep an active household going. "I like doing that kind of work and I wish I had more time available to do it."

The challenge for managers is to judge employers on their contributions rather than their physical presence at the workplace. Solid accomplishment must be the key to career advancement, rather than the old notion that burning the midnight oil equals a promotion or bonus. But, part-time work like job-sharing, has fallen into disfavor in many workplaces, partly because of the benefits question—"Can we afford to provide benefits to someone who works far fewer hours than regular employees?"—and partly because of communication concerns—"How does a part-time employee let others know how and what he/she is doing?" But these problems can be solved, and part-time employment can continue to make it possible for valued employees to participate both in the workplace and at home.

Ann Cardwell, an office manager for a West Coast research firm, had to make a hard decision. When her employer insisted on turning Ann's three-day-a-week position into a full-time job, she quit, citing her need to spend time with her preschooler. Everyone lost in this decision. Ann's employer lost a valuable, seasoned employee, and will have to spend additional resources training her replacement. Ann missed the lost income and felt isolated from the work world. Fortunately, she soon found another position at a firm with a four-day work week option. This allows Ann an adequate income, professional stimulation, and additional time to spend with her young son.

Flexible Workplaces

Being able to work at home is a valuable benefit for many. Telephones, facsimile machines, and computers make this a workable option in many jobs. The choice to work at home falls into the alternative work schedules or "flexplace" plan. "Flexplace" opportunities, often called "telecommuting" allows employees to do all or a major part of their work at home using a telephone and personal computer to stay in touch. Among firms trying it is Levi Strauss in San Francisco. Telecommuting might be a way to eliminate extended maternity leaves without weakening the benefits of a mother being at home with a newborn. It definitely gives commuters more time to be at home and/or to devote to work and can also be the answer to accommodating workers with children or dependent parents who are occasionally sick.

In the early '80s about 15,000 workers had home work stations; however, it is estimated that by the late '90s as many as 10 million workers will have them. This practice gives workers a lot of discretion in scheduling their work hours, reducing not only work/family conflicts but also costs related to child care, commuting, and office space. Researchers, writers, data clerks, financial analysts, real estate salespeople, word processors, and computer programmers are just a few of the careers ripe for exploring this option. Telecommuting is particularly attractive to those employees who are self-disciplined and self-directed. There are, however, some risks in this option: loneliness and feelings of isolation on the part of the worker can decrease motivation. Loss of control by the supervisor may make it more difficult to monitor and evaluate the employee's work.

Special Problem Help

Often, stressed workers have problems in a number of areas. This is where a general counseling and referral program is extremely helpful. Several large companies began offering this type of program years ago to deal with alcoholism among employees. The focus has changed a great deal, although most programs still include alcoholism referral and treatment.

Financial problems, job stress, domestic violence, drug or alcohol abuse, mental disorders, or problems involving a worker's adolescent youth are now commonly dealt with through company employee assistance programs (EAPs). Difficult problems such as these are often compounded and can drain the resources of any worker very quickly. Setting up an EAP does not mean that the employer becomes the counselor or is expected to solve the employee's problems. It does, however, provide support for solving one's own problems, as well as offering alternatives for receiving professional help.

Control Data Corporation, a Minneapolis firm with 47,000 U.S. employees, takes the basic EAP concept a step further. They provide an EAR, employee advisory resource, a 24-hour counseling service available to employees or their families. Since 1984, EAR has provided advice in marital disputes, drug and alcohol problems, family financial concerns, or work-related difficulties. Control Data also recognizes the complexities of modern family life in its provision of an employee services network (ESN) and Wiser Ways Program. ESN is a tape library available by phone on topics ranging from buying a used car to retirement planning. Wiser Ways is a sophisticated discount buying program designed to save employees money on everything from eyeglasses to home appliances. Control Data enjoys low employee turnover and high morale as a result of their comprehensive employee benefits program.

Relocation is a special problem that requires specific kinds of help from employers. The stress and logistical challenges encountered in relocating when a family is transferred to another community are especially difficult for two-paycheck families. Selling one home and buying another, regardless of the market, finding the "trailing" spouse a new job, acclimating children to new schools, and the family to new medical and service professionals can be very costly, both financially and emotionally. Some couples are settling for a commuter marriage where they live in different towns and visit each other as frequently as possible. In addition to heightened stress on the marriage, this arrangement often results in counterproductive workaholism, where employees work to relieve the loneliness of not being with spouse or family.

International transfers can be especially difficult. Executives eligible for international transfers are often likely to be part of a dual-career partnership. Immigration laws often make it very difficult, if not impossible, for spouses to find work. Cultural differences can also take their toll on adolescent children who need to identify with their peers.

Employees need considerable help in making these adjustments. Currently more than one-third of America's major corporations are providing some form of spouse re-employment assistance. Corporate relocation assistance can range from assisting a spouse in updating a resume, to a full-blown career skills program that helps the individual identify career objectives and job opportunities.

Costs of spouse employment assistance vary. Fees for a relocation consultant can range from $150 per hour to $4,000 for a complete individualized program, with an average price around $2,500, according to Sharon Gadbury, Ph.D., president of Transitions Management Group in San Francisco. IBM is among the first firm with a good track record of providing comprehensive spouse employment assistance.

Recent worker trends indicate many upwardly mobile young professionals are dropping out or refusing promotions if they involve relocating. Today less than 70% of potential transferees accept relocation generally due to the negative impact on the career of the spouse.

Baxter Travenol Laboratories prepares special kits for children of employees being transferred by the company. Materials in the kits address relocation concerns from the perspective of children at a variety of ages. Each box contains a T-shirt, scrapbook to record progress of the move, crayons, and a tote bag. Older children get T-shirts, binders, stationery, key chains, and address books. The company, which transfers less than 5% of its employees every year, reports that the kits are very popular with relocated families. This kind of sensitive response indicates to the employee, spouse, and children that the firm cares about them and their needs.

Those who are educated in the art and science of family development are part of a very rare breed. Some adults, both male and female, are natural family managers, but most Americans grow up without even thinking about family life—let alone balancing work and family—before they are in the midst of it. So, like other basic skills that are bypassed in the school curriculum and for which there are few effective role models, *family life education* needs to be a part of the achieving adult's remedial program. Family life and parenting programs are springing up in workplaces throughout the country. These work-site programs are designed to help parents know how to balance work and family life, how to discipline effectively, how to help children or elders cope with crisis or trauma, etc. The assumption is the more skills you have to be effective as a family member, the more productive you will be as an employee. Employers also benefit from this visible demonstration of concern for the needs of workers as family members responsible for child care or eldercare.

INAPPROPRIATE CORPORATE RESPONSES

Horror stories affecting working parents have begun to be documented in the popular press: the pregnant employee who gets fired; the new mother who returns to work to find her responsibilities diminished; the waiting lists for slots in company-sponsored child-care centers; the abysmal care provided at some contracted eldercare programs. Of a much less severe impact but also inappropriate is an action taken by an East Coast retail establishment. When one of its workers is forced to work extensive overtime, they send the spouse (read "wife") flowers. (We don't know of any husbands who have been sent this bouquet.) Of course, management thinks this is a gracious gesture and some may genuinely appreciate it. We find it an archaic remnant of old-style thinking. What a spouse needs in this circumstance isn't a bouquet, it's more time for the family to be together. In the case of a family with young children or a disabled relative at home, the absence of the spouse has no doubt caused the other spouse additional work or additional expenses in the form of a babysitter or respite care worker. What the employer should do is give the worker compensatory time off or a cash bonus. These are likely to be much more appreciated than posies.

IN SUMMARY, HERE IS WHAT FAMILIES NEED:

- A living wage
- Job security
- Help with dependent care
- Health insurance
- Some flexibility on work hours/days
- Flexible workplaces
- Special problem help
- Family life education
- Supportive supervisors with family-friendly attitudes

3

NOT FOR WOMEN ONLY—BUT. . .

IF THE SHOE FITS

When we first began writing this book we were determined not to harangue on women's issues. We both felt strongly that the concerns of family that would be put forth by both the employees and employers are truly unisex issues. The more information we gained, however, and the more we explored the underlying reasons for American business and governmental policies lagging so far behind those in the rest of the civilized world, it became evident that old attitudes and practices centering around *women* played a major role.

WOMEN IN LABOR FORCE: GROWING FAST

Between 1950 and 1985, the number of women in the labor force increased by 178% while the number of male workers increased by only 47%. More than half of all women with children under age one now work for pay, as do 70% of all women with children between the ages of six and 17. More than 5.3 million working mothers are single parents. Fifty-seven percent of married women with children under age six worked outside the home in 1987, compared with only 12% in 1950. Almost 75% of the care of an elderly relative is provided by a woman. By 1995 women will fill more than 67% of new jobs created and 80% of them will become pregnant during their work lives. Finally, the percentage of U.S. families with both mother and father working had risen from 43% in 1975 to 63% in 1988, according to the U.S. Bureau of Labor.

A WOMAN'S PLACE

The demographic prediction of the '90s says it clearly: by the year 2000, 80% of women in their prime childbearing years (25–44) will be in the labor force. According to the Small Business Administration, women are the fastest growing segment in the labor market.

What do all these numbers mean? Fierce competition for good workers will drive employment policies during the decade. Not only will the pool of new workers be substantially smaller, the majority of these new workers, three out of every five, will be women. Mothers of children younger than three years of age have been rapidly entering the job market. Women in the last decade have demonstrated their commitment to their careers by delaying marriage and childbirth and by returning to work sooner after having children. Adding to the complexity of this situation will be a huge percentage of the U.S. population over the age of 75. Thus, America will have a generation of women workers facing the dual demands of child care and eldercare. A 1990 *Newsweek* cover story, "The Daughter Track," headlined the facts that the average American woman spends 17 years raising children and 18 years helping aging parents. Coupled with shouldering these responsibilities, women still do most of the work around the house, while putting in at least eight hours a day in the labor force. One might well ask whether this is humanly possible. It is—but it is not easy, and the stress takes its toll. And many women are paying a price for their workplace contributions. A recent survey reported that 71% of corporate women believe that high-achieving women have to forgo having children to stay on the corporate fast track. Of women in executive positions in the early 1990s, 50% were single and 50% of those who did marry had no children. For some this is a considerable sacrifice, especially when compared with their male peers, 95% of whom are married with children.

Single parents, who are mostly women, are in the most vulnerable position. Almost 11 million families were headed by women in 1989, compared with 6.6 million in 1972. The stresses caused by both roles as worker and sole caregiver are particularly intense and likely to have a continued impact on workplace productivity—to say nothing of the mother's own health. Compared to the average $871.00 per week earned by a dual-career couple, the single female head of household makes only $361.00 per week. The divorce rate is not declining. More than half the children born in the '80s are or will live with only one parent before reaching adulthood. The dual-role stress, teetering on the brink of poverty, puts single mothers in a very precarious position . . . both as employees themselves and as healthy role models for the next generation of workers.

Donna Klein, director of work and family life for the Marriott Corporation, says that her company became active in work and family programs because women make up half of their 230,000-person work force. "The labor shortages predicted for 2000 are very real to us," she says. Indeed, in the worlds of hospitality, retail, banking, and health care, labor shortages have begun to hit hard. Vacant positions for radiology technicians, physical therapists, bank tellers, data entry operators, sales clerks, and hotel maids confound human resource managers from coast to coast. Many of the workers eligible for these positions are women with small children or elderly relatives needing care. They need an employer who not only will be flexible, but also will be *proactive* in offering benefits to help that sought-after worker meet her family obligations.

But until recently, U.S. businesses weren't too concerned about female employees. If a woman quit to have a baby or stay home with her family, she was doing "the predictable thing." During the '70s when the work force grew by 3 million a year, an employer could easily fill her slot with

---

WOMEN'S DISPROPORTIONATE BURDEN

Six years ago the *Wall Street Journal* asked executive women working full time how they and their spouses handled home responsibilities. Recent studies indicate the picture has not changed.

- 52% of women did the family laundry
- 47% of women said they had primary responsibility for grocery shopping while 41% shared the task with their husbands
- 70% were the sole or primary parent in shopping for the children's clothes
- Only 5% of the husbands assume chief responsibility for any duty involving children
- Women who do not work outside the home spend 55 hours per week on household tasks, compared to 26 hours for women employed full time

A current study reports that 70% of the total time spent on household chores was contributed by women, 15% by men and the remainder by other members of the household

another worker. The prevailing view was that women were not "serious" members of the work force. They worked for "pin" money—extras for their families—and were economically reliant on their husbands, not their workplaces. Other pervasive myths were that women would marry, have children, and drop out of the world of paid employment, or that they weren't working for that same sense of psychic satisfaction men were—that they got their rewards from nurturing their husbands and children. While these opinions may have been true of some women in the past, statistics now reveal that most women work because they have to earn a living. In addition, educated women, married or single, don't view their degrees as ways to find husbands, they see their education as investments in a life-long career path. The reality is that many women view work both as a source of personal satisfaction and as an economic necessity. Single women with or without children comprise a significant percentage of the work force; married women with children and husbands in low-paying jobs reject the notion that they are merely working for "extras."

Even as women's attitudes and needs have changed regarding the world of work, corporate America has by and large been stuck in the '50s with a TV image of "Harriet" keeping the home together while "Ozzie" goes off to the office or plant. The fact of the matter is that "Harriet" has now taken on both roles.

ROUND-THE-CLOCK WORKERS

While child care may be becoming a shared responsibility, other family responsibilities may not be. In a nationwide survey analyzed by sociologist Catharine Ross, 76% of women employed full time still do the majority of housework. This disproportionate burden means that women have 25% less leisure time according to a 1987 survey of 600 women and men with incomes over $25,000. While this is burden enough for women with nine-to-five jobs, it is even more exhausting for women with management- or executive-level positions who bring work home to do on evenings and weekends. One entrepreneur confided in us: "Something's got to give. I need either more help at home or more help at the office, but I can't continue like this. Sometimes I think I get sick just because my body needs a break."

Waiting for men to voluntarily take on their share of family responsibilities is a major irritant for most women today. According to the 1990 Virginia Slims Opinion Poll, this frustration is second (only to money) as a cause of resentment toward male partners. Seven out of 10 women polled felt that more help with household and child care would greatly relieve the day-to-day stress they feel.

Do women "do it all" because they have to, or because they fear or resent asking for help? Many women are still trying to run their households like their mothers did, although most of these mothers didn't work outside the home. The woman hesitates to ask her spouse to do more, because she didn't see her father cleaning or cooking. These inequities must be renegotiated both at home and in the workplace. The impact of more males participating in home/child tasks is great. When politically powerful male workers join the chorus for more flextime and variable benefit packages, management is more likely to respond.

John P. Fernandez points out, in his book *Child Care & Corporate Productivity*, "the unique and comfortable position in which many of the married men in management found themselves; but that comfort may be short-lived. As career opportunities for women increase and as the pressures on their careers intensify, wives will become increasingly intolerant of the extreme imbalance in responsibilities at home, and more and more married men may find themselves no longer immune to dealing with family problems in the workplace."

When this subtle but perceptible shift in attitude occurs among men, and they recognize the importance of housework and family caregiving activities, social values begin to change. Some men are now realizing that certain of these nurturing activities can be immensely satisfying.

MONEY TALKS

The element of pay equity must also be considered. One new working mom stated: "I feel guilty asking my husband to do more around the house, he works just as hard as I do, and he brings home more money." This last revelation is a critical one for many women. Their rationale goes something like this: "He earns more than I do, so his job must be more important, therefore it's up to me (the one with the less important job) to devote my nonwork hours to taking care of him, the kids, and the house." Nowhere in this line of reasoning is there acknowledgment of the fact of sex discrimination manifested in pay inequity in this country.

Women earned 63 cents for every dollar men earned in 1939. The 1990 figure is 67 cents to every dollar. Pay equity seldom exists on U.S. college campuses, at government entities, or in private business. The U.S. Equal Employment Opportunities Commission recently sued a Baltimore television station because management illegally underpaid an anchorwoman almost $40,000, compared to her male colleagues. Then they fired her for complaining. This is just one of thousands of discouraging examples of women being robbed of what's due them.

The wage disparities between male and female workers, while diminishing, are still quite apparent. Money was cited as the number one source of dissatisfaction with their jobs by women responding to the Virginia Slims poll. Sixty-three percent felt it was the greatest source of stress and resentment. Having the opportunity to earn more was seen as definitely making their lives better, but old-boy biases make this very difficult. In 1988, the average income for families headed by a single mother with children under 18 was $11,989, compared with $23,919 for those families headed by a single father and $40,067 for those families with both parents present. This gap affects all female workers from assembly line workers and cooks to clerks and executives. One explanation has been described by some as "the glass ceiling," the invisible barrier that keeps women from rising to the top decision-making levels in their companies. Lack of access to the uppermost executive ranks also denies women access to the highest salary levels. Most women who are highly motivated by money find that they have to take the risk of starting their own business in order to fully utilize their leadership potential and earn "real money." At some firms, however, this is changing. For example, at U.S. West women hold 21% of all the jobs in the company's top 1% salary level. The firm has a goal of raising the percentage of women holding top jobs to 35% in this decade.

The fact that few women are in upper-level management, even after 25 years of female involvement in lower- and mid-level positions, is often the reason for lower pay. It also says that the important and relevant characteristics of most women's leadership style is not being acknowledged. Industrial age minds are still screening the image of a woman out of the corner office. Although a glass ceiling or invisible barrier barring females from the uppermost echelons truly does exist, and a lack of promotional opportunities is causing significant numbers of women to drop out of the work force entirely or start their own businesses, there are more complex reasons for so many fast-track women deciding to quit.

A federal district judge recently pronounced a "guilty" judgment against a well-known Philadelphia law firm. A female associate was refused a partnership and charged the firm with sex discrimination. The judge indicated the firm was applying tougher standards to women than men who seek partnerships. Also strongly influencing a number of these women who leave their former employer in disgust is a lack of adequate dependent care and flexibility in hours to meet family responsibilities. However, in the minds of many women, and most men for that matter, it is still viewed as "not OK" to *verbalize* these family concerns. These workers feel that they will be viewed as less than serious about their careers, or complainers, or expecting too much in this recessionary economy. We also suspect that those firms who haven't changed their culture to be family-friendly are also those firms where the glass ceiling is most firmly in place. There seems to be a circular pattern of defeating actions.

One Midwest public relations executive told us, "I had been frustrated for quite some time—feeling that I wasn't going anywhere in the company but putting in lots of hours, constantly traveling, exceeding my division's goals, bringing work home every weekend. Then after I had my first child, it just became too much. They still expected just as much effort from me without any flexibility in my work schedule and still not holding out any hope of a senior VP slot. I quit. I have two kids now, am working free-lance around their schedules, and am glad to be out of that pressure cooker." Few of this woman's needs as an employee were being met, so it's not surprising that she made the decision she did. However, it's more likely that she and others like her would tell the exit interviewer or inquiring reporter, "I left due to lack of promotional opportunities" than, "I really missed my child; she was growing up without me; I felt exhausted, angry, and guilty."

Much harder to assess is the phenomenon now called, "the mommy track." It was recently suggested, by a prominent work/family advisor, then explored extensively in the press, that women who needed to give more emphasis to family concerns during certain periods of their lives, be segregated out and put on what was labelled a "mommy track." This category would purportedly afford more flexibility and family-type benefits for participants, but would foreshorten their opportunities to advance in the company. Whether or not the mommy track exists, it represents a spurious way to categorize employees. A similar "daddy track," where fathers would be asked to stand on one side of the line and be relegated to less interesting assignments, little chance for advancement, and perennially lower pay is hard to imagine. It is true that for relatively short periods of time, some workers, mainly women, may choose to earn less pay via reduced work hours or turn down a promotion that requires lots of overnight travel or take a sabbatical to care for a young child or elderly relative. Yet we are reminded that such choices are generally of limited duration. Many workers continue to make vital and significant contributions to their organizations during these times of work flexibility. That should be the focus, not what they're choosing or obligated to do for family members.

A partner in a large accounting firm came to us, saying, "I need your advice. I've got a woman who just returned from an extended maternity leave, is working a four-day work week, and wants to be made partner. What should I do?" We waited. Finally, one of us said, "You still haven't given us any relevant information. Is she performing? Is she a leader? Is she meeting or exceeding the goals established for her division? These are the criteria you need to use to evaluate her for a promotion, not how many hours she is physically at the job site in a week, a month, or even a year." He walked away looking thoughtful and somewhat perplexed. Yet nothing we told him deviated from classic management advice à la management gurus Peter Drucker or Tom Peters: Judge employees by how they perform, what they produce, achieve, and contribute. Performance-based pay and promotion must become a hallmark of management in the '90s. Of course, none of this is as "sexy" as the catchy media label, "mommy track," which appears to pit women who do choose to have children against those who don't. We'd prefer to see the whole concept permanently put to rest.

Many company executives seem to agree. The managers we interviewed staunchly denied the existence of a mommy track, refuting any suggestion that employees who availed themselves of their work/family programs in any way compromised their chances for career advancement, or the opportunity to get a plum assignment or top account. Yet we only interviewed and studied those firms that had taken the leadership to make it easier for employees to work and parent. Even at these firms, off the record, we had employees express doubt about their ability to reach top corporate ranks after they took extended maternity leave or reduced their hours to care for a disabled spouse.

Time will tell. Many of the initiatives we report on in this book are still quite new. Women are also relative newcomers to the mid-management ranks of some of these firms. More study is warranted to see what happens to those pioneering women and men who helped craft work/family programs and then actually took advantage of them at some point in their careers.

Another future challenge is how to work fairly with the small, predominantly female-owned cottage industries springing up in this country to deal with the needs of the two-career or single-parent families. These women-owned and operated housecleaning and catering companies are joining the ranks of in-home child-care centers as major new employers. Many of these very small firms do not offer benefits of any kind to their employees. So how do these workers meet the needs of their families for child care or eldercare?

According to the Children's Defense Fund, it costs on average $3,000–$5,000 per year per child for full-time child care. However, the average salary of a child-care worker is $10,000 per year. While this is clearly an inadequate income, even paying this becomes a hardship for most working families headed by women. Forty-five percent of families with children under six years old earned between $15,000 and $40,000 per year, so they really can't afford to pay their child care, eldercare, or household worker more. This mitigates in favor of some sort of government and/or employer assistance in subsidizing a decent salary for child-care workers who take care of our nation's most precious resource. Some other ideas are discussed in chapter 5 dealing with the unique dilemma of the small firm.

MEDIA MIND-SHAPERS

Societal attitudes are both shaped and reflected in the news media. Popular magazines recorded the "mommy track" controversy and coined the "daughter track" idea. From these writings it is obvious that spirited debate is taking place in regard to women's roles and work equity. Bookshelves hold many more publications on family policy and family problems than was evident in the '80s. Major newspapers are quicker to point out the prevalence of family dysfunction such as domestic violence, child abuse, malnutrition, and homelessness. They are also reporting, with marked approval, the actions being taken by business and the private sector to remedy these problems. Ideas for a better world are being propagated.

What bothered us as we reviewed the media impact, however, was the line-up of current television programs. They seem to lack honest, instructive role models for women who are trying to balance both work and family. Gone is Mary Beth Lacey and the constant tension she felt between doing her job as a New York policewoman and meeting the needs of three kids and a husband. In her place is Roseanne Connor, whose work is unimportant to her, and Claire Huxtable, an attorney who is obviously too busy at home to ever be seen in the courtroom. Those strong female professionals portrayed in "Murphy Brown" and "The Trials of Rosie O'Neill" go home to empty apartments and their own existential angst, much like the characters Joan Crawford portrayed in the '40s. Where are secretaries who pick their children up from day care and rush home to fix a 30-minute meal? Or, the fast-track market analyst who discovers that she really wants to stay at home for a few months with her newborn? Or, the single mom whose profession often takes her out of town to work with clients and finds that child care is always a struggle. Television producers are doing today's families a disservice by pretending that these people do not exist. Their characters could be much more dramatic, relevant, and instructive than watching Roseanne drink a beer at the kitchen table. And, in the long run, television could add integrity to its status as the number one educator in the country.

We do laud the writers, producers, and actors on shows such as "LA Law" where two men, one with a developmental disability and the other with Alzheimer's disease, are brought into the fold and given jobs. This is also the show that depicted a married couple who were lawyers, juggling the vagaries of child care, resulting in both bringing the child to the office when their support system broke down. We think that honestly dramatizing these struggles on the TV is both encouraging and validating for the rest of us in the viewing audience, as would more programs devoted to these real life dilemmas and how they are resolved by other families or employers.

SPECIAL CHALLENGES FOR WOMEN OF COLOR

The fact that employers have a tendency to hire, especially for management positions and above, people who look like themselves, has been well documented. Because most organizations are still run by white males and no one looks less like a white male than a woman of color, this phenomenon definitely stifles her opportunities to get hired into a leadership position. Subtle signs that women of color hardly exist in the minds of employers exist everywhere. One example is the phrase "women and minorities." It is used in many labor reports and has become "standard expression" in spoken language. Where do women of color fit in that phrase? It appears to be a convenient way to pretend that they do not fit—period. Yet 58% of black women (6.5 million) and 52% of Hispanic women (3.4 million) were in the labor force by 1987, according to the U.S. Department of Labor. But when enlightened recruitment policies do result in a woman of color being hired, she faces another dilemma. She may often be perceived as a token, being the only non-white person in the work group. We know that being able to see a model or have a mentor can be a very positive career growth experience, but women of color most often go without these aids.

Many family-related stresses are also magnified for the nonwhite female worker. African-American women form the largest group of female heads-of-households. They often carry the entire responsibility for their families on their own shoulders, as well as the challenge of getting training and meeting their employer's demands. Significant numbers of women of color come from cultures where they are the least likely to receive training or an education, compounding the difficulty of getting jobs with top pay or opportunities for advancement.

Because many ethnic cultures have more conservative ideas about family roles, many non-white women are now fighting the same stigma that white working women pioneers suffered in the '50s and '60s. Their husbands are threatened by their worker role and the perceived independence it brings, stay-at-home neighbors are critical, and extended family members suggest that the working woman is foolishly letting her family down. That's pressure—and it's very stressful.

Finally, the women of color who have made it into the executive suite or as entrepreneurs also feel the pressure to "be an active role model" and "help the other sisters," as one business owner told us. Expectations to speak to community and women's groups, be ever-available for media interviews, and be constantly singled out for praise or criticism, may add to her burden.

While some firms are starting to recognize the special life/job stresses for women generally, what is not so often addressed by many firms is the triple challenge faced by many minority women. These women of color struggle to balance not only work and family but also the often unspoken obligation to be the "keepers of culture." They put in long hours on the job, then go home to feed, clothe, and otherwise care for family members and somehow have to find time to teach their children the family's ancestral language, culture, and traditions. Observing cultural and religious holidays and being active in a community of ethnic peers is also on these women's "to-do" list. Employers who take the initiative to recognize and deal with these stresses will have an advantage over the competition in the employee recruitment sweepstakes. Methods to deal with these needs might include an expansion of training to deal with issues of cultural sensitivity and sex-role obligations, flexible work schedules, and "floating days" off that could be taken to observe cultural or religious holidays.

Optimistically, recent research on the perceived self-images of women and young girls shows that younger women of color, especially

African-Americans, see themselves more positively than their white peers. The self-concept of all girls starts to seriously erode in the span between ages eight to 14, but this loss is less severe for African-American teens. This appears to be due to the positive role models of women all around them, working outside the home and nurturing inside the home.

The moral of the story is: As business enters this new era of competition for skilled workers, it needs to pay special attention to family needs, especially the needs of women of all backgrounds in those families. Jobs will have to accommodate the changing roles for women, as well their spouses who are being forced to take a more active part in family responsibilities as Mom begins bringing home the bacon. It is also a time for business to acknowledge the strengths that people of various ethnic, cultural, and religious backgrounds can add to the workplace. These assets include the strong family values that most black, Asian, and, Hispanic workers bring to the job. This diversity can enhance the U.S. business environment. This is a most unusual consideration for the typical white male executive to make, since he has been brought up in the traditions of the American business world. Consequently, help will be needed.

Many companies are now hiring consulting firms and family/work specialists to design and direct programs for them. Others are seeking out members of their own staff whose life experiences or sensitivity have helped them identify the emerging crunch of new workers and relationship of family support policies to giving the business a competitive edge. Then, there are those few CEOs and managers who know that a business doesn't stay healthy over the years if society is crumbling around it. Since "family" is the basic unit of society, it only makes sense to attend to its needs. Whatever the motivation, the picture for the '90s is clear. Business will be highly involved in family matters.

4

WHAT BUSINESS NEEDS

Business needs to stay in business. Profitability and a good image are primary factors in making that happen. A profitable status and an impeccable reputation are products of fine management techniques and visionary leadership—both skills generally attributed to those in charge of the company. Their ultimate success, however, is heavily reliant on the behavior of company employees. Business is a fundamental social institution. Management depends on its employees to produce, to be loyal, to be there and be on time, to speak well of the company, and to give the best they have to their work.

All these attributes were an inherent part of the European tradition of apprenticeships. They resulted in lifelong commitments to one's craft, trade, or profession, but these traditions are almost nonexistent in the United States today. Job hopping, career switching, retraining, and dropping out have become the rule rather than the exception. Companies suffer great monetary losses when trained workers leave, and again when replacements are sought. Low morale and lower productivity are the result of absenteeism, lateness, or stressed-out employees. Consequently, what business needs in order to stay profitable and well thought of are policies that will increase employees' productivity, lower absenteeism, assure retention, and keep morale at a high level. These policies are closely related to the ability of the business to be "family-friendly."

PROFITABILITY

Economists have obfuscated the term "profit motive." If examined with a critical eye, all the key questions that revolve around the "profit motive" end not with some description of "the bottom line," but with a recognition of the simple fact that people seek to live as comfortably as possible, providing for themselves and their families. Corporations can write motivating mission statements with phrases relating to "acting rationally with an eye to costs and benefits." Managers and stockholders can deliver diatribes on price/earnings ratios, minimizing costs of capital, and optimizing profits. However, the reality of every business organization, from sole proprietorship to multinational conglomerate, is that it is made up of people who work in order to live well. Thus any quest for profitability has to address not only the question of how much money is left after costs, but also how those profits are going to be experienced by those who had a hand in creating them. Demographic changes and labor shortages of the '90s are making the workplace a buyer's market. Questions of company profitability and employee needs have become inextricably linked. Happy employees who work for an unprofitable employer will not be happy for long. But unhappy employees working for a profitable employer is a situation where both are doomed as well.

Understanding how to address the profitability aspect of creating family-supportive benefits can be a problem for company leaders. Douglas Phillips, senior director of corporate planning for Merck & Co., Inc., may have developed a way to do this. He claims that "value-added profit and loss statements" are a method for translating family support programs into dollars. Perhaps in the future we will see financial reports that recognize these realities. In the meantime, common sense tells us that recruitment advantages, retention, productivity, good public relations, low absenteeism, and high employee morale are what business needs to be profitable and healthy. In this chapter we will highlight the results of recent studies in these areas.

A GOOD IMAGE

If the actions of some businesses in the '80s epitomized the media slogan, "greed is good," then the '90s may well be known as the era of "responsible is beautiful." Scores of firms are scrambling to improve their public images in the face of increased public scrutiny and pressure from consumer watchdog groups. In an edition that has sold 800,000 copies, the Council on Economic Priorities issues ratings that grade firms based on records of their practices in affirmative action, child-care leave, employee profit sharing, environmental conscience, charitable donations, and worker safety, among other concerns. In 1991, top listed firms included Colgate Palmolive Co., General Mills, Kellogg Co., S.C. Johnson Co., and Supermarkets General, owner of Pathmark and Purity.

Businesses are finding that socially responsible actions not only enhance their images, they can increase profits as well. A recent Roper poll of 1,496 U.S. consumers revealed that 67% shop with an eye towards a firm's social performance and 52% said they would pay 10% more for a socially responsible product. A British cosmetics firm, the Body Shop, has experienced sales growth during the last decade of 50% annually to $143 million. The firm uses no animal testing in their products, doesn't advertise, and spends its profits on environmental clean-up projects. It also extensively educates its consumers both on its products (rejecting excessive beauty hype) and in its global activism. A Canadian grocery chain, Loblaws, has seen a 10–60% increase in a product's sales after it is labeled with the chain's environmental seal. Kinder, Lydenberg, Domini & Co. introduced the Domini Social Index or DSI of 400 U.S. companies that passed their screening on social issues. This fund's companies performed comparably with Standard and Poor's 500 Index from 1986 to 1990. Thus, it appears that the sometimes higher up front costs of acting responsibly are offset by increased sales volume of the socially responsible firms.

Corporate social responsibility is a term that has come to signify the dependence of a healthy society on actions taken by the private sector. It has evolved to be the criterion by which a company's public image is formed, linking workers, their families, and the community at large. Johnson & Johnson, the largest health-care company in the U.S. reflects this awareness in their credo, which reads in part:

> We are responsible to the communities in which we live and work and to the world community as well. We must be good citizens—support good works and charities and bear our fair share of taxes. We must encourage civic improvement and better health and education. We must maintain in good order the property we are privileged to use, protecting the environment and natural resources.

Philosophies such as this, followed by humanistic actions, result in a positive public perception that every company needs. Logan Hottle, director of "Live for Life," J&J's nationally acclaimed wellness program designed to improve the physical fitness and health of their employees, volunteers several hours of her time each week to help an adult learn to read. She said this kind of commitment is expected and is widely practiced at J&J.

Another firm practicing good citizenship is the Physio Control Corporation, a company in Washington state owned by Eli Lilly, where medical electronic products are made. As a matter of policy, Physio donates 3% of pretax profits to philanthropy, a rate that is three times higher than the average U.S. industry. But they are not alone. Levi-Strauss has been a pioneer in its efforts to contribute funds to fight the spread of AIDS in the Bay Area and has a "Social Benefits Program" designed to encourage employees to join in community activities. Levi-Strauss will give grants from $500 to $1,500 to organizations in which employees are active, depending on the organization's budget size. ARCO's social conscience is reflected in its donations to social service organizations and its matching funds program. It matches employee and retiree gifts up to $20,000 on a two-for-one basis. It also publishes a summary of its social responsibility activities, as does KIRO, Inc., a CBS–affiliated radio and TV station in Seattle. In 1982 employees of J. C. Penney in Dallas raised money to publish a cookbook of employees' recipes. Proceeds from the sale of the book went to the local chapter of the Salvation Army. Each year, managers at General Mills, Inc. in Minneapolis must state their plans to get involved in the community. Those that do will be eligible for the company's executive compensation incentive plan, a bonus of up to 20% of regular salary. Control Data Corporation is another Minneapolis-based company with a social conscience. Chairman William Norris defined his company's mission in part as "addressing society's major unmet needs as profitable business opportunities." This concept appears throughout the company's literature and is lived out in their commitment to hiring new employees from a once depressed area of the inner city, now the site of a thriving Control Data production plant.

The firms mentioned here are but a few that realize that human capital is the asset vital to a business's success in the '90s. Employees don't raise their families in a vacuum. Prosperous companies rely on productive workers who come from strong, stable families, which in turn are bred by strong, stable communities.

RECRUITMENT ADVANTAGES

The years of free-choice-in-hiring are over. The slash in birth rates after 1960 has caused the numbers of young people available for jobs to decline sharply—right through the year 2010. Intense competition for workers has begun, and it is being felt worldwide. By mid-1990, 51

Japanese companies went out of business due to lack of staff—more than double the previous year's number of labor-related bankruptcies. With unemployment at a minimal 2.1% in 1990, Japanese employers now must compete for workers and assist the workers they have to be more competitive. According to the Hudson Institute, only 15% of work force entrants in the U.S. will be young, native-born white males. This means employers will be looking for women, older citizens, nonwhite, and perhaps noncitizen workers. A company's ability to recruit those who are best trained and will best "fit in," depends primarily on a combination of the salaries, benefits, and work environments they offer workers.

U.S. Sprint calls its Workplace Flexibility Program, "a cost-effective model to meet the recruitment and retention needs of our business units." The company, based in Kansas City, Missouri, has 16,000 employees in 700 locations. Their program, started in August 1989, includes flextime, compressed work schedules, part-time jobs and job-sharing. In their "flextour" program, employees pre-select an alternative start time that remains constant for intervals set by managers. Compressed work weeks allow employees to work up to 12 hours a day for three and a half to four days. Sprint cites the benefits of reduced operating expenses per employee and an enhanced ability to recruit skilled employees to work undesirable shifts in exchange for days off.

At Stride Rite, Karen Leibold, director of program development for the child-care centers, says that they help the company with recruitment and retention. "People who take jobs here stay because of the child-care center . . . It helps productivity and morale."

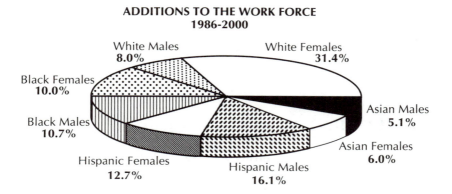

ADDITIONS TO THE WORK FORCE
1986-2000

White Males 8.0%
White Females 31.4%
Black Females 10.0%
Asian Males 5.1%
Black Males 10.7%
Asian Females 6.0%
Hispanic Females 12.7%
Hispanic Males 16.1%

Source: Bureau of Labor Statistics

As early as 1987, Arizona Bancwest Corporation realized that competitiveness was paramount in recruiting and retaining workers. As a result, the company instituted a flexible benefits plan. Don Lindner, executive vice president and manager of the Phoenix-based bank's administrative division, explained that the new plan may not save the corporation money, but costs will be offset by good employee relations. The bank's work force has changed dramatically in the past 15 years, and the bank could no longer meet individual needs with the former benefits plan.

PRODUCTIVITY

Getting workers to work more efficiently and creatively will rank among managers' top priorities for the '90s. Productivity measures work output. It affects a company's competitiveness, quality of products, and reputation for service. A measure of our nation's productivity is reflected in our standard of living and work culture. The current level of productivity of American workers is growing less than half as fast as it did in the quarter-century after World War II. Another reason for economic concern is the downward slide of the U.S.'s share of technology-based outputs in the world market—dropping from 27% to 25% during the past 25 years. Japan's share meanwhile nearly tripled from 7% to 20%.

Family/work issues play a large role in work output. The human factor in productivity is subtle and usually underestimated, if not ignored. Yet, productivity studies show that the human factor contributes from 10% to 25% to productivity growth. In labor-intensive service business and in government, people account for 70% to 85% of all costs. "The manager who ignores the human side of the enterprise does so at his own peril," said Jerome Rosow, president of the Work in America Institute, in 1977. Fifteen years later, this policy is more relevant now than ever before. Productivity is definitely in the hands of the workers.

Stress is the enemy of productivity, and the number-one stressor in the workplace is family problems. A study conducted by John P. Fernandez surveyed 5,000 management and production employees to ascertain their views on work/family conflicts. Of the sample, 41% were crafts employees and of these, 63% were women. Women comprised 40% of the management sample. Sixty-seven percent of all these employees surveyed believed that child-care problems exacted a high price in unproductive use of employees' time and minds during the work day.

- 77% of women and 73% of men with children under 18 said they deal with family issues during working hours
- 48% of women and 25% of men admitted to spending unproductive time at work because of child-care issues.

The ability of the employer to alleviate stress coming from any source—but especially stress caused by family concerns—is the major factor in managing and maintaining a high level of productivity. The state of California has discovered that employees who work from home were 3% to 5% more effective than if they had been in the office from nine in the morning until five at night. Their supervisors issued the ratings while participating in a state study on telecommuting. In addition to increased productivity, there were the benefits of reducing the need for office space in the agencies and fewer peak-hour commute trips for workers, thus affecting energy savings and reducing pollution. It also solved the after-school care need for many parents.

LOW ABSENTEEISM

If one can use absences from work as a measure of productivity, the statistics documenting missed days of work by more than 8,000 employees in Portland, Oregon, will be of interest, A. C. Emlin and P. E. Koren conducted a study of these employees and reported that:

- Women with children under 18 miss work an average of 11.9 days compared with women without underage children who miss 9.6 days
- Men with children under eighteen missed 8.6 days compared with 7.6 days missed by men with no underage children

Again, Fernandez's study has relevance here. It delved more deeply into issues of absences, reporting:

- Caring for a sick child was the reason given for missed work by 56% of the women who were absent one to three times in the previous year, 78% of those with four to six absences and 82% of those who missed more than six days of work

- Comparable figures for men were 33%, 54%, and 58%, respectively, still significant but dramatically lower
- 77% of women and 73% of men reported having dealt with family-related issues during working hours
- Employees with children under eighteen are most likely to miss work, come to work late, leave early, and deal with family issues during work hours because of family/work conflicts and child-care problems

The high rate of absences from work among women between the ages of 25 and 34 stems from the fact that such women are likely to have young children and need to take time off from work to care for them, according to the August 1990 issue of *Employment in Perspective: Women in the Labor Force*, published by the Bureau of Labor Statistics. Among married mothers whose youngest child was under age six, 11.5% were absent from work during an average week in 1989. Contrast this figure with the average rate for all working women, 6.6%, or for men, 4%. These figures have motivated many employers to start to figure out ways to help these mothers find reliable quality child care and special care for ill children.

Diane Keel Atkins, the director of corporate child-care services at Hoffman LaRoche in Nutley, New Jersey, explained, "Having an on-site child-care facility has definitely reduced our tardiness and absenteeism rates and has increased productivity. It has also been a great recruitment and retention tool for us." Their center, started in 1979, is open from 6:45 A.M. to 6:00 P.M. Fifty-five children from two and one-half to 12 years attend, but a doubling of the center's size is expected by the end of 1990.

A rural North Carolina hosiery manufacturer, Neuville Industries, established a day-care center to *save* the company money. In their field, average annual turnover nationally is normally as high as 50–100%, while locally it can range from 5–10%. Their goal was to reduce that rate to 4–8%. By May of 1987, they told *USA Today* that they had reduced turnover to about 1%, in large measure due to their child-care initiatives. They also report savings of $20,000–$25,000 in payroll taxes and have experienced substantial gains in productivity. In 1988 Dominion Bankshares of Roanoke, Virginia, reported a drop of 31% in absenteeism and a 10% reduction in turnover among employees with children in their new child-care center. They claim a workplace cost savings of over $100,000, more than offsetting the costs of running the center.

If workers are not on-the-job, the job is definitely not being done. A cohort of productivity, absenteeism is a great cost to business. S. A. Youngblood and K. Chambers-Cook in their workplace studies noted that employee absences decreased by 19% after the companies they surveyed started a day-care center. In addition, annual turnover dropped an astonishing 63% in the year following institution of these centers.

RETENTION OF EMPLOYEES

The primary reason for retaining employees is, for most employers, the positive impact it has on the bottom line. The high cost of replacing and retraining an employee—up to five times annual salary for a high-level employee, 20% of the annual salary for low-level employees—makes turnover an expensive proposition. The average cost to properly train a corporate employee for most jobs is $25,000. It takes at least $50,000 to train a highly skilled professional. Because these figures do not reflect personal costs to the employee, the overall price is even higher. Retention, then, becomes a critical factor in profitability.

There is also a high correlation between turnover and commitment to a company or employer. That commitment can be gained, according to Katherine Esty of Ibis Consulting in Cambridge,Massachusetts, by appropriate company intervention at critical points in an employee's career. Those points are at: hiring; pregnancy, for female employees; and as retirement is being considered. Intervening with attractive benefits at these points can greatly increase the likelihood of employees staying on and working hard for the company.

Many companies have found family-oriented benefits help solve retention problems. AEtna Life and Casualty Co. reports a 50% reduction in the number of employees leaving the company because of family demands after the company implemented its family leave policy. Sherry Herchenroether of AEtna told the "National Report on Work and Family" in October 1989, that the company had instituted the policy because, "We felt we were losing too many good people. With our new family leave policy, a better percentage of people will return than before we had this program." When Intermedic, Inc., a Texas-based medical instruments firm, opened a large employer-sponsored day-care center, its first-year employee turnover fell 23% and 15,000 fewer hours were lost to employee absence. In another example, at Nyloncraft, Inc., of Indiana, 85% of their employees are female. They were experiencing turnover rates of 57% in 1979, but after spending $250,000 on a day-care center, turnover immediately dropped to 31%, and by 1988 it was down to only 3%.

Some employers are finding employee housing assistance also helps retention, enabling commuters to move closer to the workplace or providing an incentive for employees to stay with the company when relocation is required. Currently more than 300 companies are providing housing assistance to non-management employees at one or more locations according to a recent Rutgers University study. Colgate-Palmolive Company allows employees to designate a portion of their benefits package to contribute to closing costs on a home purchase, a benefit offered at no additional cost. It also has a group mortgage origination program that has achieved a discount based on pooling funds, saving participating employees about 1% on home mortgages: First Fidelity Savings and Loan of Raleigh, North Carolina, offers $6,000 in down-payment loans to employees, forgiven at a rate of $2,000 annually in order to encourage longevity. It is thus reducing the high turnover rate among entry-level employees. Church and Dwight, Co., the parent company of Arm & Hammer products, has a similar program of forgivable down-payment loans. These firms have calculated these loans to be a no-cost benefit because they would spend much more than the amount of the loan in recruiting and training fees to replace an employee. Other companies are offering purchase guarantees to home builders, resulting in discounts that can be passed on the employees. David C. Schwartz, director of the American Affordable Housing Institute at Rutgers University, predicts an explosion of interest in employer-provided housing in the near future, including potential federal legislation by 1992.

BENEFITS OF FAMILY FRIENDLINESS

There are four clear-cut ways business can meet its needs for profitability and a good image in the '90s, by: (1) meeting employee's family needs, (2) providing ongoing job training, (3) increasing participation of employees in problem solving, and (4) exercising corporate social responsibility. We have seen what employee's family needs are and how they can be met. The following are examples of the relevance of these programs to meeting business needs as well.

In a report on family benefits the U.S. Chamber of Commerce asserts that responsiveness to workers' needs in the home front "can yield higher employee morale, productivity, recruitment and retention potential, as well as stem excessive absenteeism." Steven Shanker, a vice president at Union Bank in Monterey Park, California, agrees: "There is

---

WORK & FAMILY BENEFITS

PROVIDED BY 837 MAJOR U.S. EMPLOYERS IN 1990

- 64% offer some kind of child-care assistance, of these:
  - 89% offer dependent-care spending accounts
  - 41% offer resource/referral services
  - 9% offer employer-sponsored child-care center
- 32% offer some kind of eldercare assistance, of these:
  - 88% offer a dependent-care spending account
  - Only a small percentage offer counseling, resource/referral or long-term care insurance
- 54% offer flexible scheduling arrangements, of these:
  - 76% offer flextime
  - 67% offer part-time employment
- 44% offer unpaid parental leave
- 5% offer paid parental leave
- 23% offer paid leave to employees to care for sick family members
- 21% offer unpaid leave to care for sick family members
- 12% offer adoption benefits in the form of reimbursement assistance

Source: Hewitt Associates, October 1990

---

a direct connection between the existence of the (Union Bank) day-care center and my job performance." Union Bank provides $150,000 the first year to subsidize the start up and operation of the child-care complex with classrooms and play areas. It would normally cost Shanker $700 per month at another local quality facility; he now pays only $520 via a convenient payroll deduction pretax dollar plan. He can also visit his children during his lunch break and is close by in case of an emergency. In its first year alone, California Union Bank's on-site child-care center reported more than $200,000 in savings directly attributable to the center. Those using the child-care center averaged 1.7 days fewer absences than parents not using the center. Employees out on maternity leave returned 1.2 weeks sooner because the center was accessible and available for newborns. Union Bank also claims they got $40,000 worth of free public relations because of their on-site child-care center. It was featured in television news spots, a radio show, and in a plethora of news articles.

A study by the National Council of Jewish Women also found that the benefit of child-care supports may outweigh the costs. Their research revealed that the percentage of women with problems arranging child care fell from 55% to 2% when employers offered four or more child-care supports in their benefits package. At SAS Institute, a computer software firm in North Carolina that provides free on-site child care, the turnover rate is only 7% annually, compared to the software industry averages of 25% per year.

A 1984 survey reported that providing child/eldercare benefits gives employers an edge:

- 90% reported improved morale
- 85% reported enhanced recruitment
- 65% reported decreased turnover

Child-care considerations definitely have a positive effect on a company's image. The Bureau of National Affairs surveyed 691 employees whose children attended company-operated or -sponsored child care and found the following:

- 63% had a more positive attitude about their company because of child-care assistance
- 69% were encouraged to stay with their company because of child-care assistance
- 50% recommended their company to others as a place to work because of child-care assistance
- 38% selected their company because of child-care assistance

At Chubb & Sons, Inc., job-sharing is improving retention and allowing valued employees to stay in the mainstream of the corporation, even though they are taking some time off for family responsibilities. Two underwriters divided the client pool and each worked three days per week, allowing a day overlap for communicating. Each received a full benefits package and two-thirds salary during the year the job-sharing agreement was in effect.

The computer industry, which has an estimated 12% to 18% annual turnover rate, can definitely benefit from programs which reduce loss of employees. SAS Institute, Inc., in Cary, North Carolina, has found that an on-site child-care center has reduced turnover in this software company to less than 6.4% in 1988. The care center concept has been part of the company's operation since 1981. The lower 6.4% turnover rate is impressive given North Carolina has only a 3% unemployment rate, and competition for qualified workers is intense.

The wide range of work- and family-life support activities provided by Merck & Co., a New Jersey pharmaceutical firm, yields an employee turnover rate that is 50% below the industry average, which translates into a savings of $60 million a year. In addition, Merck has 35 applicants for every job opening, instead of the average five applicants seen by most American businesses in the late '80s. Douglas Phillips, senior director of corporate planning for Merck, says the decision to invest in a new position valued at $25,000 annually is equivalent to a capital investment with a net present value of $1,000,000. "Effective family issues management adds to the organization and to shareholder value; human resources should be considered an investment, not a cost," Phillips told a 1988 conference sponsored by the Institute for American Values. Phillips has called family issues management "the sleeping giant of productivity improvement."

Workers who resign from companies that are not family-friendly will probably not leave the work force entirely. Rather, they will join a firm whose policies on flexible hours and/or child-care and eldercare benefits more closely fit their own needs. Several factors in determining whether or not a firm has progressive work/family policies is the firm's attitude about women's roles in the world of work, the belief by that firm in the importance of children to the overall social and economic well-being of the society, and the extent to which that firm has already been impacted by the burgeoning labor shortage.

ON-THE-JOB TRAINING

In addition to the family-friendly policies that give a business an edge in attracting and retaining good employees, there are other ways it can improve workers' job satisfaction and performance. Key among these is on-the-job training.

Forty-five billion dollars were spent on formal training programs by American business in 1990. The necessity for this expenditure is made clear by the projection that unless American business continues, and indeed enhances, this investment by 2010, about 23 million jobs will go unfilled, many due to educational deficiencies. In the '80s employers provided a variety of programs for their employees, including such topics as:

- Management Skills Development
- Technical Skills Knowledge
- Communication Skills
- Basic Computer Skills
- Customer Relations
- Personal Growth
- Employee Relations
- Wellness/Fitness
- Balancing Career & Family
- Remedial Basic Education

Training methods varied from use of lectures, videotapes, slides, role plays, games, simulations, and self-assessment, to video-, telephone- or computer-conferencing.

The reason for this significant expenditure of time, effort, and money is recognition of the simple reality that American business became so consumed with complex management techniques and bean-counting by newly minted MBAs that it forgot about people—employees and customers. And America has paid a price for that in increased foreign competition and diminished share of the global market. A belief in the people who work for business must translate into an investment in them. If respected management expert Warren Bennis is right when he says, "American organizations have been overmanaged and underled," then the '90s should become the era of leadership. Workers want and deserve managers who will lead, motivate, coach, counsel, and teach them the skills they need for their own self-empowerment and on-the-job success.

The U.S. is in the midst of an information revolution demanding workers with expanding knowledge of techniques and markets as well as an ability to meet consumers' expectations. On-the-job training is key to imparting these necessary skills. This training can take the form of the formal seminars and less formal workshops, but it can also be powerfully accomplished by "mentoring." Employees who are allowed to "try it out," "take a risk," or "use their instincts" while having a senior adviser, coach, and confidant, will develop into the loyal innovators that build sales and reputations. "The best way to really train people is with an experienced mentor and on the job," explained Bim Black, leader of Teleflex, a $150 million engineering applications company. When mentoring can take place one-on-one, it can signal an attitude in a company that people believe in each other. This is the key to the success of Tandem Computer, according to founder James G. Treybig. His philosophy is that "(1) all people are good; (2) people, workers, management and company are all the same thing; (3) every single person in the company must understand the essence of the business; (4) every employee must benefit from the company's success; (5) you must create an environment where all the above can happen."

"The critical limitation to companies achieving their goals," explains Claudine Paris, former training director for Big M, Inc., an East Coast clothing retailer, "is their failure to develop and train their people. You can have all the computers and hi-tech equipment and facilities and plans in the world, but if you don't develop your people, you won't be successful." Her thoughts are amplified by Tom Peters and Nancy Austin, authors of *A Passion for Excellence* (1985). They advocate what they call "overinvestment" and "upskilling" as the needed goals in employee development:

> Businessland, in an across-the-board terrible year in the personal computer industry, found it could afford a 540-person direct sales force in addition to those in their retail outlets. Moreover, the company saw fit to invest $600 a month training each already highly qualified person. The reward: 198% sales growth to $267 million in 1985.

In another instance, Metal Forming and Coining of Maumee, Ohio, employs only 70 people yet, for the past seven years they have provided an education benefit to its employees both hourly and salaried. The company grossed $12 million in 1990 and their chairman and president Mike Czerniak credits half the company's sales increases to its education investment.

One way to try to create this rewarding and successful environment is to offer opportunities for peer training. One retailer found that as her company grew, employees jumped at the chance to train newcomers. This enthusiasm has improved not only the quality of training for the new workers, but the morale of the seasoned workers who were chosen or allowed to train. This leads also to greater feelings of employee participation and ownership—ownership in their work, the outcomes, the products or services and, ultimately, the profitability of the entire firm.

INCREASING WORKER PARTICIPATION

The 1990s will also see an increasing number of businesses embracing the idea that a way to boost productivity and retention is to increase worker participation in corporate planning and decisions. Using one method, the work-team concept, teams of five to 12 multi-skilled employees work under little supervision at a specified task. About 36% of U.S. companies report more participatory workplace practices, up from 18% in 1987. A recent survey of 476 Fortune 1000 companies found 46% had some employees in self-managed work teams, compared with 27% three years ago. Procter & Gamble, Boeing, Digital Equipment, and GE are among those firms that claim this approach elevates worker knowledge, commitment, and output. While manufacturing applications are more prevalent, some service providers are trying the work team approach. AT&T Credit Corp. in Morristown, New Jersey, found that using whole teams to process leave applications doubled daily production. Team members at the Shenandoah Life Insurance Co. in Roanoke, Virginia, were able to increase their volume of work by 33%, reducing staffing needs and cutting costs by $200,000 a year.

For example, at Johnsonville Foods in Sheboygan, Wisconsin, workers have the authority to hire and fire each other, buy equipment, and plan the budget. This level of employee self-determination came about as a result of prior poor performance, workplace accidents, and other costly errors. CEO and owner Ralph Stayer decided eight years ago to change the way his firm was doing business. He told the Associated Press, "It isn't a soft or crazy deal. I'm a real hard-nosed pragmatic guy. . . . Teach people to do for themselves, this way you get a far better performance." Since 1982, Johnsonville sales have increased more than 20% annually and productivity has increased 50% since 1986.

Firms like General Mills, IBM, and Goodyear have employees working in teams without bosses to set profit goals, write schedules, develop products, meet customers, and write budgets. General Mills manager Pat McNulty expects productivity to be 30%–40% higher than at traditional plants. He explains, "Nobody knows the job as well as those doing it. If you empower those people to make the decisions, they make good ones." A General Mills worker, Rhonda Lunsford, adds, "You feel like you're going to your own business, not like you're going to do something for somebody else." Workers at Chaparral Steel in Midlothian, Texas have traveled the globe to evaluate suppliers and make purchasing decisions. Who better to decide what equipment should be purchased than those who will be using it daily? One lathe operator found a machine that cost half the $1.5 million budgeted for it. Clearly, these new work arrangements are not confined to white-collar or professional jobs. NUMMI, a joint venture of Toyota and GM promotes partnerships with employees, restructuring to operate more efficiently, and actively tapping employee ideas in the process.

There is a downside to this management approach: Workers have to want to take a leadership role. They can't just be the kind of person who wants to sit back and be told what to do. Managers have to learn how to give up authority and be willing to reward this kind of initiative and decision making. Some labor officials have also bemoaned the reduction in promotion possibilities inherent in a peer team approach, and in some instances, seniority rights are lost. Johnsonville now provides no cost-of-living increases or seniority raises. Employees receive additional salary only if they assume more responsibility, though the company paid out 28% of pretax profits in employee bonuses. "I don't get a lot of pressure from above," said worker Michelle Stock. "I'm not just standing there doing my thing. I'm paying attention. You're thinking about what's going on. You're thinking about the results." While such an approach may shake up the status quo, clearly there are rewards for employees and employers alike when you hear workers talking like this and see positive bottom-line results of the sort experienced by Johnsonville, General Mills, Chaparrel Steel, and many others.

This trend towards participatory management bodes well not only for increased corporate productivity but also signals an atmosphere where employees' work/family concerns can be aired and resolved with less fear of reprisal. As workers take more control over how they are to do their jobs and how they are to be held accountable, issues like hours punched into a time clock become less important. Even the most skeptical manager is less likely to be concerned about an employee's

---

WHAT ARE EMPLOYER INCENTIVES FOR BEING FAMILY-FRIENDLY?

- A boost to commitment and morale
- A good image/favorable free publicity
- Recruitment advantages
- Increased productivity
- Less absenteeism & tardiness
- Retention of employees/reduced turnover
- Greater flexibility in employees' available work hours
- Less stress for working parents
- Shorter maternity leaves

leaving work early to pick up an ill child, if he/she sees that person as a productive worker meeting mutually arrived at production/service goals.

THE UNIQUE DILEMMA OF THE SMALL FIRM

Almost one-half (26.2 million) of all American workers are employed by small businesses of fewer than 100 employees, according to the U.S. Small Business Administration. Employers of fewer than 25 persons provide jobs for 17.9 million workers, or 30.3% of the work force. Forty-four percent of the workers in firms with fewer than 100 employees are women. Many of these workers are without important workplace benefits. In 1983 only 38.7% of businesses with fewer than 25 employees offered employees a health plan. An even smaller number offer comprehensive work/family programs. This puts small firms at a competitive disadvantage. In its May 1985 publication, *The State of Small Business: Report of the President*, the SBA reports that "A small business's ability to attract and maintain a quality workforce is directly related to the benefits it offers. . . . Firms offering equal wages but better benefits are better able to attract more productive workers and, as a consequence, increase their competitiveness in the marketplace."

It is clear that small businesses are concerned about family issues for the same reasons large firms are—to be competitive. Hal Wood, president of The Little People Day Schools in Norristown, Pennsylvania, told *Entrepreneur Magazine*, "In many areas of the country, including ours, unemployment is very low and competition for workers can get fierce. Companies offering some type of daycare program will have the competitive edge when it comes to attracting and retaining a stable workplace."

Smaller firms not knowing where to begin in providing family assistance, may wish to get some advice from a child-care consultant. These professionals can help assess employee child-care needs, conduct a cost/benefit analysis, explain all the options, and assist in developing a model appropriate to the smaller company's short- and long-term needs.

The easiest way for a small firm to help its employees with child- or eldercare needs is to set up a flexible spending account, also called a pretax dollar account or dependent care assistance program. Employees put a percentage of each paycheck into a fund maintained by the employer. The employer then uses the monies in this account to pay dependent-care expenses up to $5,000 per year, the maximum allowed for married couples filing jointly. It is an ideal plan for a small business because it is relatively simple to set up and only involves the initial start-up and regular bookkeeping fees. The funds in the account are exempt from federal and state taxes (in most areas) as well as Social Security and FICA.

Two other suggestions that may benefit smaller firms with child-care concerns are voucher or vendor programs. Those involve a bulk-rate purchase of day-care center slots by the employer that can be sold to employees at a substantially reduced price. Small businesses that don't have enough employees to justify establishing their own child-care center can also work together with other nearby small businesses and develop support or run a cooperative facility. In Tyson's Corner, Virginia, a consortium of 22 local area businesses funded a nonprofit, tax-exempt center near their offices. The Tyson's Corner Play and Learn Childrens' Center is operated by a board comprised mainly of parents. The founding members' firms can continue to reserve spaces for their employees by contributing $1.00 per space, while new businesses can join by contributing a higher amount per employee to the center's operating budget. The initial $100,000 contributed by the founding firms has yielded such a popular and successful result that it has become a model for three other child-care centers. Seven TV and radio stations in the Washington, D.C., area created the Broadcaster's Child Development Center in a conveniently located school. Eight employers including Lockheed, NBC, Columbia Pictures, and Universal Studios responded to a $10,000 solicitation from the Burbank California Unified School District. Together they renovated an empty school building for child care. In return each employer received 20 child-care slots for their employees' children.

Small business may, under current federal laws, deduct payments to dependent-care consultants, payments to center providers, subsidies to parents for child/eldercare costs, referral agency fees, or the annual costs of operating a dependent-care center. Capital expenditures for buildings, equipment, and renovations can also be depreciated.

We found that many small business owners to whom we spoke were willing to go to great lengths to keep a valued employee, thus agreeing to parental leave, a reduced work schedule, or establishment of a pretax dollar dependent-care account, if it meant keeping that person with the firm. Often these arrangements are not part of formal policy but are negotiated on a case-by-case basis. Indeed several representatives of small firms admitted to opposing state or federal legislation that would have mandated any of the above benefits, citing concerns about governmental interference in the financial viability of their business. We believe that these concerns may be unfounded. This opinion is confirmed in the survey findings of Barbara Butler and Janis Wasserman, researchers who interviewed 30 small organizations in New York and New Jersey and concluded, "The fact is that small businesses choose their workers carefully, have little overlap of personnel, and value good workers highly, so highly that they are generally more than willing to negotiate an arrangement that will satisfy a valued employee's need to spend some reasonable amount of time parenting, as well as the employer's need to have that person back as soon as possible. There is little evidence that firms in states with legislation mandating disability leave or those in the majority of nations of the world with paid infant-care leave policies have suffered financially."

The financial worry most mentioned by many small business owners is that they will wind up paying two salaries for one job: that of the original worker on leave and that of the temporary replacement. These costs may not be as high as presumed at first glance. The costs of both the original and the temporary workers salaries may be offset by the probability that the employee not granted the leave might choose to withdraw from the work force. This would cause the employer to bear the cost of recruiting and training a new employee. While the original employee is on partial salary during leave, a terrific employee incentive to return, often a replacement worker is available at a lesser cost. Smaller employers also stand to benefit the most from proposals to establish employer-employee contributions toward a disability insurance fund that would defray some of these salary costs.

EMPLOYEE BENEFITS IN THE YEAR 2000

Managers of both large and small firms used to be warned not to ask about an employee's home life. Now they are encouraged to use surveys or focus groups to find out if workers need child care and other work and family benefits. The reason is simple—more intense competition for workers due to growing labor shortages in key businesses. Citing this shortage, a survey done by the International Foundation of Employee Benefit Plans predicted that employers will respond to this concern by implementing more family-friendly benefits by the year 2000 (see page 74).

Business needs to help generate strong families. While companies are attempting to both be profitable and project a good image, workers want

NON-TRADITIONAL BENEFITS FOR THE WORK FORCE OF 2000	THOSE CURRENTLY OFFERING	WILL OFFER BY YEAR 2000
Offering child-care resource and referral service	29%	75%
Subsidation od child-care expenses	12%	52%
On- or near-site child-care facilities	7%	35%
Sick child-care facility/ home-based care	3%	28%
School/camp advising services	3%	14%
Off-hour babysitting	1%	9%
Eldercare resource and referral service	11%	64%
Subsidization od eldercare expenses	3%	23%
Elder respite care	1%	19%
Part-time employment	80%	94%
Flexible hours	52%	86%
Family leave	49%	84%
Job-sharing	24%	67%
Telecommuting	15%	52%

Source: International Foundation of Employee Benefit Plans

to keep their families together and contribute to the larger community. The needs of both groups can be answered simultaneously. When family-friendly practices are in place, both sets of needs have a good chance of being met—and both sets of goals can be achieved. In changing the benefits and policies paradigm from the outdated model of the '50s to strategies and practices that embrace the character of the worker of the '90s, if females, minorities, and family-oriented males are not considered, business hardly has a chance of "staying in business."

5

WHAT BUSINESSES ARE TRYING— MODELS FOR THE '90S

Historically, American companies have met society's demands for profitable business enterprises. Where perhaps American business and government have fallen down is in response to the greater societal need for help in achieving family stability. While many Western countries depend on their governments to provide the supports needed for families, the United States is increasingly dependent on private business to answer workers' needs. Some firms have risen to the challenges impressively.

This chapter introduces 14 companies that are leading the way through innovations in family caretaking. We tried to select a representative cross section of those firms embarking on work/family initiatives in terms of the following: geographic location across the United States; size; diversity in type of firm—service, manufacturing, and product-based—and age, ranging from established firms to high-tech ventures. From those headquartered in the East we feature Merck, Time Warner, Ernst and Young, Johnson & Johnson, AEtna, IBM, and Stride-Rite; from the West and Northwest: Levi Strauss, Security Pacific Bank, Microsoft, Carver, and St. Francis; and from the Midwest: Hewitt Associates and 3M Corporation. The firms we selected range in size from fewer than 200 employees to more than 50,000 workers in the U.S. They produce goods and services from books to bandages, consulting services to software packages. They also show a great diversity in internal organization, from traditional labor/management-strong union models to innovative, nonhierarchical team orientations.

The common thread among these companies is a commitment to viewing the individual worker as a valued resource and a recognition that the individual doesn't come to work out of a vacuum. These firms recognize that workers are part of families and that families are changing. With these changes come needs heretofore unrecognized by American business in any organized fashion. These firms have created new organizations. The structures take many forms from relatively simple programs of flexible work hours and cafeteria benefit plans to capital-intensive company-sponsored child-care and eldercare centers to comprehensive work/family awareness training programs.

Other corporate giants such as Exxon, Du Pont, and Kodak are offering employees new options and services over and above the usual benefit packages of health insurance, retirement funds, and bonus checks. They are investing in programs such as child care or eldercare, flexible scheduling, job-sharing, extended leaves, and a smorgasbord of other employee benefits. They are doing this partly to maintain a recruitment edge and insure their ability to get the best workers, and partly to keep the bargain made by American businesses in the '40s—to take care of their workers. Small businesses are having a harder time developing benefits that help relieve family stress. They are, however, building new coalitions and inventing creative ways to provide many of the same support systems to employees that the large companies now have.

A number of model programs are described below, as are the attitudes and effort involved in making them work. We also examine the results. Employers are finding that it truly pays to meet the real needs of employees and their families. Those listed here provide illustrations that we hope will both inspire and teach. Many other businesses have similar programs or are trying other routes. However, these companies serve as fine examples as to the motivation, processes, and results being achieved by management that is forward-looking and socially conscious. They offer models that can be transferred to other settings and ideas that can be adapted to different times and places. These organizations have been trendsetters as *companies that care.*

A LONG HISTORY OF WORK/FAMILY SENSITIVITY

Merck & Company, Inc.

Merck & Company, Inc., is the largest manufacturer of prescription drugs in the United States. It is also viewed as a premier research institution, devoting 12% of total sales income to this effort. The company has been a leader in developing anti-inflammatory medications; Merck scientists also discovered vitamin B_{12} and streptomycin. It is not just in the scientific area, however, where Merck is a pioneer. Its policies on pay, benefits, working hours, leaves of absence, and child care have made the company one of the nation's leaders in helping employees balance work and family life.

Fortune magazine recently ranked Merck first among the 10 most admired companies in America. They received this rating for their quality of management, wise use of corporate assets, quality products, long-term investment value, financial soundness, and the ability to attract, develop, and keep talented people.

Merck is no newcomer to work/family sensitivity. The firm has a 30-year commitment to maternity benefits and over the years has developed an entire package of employee inducements, not just those related to child care, that make it a progressive employer. It is one of the premier firms in the nation in terms of pay, pension, and health benefits. An excerpt from the company's position paper reveals how this employee-oriented attitude came about: "It is Merck's strong belief that family support policies and practices can help significantly to reduce the stress the employee feels from the increased demands of a fuller lifestyle. The reduction of stress has an obvious benefit to the employee; it also can positively affect the employee's productivity on the job."

In 1979, Merck established an innovative program to help all employees rethink their attitudes about women and minorities. The educational program consists of seminars in affirmative action, a training program for all production supervisors, shop stewards, and union officials. All of Merck's 19,000 U.S. employees have spent a day reviewing case studies and watching films representing real-life examples of sexual harassment and racial stereotyping relating to the hiring, treatment, and promotion of women and minorities. Five hundred senior managers were initially trained and then became trainers for the rest of the work force. This educational program has won numerous awards and is now being replicated by more than 50 major firms in the U.S. It has also started to pay off with women in top jobs jumping from only 1% in 1981 to 7% in 1990, with a target of 20% by 1995.

Another innovation of Merck & Company, introduced in 1980, is its donation of a large sum of money to a group of employees to start a near-site day-care center. Located just a mile from the company's headquarters in Rahway, New Jersey, the center receives office services such as telephones and printing from Merck, but the facility is self-supporting and is governed as a non-profit organization by a board composed of parents. There is normally a sizable waiting list of parents wanting to get this excellent, convenient care for their infants and toddlers. Merck recently committed an additional $500,000 to expand the center. This is the kind of family-friendly thinking that results in a tangible benefit badly needed by many working parents.

"The center was expected to be self-sufficient in three years, but it was self-sufficient in 18 months," said J. Douglas Phillips, senior director of corporate planning. Phillips believes that family issues management is "the sleeping giant of productivity improvement. Corporations have to realize that people don't leave their home problems at home and their work problems at work." These work/family options engender a feeling of job security by employees that is often cited by Merck managers as the reason they are known as a company with strong employee loyalty. One Merck employee, Diane Dalinsky, summarized well the feelings of many at the company, "With all the benefits you have here, it makes you think twice about going anywhere else."

Flexible hours are another concession to the realities of family responsibilities. Workers can come in as late as 9:30 A.M. or as early as 7:00 A.M. Part-time work and telecommuting for new mothers are also being tried in the company. Merck grants its employees two parental leave options: a six-week child-care leave with full pay and six months' leave with job security and benefits, or eighteen months' leave with benefits and the chance to return to the same or similar position if an opening exists. Some divisions pool employee responsibilities, having previously engaged in cross-training to assure all jobs get done. At other times temporary workers are utilized to do the jobs of those on parental leave or off the job with some other sort of temporary disability. Merck has gained recognition for its innovation among those who study corporate benefits and is included in the book *The Best Companies for Women* by Baila Zeitz and Lorraine Dusky.

A COMPREHENSIVE FAMILY-FRIENDLY PACKAGE

Time Warner, Inc.

Time Warner, one of the world's leaders in publishing, motion pictures, and communications, has a comprehensive package of benefits for families, including flexible hours and workplaces and part-time work. A flexible benefits plan includes parental leave, counseling, lunchtime workshops, dependent-care tax deductions, and a referral program for child-care or eldercare needs. After a standard paid maternity disability leave of eight weeks, a new parent can take up to six months' unpaid leave with full health benefits and no loss in seniority. A job of equal status is guaranteed on return. The firm also provides sabbaticals for an employee after 15 years of service, generous vacation leaves, and up to $2,100 reimbursement of the total cost of adopting a child. In addition, the company performs annual comparable worth surveys on salary and equality of treatment in the workplace. It also has programs for tuition reimbursement, job posting, specialized training, and succession planning to assure female representation in the next generation of company leaders.

Twenty-four percent of the employees in upper management at Time, Inc. Magazine Company are women. In 1987, 47% of those enrolled in the firm's management training program were women and the number continues to grow. These figures testify to Time, Inc.'s commitment to and leadership in promoting women.

In late 1989 Time Inc. Magazines (before it became Time Warner Inc.) joined with seven other major New York area firms to provide emergency child care in employees' homes. "Balancing work and family responsibilities is often difficult, but especially when emergencies arise," explained Karol Rose, manager of Work and Family Programs and Training at Time Warner, Inc. "We understood that these emergencies, such as an ill caregiver, mildly ill child, or unexpected changes in work schedule make it difficult to manage. That's why we are pleased to announce this pilot project to provide trained in-home caregivers for infants through 13-year-old children." Ms. Rose explained that Time, Inc. Magazine's family-friendly policies reflect the company philosophy: to help employees and their managers respond to changing needs, as they handle the demands of balancing work and family.

Another innovative benefit to working parents is the company's subscription to a special publication, *The Work and Family Life Newsletter*, produced by Bank Street College of Education in New York City, an independent graduate school of education and a leader in the area of work and family life. It is available at Time's Work and Family Office and at their monthly lunchtime workshops; it contains excellent articles on topics of interest to working parents. To give a sense of the kind of practical articles they include, the November 1989 issue contained features on the changing composition of the work force, sharing responsibilities for eldercare among siblings, curbing fighting among children, family health issues, and some guidelines for choosing children's toys.

Completing Time's comprehensive array of employee services are scholarship funds for employees' children through the Academic Award Program and support matching grants for education and the arts. An employee bookstore carries a wide range of books, records, videos, and gifts appropriate for children of all ages and biweekly newsletter advertises special child-care or eldercare needs. Time's innovations are paying off in employee loyalty and its reputation as an exciting and flexible place to work.

THRIVING ON ALTERNATIVE WORK SCHEDULES

Levi Strauss & Company

In a sprawling campus of red brick buildings that more resembles a university than the world's largest clothing manufacturer, a legion of jeans-clad employees are reaping the benefits of a company that is family-friendly. Headquartered in San Francisco, Levi Strauss employs more than 27,000 people in the United States. In San Francisco, 30 employees have embarked on an experiment called telecommuting where employees will be provided a personal computer to work from their homes. While this represents a tiny fraction of the entire Levi Strauss work force of 39,000 people worldwide, the results of this pilot project will be closely followed by workers at their plants across this country. More than 51% of the Levi Strauss work force is composed of women and the firm has been a leader in developing family-oriented policies throughout its history. It is also recognized as one of America's top companies in terms of exercising its social conscience. Chief Executive Officer Bob Haas is a founder of one of the first major foundations to benefit AIDS research and education.

Levi Strauss has created a variety of working arrangements facilitating work and parenting responsibilities. It provides five months' unpaid maternity or paternity leave for both birth and adoptive parents. Alternative work schedules such as job-sharing, part-time positions, flextime, and a compressed work week all are encouraged "to meet changing company and employee needs." These benefits are the result of a hard-working task force that included Mr. Haas himself. Further testimony to the firm's work/family commitment.

Jenny Crowe-Innes, director of employment, employee relations and equal employment opportunity is quick to explain that "There's nothing built into the system that says if you go onto an alternative work schedule, you're not a fast tracker. For example, Donna Goya, one of nine senior managers with the company, took a year off, worked part time, did a job-share, and still earned a top management position. While I'm not aware of any men who have yet taken advantage of alternative work schedules, it's something that we're educating about and will come someday soon. These men are married to women who also have careers; the expectation today is that a child is raised by both parents so we are now seeing men who are experiencing family demands at work." Donna Goya is now Levi Strauss's full time Director of Personnel, but when she was on her three-day work week she decided to use her two days off as a developmental tool for her subordinates. They took turns assuming her responsibilities.

Savvy and *Mother Jones* magazines have listed Levi Strauss among the best places for women to work. It is also featured as a desirable workplace in Lisa Birnbach's book titled *Going to Work* and in *The 100 Best Companies To Work For In America* by Robert Levering, Milton Moskowitz, and Michael Katz.

A measure of the extent of the company's commitments to its innovations is evidenced in an amendment to their mission statement written when the company went private in 1985. At that time, the company put in writing its goal to help employees achieve balance in their personal and professional lives. "I've been here 10 years; it's a great company, a progressive company and we're having a record-breaking year," says Crowe-Innes. "We have a true belief that employees are better workers and better people if given options in their work schedules." In addition to providing the alternative work arrangements listed above, the firm provides regular counseling, videos, and written information on how to find good child care. A program to reduce taxable income by allowing pretax dollars for child-care expenses has also been established.

The company proposes to do a survey of all employees at each of their locations in the U.S. to ascertain further needs of workers. "When our production goes up we ask people to work overtime. It really impacts family life. We want to take a new look at what these workers and their families need," says Crowe-Innes. The desirability of providing on-site child care, will also be examined in the survey.

Queried about the projected coming labor shortage and how this may affect company operations, Crowe-Innes responded that the firm's primary focus now is preventing burnout and retaining workers. Attracting new workers will also become more important in the next decade with the coming shortages of skilled labor. "Compounding these issues are the numbers of our current work force in their thirties who may have responsibilities both to young children and aging parents," she noted. Questions about the impact on work life of eldercare demands will be included in the upcoming all-employee questionnaire.

Crowe-Innes concludes, "The values of our company come through in the benefits we now provide or plan for the future. We are a large company that thinks small in terms of our employees. Many of our plant operators and production workers have been with us for 30 years. They value their association with Levi Strauss and because we benefit from this longevity, we constantly strive to find ways to communicate that we value our workers." This attitude is well typified in the slogan that appears on the company's logo, "Quality never goes out of style."

EXTENDED PERSONAL LEAVE—CREATING CHILD- AND ELDERCARE RESOURCES

International Business Machines Corporation
If there is competition for the top of the list of family-friendly companies, IBM is a serious contender. The firm, based in Armonk, New York, offers 28 options on a list of work/family balance programs. These range from an employee assistance plan and eldercare referral service to a family video library and a retirement education assistance plan. IBM was the first company to establish a national network of resource and referral organizations for eldercare needs. In 1989 they expected at least 10,000 employees annually to take advantage of this year-old service. This eldercare program alone is expected to reduce by 50% the time employees might be off the job seeking care for their relatives.

Adding to their impressive roster of benefits are a child-care referral service, relocation plan, adoption assistance plan, special care for children plan (to help with the expenses of a mentally, emotionally, or physically disabled child), parenting seminars, flextime, home terminal program (making computers available for at-home work for a temporary business need), a pilot work-at-home option, and community service assignments or faculty loan program where IBM pays the salary of the employee working as a volunteer or teacher. Finally, they offer an array of health benefits that includes a voluntary health assessment, personal health account (for items like vision care or immunizations), a Plan for

Life health promotion program, and comprehensive medical, disability, and life insurance plans. Their Retirement Education Assistance Plan provides tuition reimbursement of up to $2,500 each for courses taken by employees or their spouses to prepare for retirement.

Two of their benefits, however, deserve special mention for their innovation and their long-range benefits to the firm and its workers. The Extended Personal Leave Plan expands personal leave time from one to three years. Employees are guaranteed a job on their return and continue to receive their regular benefits package. What a way to guarantee employee loyalty! Employees may work part-time at IBM during the first year and are required to "be available" to work part-time the last two years, if needed by the firm. A boon to workers with young children or elderly relatives to care for, this plan is available based on job performance, reasons for leave, and business needs. Michael G. Shore, a spokesman for IBM, explained, "The single largest reason for the leave is child care." IBM employs 228,000 U.S. workers, of which 67,000 are women. On any given day approximately 2,000 employees (three-quarters of them women) are on this extended personal leave. Shore explains that new programs were added after surveys, focus groups, and manager/employee discussions showed a strong employee need for more work flexibility.

The second noteworthy IBM initiative focuses on its commitment to create more and better child-care options. According to a recent *New York Times* article, the firm committed $22 million over five years to establish a fund designed to help better meet its employees' child-care needs, "the largest financial commitment by any American corporation for childcare." J. T. Childs, Jr., director of IBM's Work/Life Program, described the company's decision as "a long-term investment in our economic and competitive health." He noted that the child-care referral service had been stymied by the limited supply and inferior quality of child-care programs in many communities. He went on to say that although the new centers and training programs for workers will help IBM employees, local communities will also benefit through access to the centers and providers. In the article IBM announced that it would "spend $3 million during 1991 to build five new childcare centers near its offices and plants around the country to serve 530 preschool children," spending "an additional $500,000 in communities that have large populations of IBM workers to improve existing daycare centers and to recruit and train people who care for children in their homes."

IBM will also launch several new child-care centers in partnership with other corporations, including American Express, Duke Power

Company, and Pepsi-Cola. This cooperative approach has also been advocated for smaller companies, as a way to minimize costs and maximize access.

IBM, like most other firms, does not release data on costs or cost savings for their work/family innovations, though company spokesman Shore cited improvements in morale, loyalty, and productivity. The only possible disadvantage he admitted was that in some instances greater flexibility might make supervision difficult for managers. He noted, however, that proper delegation, advance planning, and cross-training go far to mitigate these potential problems.

JOB TRAINING

Security Pacific Bank of Washington

John Getzelman, president of Security Pacific Bank of Washington and Security Pacific Bancorporation Northwest, is a man who exudes energy. He is also a person who is utilizing that energy for the betterment not only of his 5,500 employees, but also the general citizenry of the Pacific Northwest. The bank is taking both its corporate and community missions to new levels. When asked about the competition for workers in the Northwest's booming economy, Getzelman launches into a discussion of "linkage." "Look, we're involved in this region, in the people. We're connecting our philanthropic efforts in the United Way giving campaign to the reality that we can't find enough computer keypunchers. Downstairs, there's a workshop going on now for participants in the Governor's Family Independence Program, training welfare recipients for jobs. We're just one of 80 corporate sponsors. This is an opportunity, not a burden. I have hundreds of jobs that need to be filled. The cost involved in not utilizing these people is tremendous—not just to the business but to all of us." The bank gets needed workers; people get off welfare and into good jobs giving them salaries to buy goods and services that then add to the Northwest's economic boom.

Getzelman further explained that the need for new employees is significant and growing with competition for both clerical and technical staff from Boeing and rapidly expanding hi-tech firms like Intermec and Microsoft. Sydney T. Brown, senior vice president and human resources manager for the bank, amplified his point: "This need for employees is coming not only from our economic boom, but also from a greater emphasis on customer service. Our labor shortage is real and it's hitting us now. We have more than 250 current openings: that's 5% of our work force."

Security Pacific Bank is responding through The Family Independence Program, which is creating new workers, and by providing internships for minority students to whom they've awarded scholarships. These initiatives link the company's social and economic concerns. The bank seeks to retain current workers by providing on-the-job training and retraining. Further, bank heads are trying to change the company's mindset as to who can perform different jobs. "We want to keep people in the company because they are a known quantity—we have an investment in them," explained Brown. The firm is therefore beginning to utilize flextime, job-sharing, and part-time workers.

The opportunity for part-time work was born out of peak-time customer activity in branches. "We needed additional staff only at certain hours, so we offered part-time positions," explained Getzelman. "A business-driven change is being viewed as an attractive benefit by employees with family concerns. Our part-time numbers are now greater than they've ever been. If a person works more than 20 hours per week, they get full benefits. We think this will continue to be a draw to workers with child-care or eldercare needs. We're also launching a child-care study. We view child-care issues as being more important to retaining employees, but it may well become a recruiting issue as well. We're in an employee, not employer-driven, market now."

In light of the bank's concerns about keeping workers, they have established a pretax program, known as a "Dependent Care Assistance Plan Account," where up to $5,000 of a worker's salary per year can be earmarked for costs to cover the care of a child, elder, or disabled spouse. "We also think there is an opportunity to include child care as a benefit in a flexible benefits plan," said Getzelman. "You can choose to use your dollars for child care while someone else may choose life insurance, or a certain medical plan. It doesn't hurt the company by costing any more—we're planning to spend a set amount on benefits, but it gives employees the option of deciding how those benefits can best meet their families' needs. It's also a win/win for two-wage-earner families: one spouse's employer picks up health benefits while the other covers child care."

While Getzelman and Syd Brown agreed that work and family issues have financial implications for the company, neither saw them directly linked to the bottom line. "Our economic needs coincide with our social needs: we need good people. It's just plain logic that doing the right thing helps us get and keep those good people. Then when the pendulum swings back and perhaps the economy isn't quite so strong, these family-oriented benefits will be in place and ingrained in the company," exhorted Getzelman. "I want us doing these things because they're right, not because it gets us 'a bang for our buck.' We're all impacted by the way babies are being raised in the '90s; we all have a stake in making it easier and better for working families."

Security Pacific is benefiting on several fronts from their work/family initiatives. Not only are they able to attract and retain workers, they are meeting the public's demand for increased customer service. Flexible work schedules for parents translate into increased banking hours for their clients. They also deserve kudos for the links they are creating between their demands for workers and community needs.

FLEXIBLE HOURS

Microsoft Corporation

One of the leading lights in the burgeoning hi-tech industry is the Microsoft Corporation, headquartered in Redmond, Washington. Its trendsetting software is revolutionizing current business practices; the firm is also emerging as a leader in treating employees with family concerns as well.

Not only are Microsoft's products forward-thinking, it also has a unique staff. "Our total work force is very young; our average age is 30," explains John Prumatico, human resources director. "We hire very bright, well-educated people, many of whom got involved early in the personal computer business or those who learned about it in college. Many of these folks haven't worked anywhere else. Their minds are geared toward successful, simple solutions. That's their orientation in considering workplace issues, as well."

Microsoft now employs 4,300 people worldwide, with 3,300 in 38 states in the U.S. Of these, 2,500 are located in or near the company's headquarters. In an environment Prumatico terms "unstructured and dynamic," solutions to work/family problems are approached creatively. "Our employees are very valuable to us. We try to customize their benefits and work environment as much as possible to meet their needs," said Prumatico. While the young work force is just now being impacted by child- care concerns, in four or five years a larger percentage of workers will be involved in family care issues, as management has noted. Benefit programs for working parents are both innovative and comprehensive. A pregnant employee can take up to three months' maternity leave at full pay and benefits. The firm handles fathers' requests for paternity leave with a similar flexibility. Explained Prumatico, "Microsoft encourages flexible hours, schedules, and personal leaves to allow the new father time off to spend with his family. We don't want any individual to be forced to choose between work and family."

"Child-care issues, including an on-campus center, continue to be reviewed by Microsoft," explains Prumatico. "Microsoft has employees located throughout the United States, all with different child-care needs. In order to maximize a parent's flexibility in choosing the style of child-care and to provide equity to Microsoft parents nationwide, we implemented a tax-free flexible spending account." This plan allows parents to pay child-care expenses with pretax dollars, resulting in considerable tax savings at year end. "We also recognize that child-care can be very difficult and time-consuming to find. Microsoft wanted to assist parents with this, so a child-care referral service is available for employees. This service provides a wide range of services—referrals for infants up through teenage children. It gets back to the very nature of the people who are attracted to Microsoft and whom we're attracted to as employees. They are a diversified, assertive and very creative group." Other corporate programs that address family life include focus groups on parenting issues and systematic feedback from employees on how well the benefit package responds to these issues, the availability of PCs for at-home work, and electronic mail (e-mail) access to shared information on caregiving and parenting.

By all appearances Microsoft is a company working very hard to be family-friendly. While some critics of the firm have reported tales of 60-hour work weeks and regular weekend sessions by bright, competitive fast trackers in the industry, management disagrees. "Sure, you can drive by here at 8:00 P.M. and still see our parking lot a third full," says Prumatico. "But what you don't see is that some of these people didn't arrive until noon because they were at home with a baby or they left for two hours to play squash with a spouse or meet with their child's teacher. In most companies it's the rule to have everybody on site from 8:00 A.M. to 5:00 P.M.; here it's the exception. We have no set hours. Because every employee has an e-mail account, this significantly reduces the number of meetings, memos, and conferences that are normally required in a more traditional workplace. It's an unstructured atmosphere where work groups are project-oriented. They move and change as needed to get the job done. We trust our employees' judgment in terms of when they're here or working at home as long as the job gets done."

While this type of trust and collegiality sounds ideal, Prumatico admitted that there are pockets of resentment against those employees who do avail themselves of Microsoft's flexibility. "While this is a supportive environment, there are employees I worry about in terms of understanding our philosophy about work/family issues. We always have our radar up and we continue to seek out opportunities to educate and improve."

A CHILD-CARE CENTER ON SITE

Carver Corporation

While many of the firms pioneering work/family programs are quite large, the Carver Corporation in Lynwood, Washington, has only 280 employees, but has provided child-care services since the day their doors opened 10 years ago. Carver manufactures high-end audio equipment, with sales at approximately $25 million per year. Six years ago a child-care facility was brought on-site to be more responsive to the needs of employees. The center is heavily subsidized, with the corporation picking up approximately $110 per child per week, leaving $40 per week per child for the employee to cover. This low fee is especially important to lower-wage workers for whom the full cost at $150 per week could prove onerous. "The day care is the main reason I wanted to get a job here," explained Pinky Doyle, a stockroom clerk, to the Seattle Times. "And it's one of the reasons I'll stay," she added. Other workers heralded the benefits of having an on-site center as allowing them to see their children more often, spending less time on the freeway, and having more energy to do their jobs.

Lynn Cederholm, human resources manager for the firm, is not only an official spokesperson for this benefit, she is a committed advocate personally. "My daughter, four, and son, two and one-half, are at the center. It has helped me include my children in my day-to-day life. For instance, one day I got really upset by some news I received, I went to the child-care center and my daughter just held me. Usually you think in terms of being close by 'to do' for your child, but on that day she was really there *for me*." Cederholm continued, "For me it was really a consideration in coming to work here. Not only was the on-site child-care center a draw, but so was the entire comprehensive package of family-friendly benefits. We have particularly seen it help with retention of upper-management employees."

Carver provides for a standard three-month paid maternity leave with all benefits. However, the firm is known for its flexibility in terms of when new mothers come back to work. Often employees in professional positions return part time or take longer unpaid leaves depending on their needs. New fathers are also granted two to three weeks of unpaid paternity leave. Telecommuting has been tried by some parents in the engineering and sales divisions, but isn't seen as viable for employees in production- related areas, according to Cederholm.

"We have the kind of team attitude that we all work together here; it's not viewed as a problem if someone has to leave early to pick up a sick child or deal with an elderly relative. If necessary, personal leave is available. We're very accommodating," explained Cederholm. "Bob and Diana Carver have grown children, but their philosophy as founders of the company have been the driving force. They don't think employees should have to choose between working for Carver and being a good parent."

The '90s will be a volatile time for this young firm as it strives to become a world-class manufacturer. "Providing family-friendly benefits is a question of business necessity," said Cederholm. "Twenty percent of our employees utilize our on- site day-care center for kids from one year to kindergarten age. We see this as a real recruitment tool to get us the technicians and assembly people we need to help this company grow." Carver's employee retention study found that even employees who didn't use the company's day-care voiced positive opinions about the program. This study also documented that those who use the day-care center stay employed at the company longer than expected, even after their children grow past day-care center age. The report further found that these employees tend to be more enthusiastic about their jobs and more productive on the job. The company is considering adding programs for care of infants, as well as after school, and summertime activities for youngsters of Carver employees. Recently, the firm was honored by a Seattle professional women's group for their work/family innovations. They are a valuable model for other small firms.

EMERGENCY CHILD CARE

Ernst and Young

On October 1, 1989, Arthur Young & Co. and Ernst & Whinney merged to form Ernst and Young. Thus the world's largest accounting, auditing, tax, and management consulting firm was created with more than 25,000 employees in the U.S. This merger also resulted in a major employer who is on the cutting edge of progressive work and family policies. Previously, both independent firms were experimenting with flexible work schedules, resource/referral services for child-care and eldercare needs, extended parental leaves for birth, adoptive, and foster parents of both sexes, telecommuting, and "cafeteria" benefit plans. By far the most innovative development, however, was the leadership of Ernst and Young, together with six other major New York City firms, in launching a ground-breaking pilot program in fall of 1989 to meet the needs of employees with emergency child-care needs.

Recognizing that U.S. businesses lose $3 billion annually to child-care related absences, these employers created a program providing licensed caregivers in the homes of employees who live within a 60-mile radius of New York City. Banding together to create this innovative pilot program with Ernst and Young were Colgate-Palmolive Company, Con Edison, Home Box Office, Inc., National Westminster Bank USA, Time, Inc. Magazines Co., and the law firm of Skadden, Arps, Slate, Meagher and Flom. Services are coordinated by Child Care, Inc., a nonprofit child-care resource and referral agency that relies on certified caregivers from two licensed home health care agencies in New York City and northern New Jersey. Seeing how successful this approach has been, two additional employers signed up to join this consortium by late 1990.

When children are mildly ill, a normal caregiver is unable to work, a child-care center is closed, or an unexpected business trip arises, parents can call for a licensed caregiver to be at home with their children under age 13. Five of the participating companies pay the full cost of the care, which will be $10.40 an hour in New York City and $10.50 in New Jersey. Ernst and Young and one other employer pay much of the cost, with the employees covering the balance.

At Ernst and Young the service is available to the 800 employees who live in the areas served by the home health agencies monitored by Child Care, Inc. During the first four months of its inception it was used 11 times according to Rosemarie Meschi, director, national human resources. "We are incredibly pleased; emergency child care has been a major problem facing working parents and their employers, causing absenteeism, lateness, turnover, and loss of productivity. We've done some rough projections of cost and we're looking at less than $10,000 out of pocket per year; considering what we normally have to pay in temporary workers and lost productivity, it's a bargain. We set this up as a one-year pilot, however, because we just don't know how widely it will be used. In this part of the country we also have to deal with people's level of comfort at having a stranger in their home during an emergency situation. Also, there is the possible pitfall of everyone trying to use the service at once during a school holiday." The program is designed to be a last resort, she explained, after workers have exhausted all other options. "Thus far it has been used as we envisioned for mildly ill kids whose parents don't want to take them out of the house and in one case when the water main burst closing their regular day-care center. We're so positive about this pilot program we want to encourage more usage, so we published a brochure based on employee endorsements and have distributed it to all eligible employees."

Meschi sees work and family innovations as a continuing concern of the firm over the long run. She also believes that the firm will be particularly attractive to women professionals because they may be offering more opportunities for part-time or flextime positions due to the fluctuating demands of tax season. "We are continuing to explore methods to meet our changing work force needs, since we are experiencing increased competition for workers from the high technology firms, as well as needing to deal with the demands of dual-career couples. This industry has had a relatively high annual turnover rate of 20%. We have always had the reputation as someplace people want to work; we're striving to stay competitive and do the right things to retain that distinction."

In order to make sure that the firm stays on top of all these changes, Ernst and Young has a Human Resource Strategic Plan addressing "Workforce 2000" issues. "Our vision and commitment should be credited to Paul Ostling, our national director of human resources," explains Meschi. "Paul has helped us all understand that the traditional career development path 'up and out' doesn't work anymore. He got us asking the questions: Why do employees have to move out? Why should we be training someone else's employee? We've invested in people, let's figure out how to retain them by meeting their work and family needs. The recent merger gave us a chance to get all of these issues out on the table—it is a great opportunity to break old traditions and create better new ones," she concluded. One of the new ones sure to have its results scrutinized is the comprehensive emergency child-care pilot program.

PARENT SUPPORT PROGRAMS

AEtna Life and Casualty Company

More than 2,000 employers across the country are offering ongoing support groups or occasional lunchtime seminars as a relatively inexpensive means of helping employees with work and family issues. One of these firms is AEtna Life and Casualty Company, which has been administering family support seminars for about four years. AEtna and other firms embarked on these programs to assist their employees who are combining working and parenting. Some of these workers experience extreme isolation and stress from limited time, resources, and even access to practical advice. These stresses are different from generations past, when a majority of families had a stay-at-home parent, or relied on the supports of grandparents, church or synagogue, and community. Today's parents not only are often geographically separated from their parents, they are also experiencing parenthood differently as a result of two-career or single-parent families. A Northwest management consultant told us, "I remember how angry I felt the day my mother remarked that she couldn't understand why I was always tired. After all, I only had one toddler and she had raised five children. Of course what mother was failing to take into account was that I was running my own business and serving on two corporate boards, as well as raising my son, trying to be supportive of my husband's career, and managing a household."

Keeping in mind these kinds of strains, the parent support programs offered by AEtna and many other firms focus on advice about day-to-day problem-solving and life management skills. Popular topics include setting realistic goals, hiring household help, evaluating the quality of child-care or eldercare centers, coping with the challenges of single parenting, selecting toys and other learning experiences, dealing with behavior problems in children and teens, and creating a nurturing family culture. More practical concerns include improving nutrition, child development guidelines, healthy pregnancies, infant care, job reentry after parental leave, CPR, and first aid.

AEtna offers its two-hour family support seminars during company time. (Most other companies use the lunch hour or special extended lunch breaks.) Late afternoon and evening sessions have been found to be less popular because they are viewed as usurping precious family time. Sherry Herchenroether, AEtna's director of family services, addresses a common concern of firms embarking on family support seminars. "In the very beginning we were nervous about whether supervisors would allow people to attend. The seminars were underwritten by the company and we would make it a big point that they were free." Encouraging key managers to attend the seminars also helped increase the program's acceptance throughout the company. As one manager who attended an eldercare seminar at AEtna said, "It's hard to believe that my company really cares about this issue. But they do and that means a lot to me."

After a seminar topic is chosen based on employee input, it is advertised widely in the company, according to Herchenroether. The most popular topics are repeated every three months. Speakers include outside consultants, specialists in other fields, and community contacts such as nonprofit organizations or government experts. For instance, a representative of the state education department spoke on zoning and funding regarding establishment of after-school care programs. Worker interaction is encouraged at all of these sessions. Many firms have seen ongoing parent networks emerge out of their seminar initiatives. While Aetna covers the full cost of seminars, other firms charge a nominal participation fee. Not only does this help defray costs, it also improves attendance, say some experts, by making workers feel that they have invested in the sessions.

OVERNIGHT, SICK DEPENDENT CARE, AND OTHER INNOVATIONS

Hewitt Associates
A suburb 20 miles north of Chicago called Lincolnshire is the headquarters for Hewitt Associates, an international firm specializing in compensation and benefits consulting. The firm was founded in 1940 by Ted Hewitt, who stated two clear objectives: provide the highest quality of service to clients and provide a satisfying work experience for associates (as all employees are called). These principles still guide the company, which is now the 12th largest consulting firm in the U.S. with 1989 revenues exceeding $200 million. They currently have 30 non-U.S. offices in 19 countries. In the U.S. they employ 2,800 people in 31 different locations, about 60% of them women. Not only does Hewitt Associates have a long history of hiring women, they promote them, with 36% of their management ranks now occupied by females.

Peter Friedes, chief executive, says that he is sensitive to the needs of working women, and single mothers in particular, because his mother was widowed when he was 11 and worked as a secretary to make ends meet. Several years ago Friedes held several internal focus groups of working parents to ask them what an employer could do to make their lives more manageable. "We learned a lot by just listening—that almost every working parent in our environment feels bad or guilty about at least one of their roles (worker or parent) and usually about both. . . . We also learned that our people were quite self-reliant—they weren't asking for much help, but said that information about child-care facilities, babysitters, laundries open after working hours, and so forth, would help. Assistance with the cost of overnight babysitting when required for work, would help. More options upon returning to work after childbirth would help. More understanding by managers would help. In addition, it's important for an organization to constantly use words that make male employees know that some of these work/family benefits are for them too."

All associates, both female and male, have access to a broad panoply of family-sensitive policies, including pretax dollar dependent-care accounts, reimbursement for up to $2,500 in adoption expenses, extended personal leaves of absence, work/family workshops, and an extensive family resource library. While the firm doesn't currently provide on-site child care, it has contributed seed money to create more near-site child-care resources. Their more significant innovations, however, include creating a family resource consultant position on staff, introducing provisions for overnight and sick dependent care, establishing Mothers' Rooms at several regional offices, and conducting informational programs for expectant parents.

Linda Foster, the family resource consultant for Hewitt, explains her position with the firm: "The Family Resource consultant surveys the family needs of associates, creates new programs where appropriate, and acts as the link between the employer and employee to assist in helping associates in the difficult task of balancing work and family responsibilities." Her position was originally viewed as a part-time role but now is a full-time position, assisting employees with both child-care and, increasingly, eldercare needs. "I help find nursing homes and financial resources, counsel on leaves of absence and on such resources as health and wellness programs," explains Foster. "We're very much a 'listening culture.' Our benefits package is a reflection of the respect we have for our associates. One of the emerging needs within our organization is the need to address the pressures facing working parents with (both) children and elderly dependents. We've taken some new initiatives to help our associates juggle the responsibilities of career and parenting."

One of the more unusual of these initiatives is Overnight Dependent Care. Associates are reimbursed for babysitting costs or eldercare costs incurred when out of town on business or working significantly later than normal business hours. For the second quarter of 1990, overnight dependent care was used by 15 associates for a total of 43 days. Foster believes this small cost is easily offset by the increased work productivity and associate loyalty engendered by this benefit.

Associates can also be reimbursed for up to five days per year of additional dependent-care expenses for a sick child or other dependent relative. Six days of basic personal/family leave are provided as well to each associate. Associates may "purchase" one, two, or three additional days as needed (or get cash back based on their salary at the end of the year for days not used). Sick dependent care in the second quarter of 1990 was used by nine associates for a total of 20 ½ days. Each associate availed him/herself of between a half a day up to five days to care for an ill child or relative. Again this cost is viewed as quite small in comparison to losing that worker, rehiring, and training a new associate.

Under a different program, associates can leave an ill child during the day in a local hospital with professional care. "I tried it with my child," said Foster, "I admit I had some reservations initially about taking my ill child out of our home. At the end of the day he didn't want to leave! He could order from the menu, enjoy their play area, rest in his own bed, and receive lots of attention from nurses. He was happy and I knew he received excellent care." She said that usage this year by associates is much higher, as they've promoted it more and as other parents and children have reported positive experiences. "Families with ill dependent elders or children can also call a social service agency who will send a skilled caregiver to their home," Foster explained. Hewitt Associates helped to develop these services in the area where most of the associates live. Associates can call anytime between 6:00 A.M. and 9:00 P.M. It just started in January 1990, but already we've had a tremendous response."

Another lament of many working mothers is the dilemma of trying to return to work while continuing to nurse their infants or toddlers. Hewitt Associates has addressed this concern in the most sensitive and sensible way. They provide "Mothers' Rooms" in almost every one of their regional centers. "Mothers' Rooms are a safe, private, secure place for women to pump their breast milk," says Foster, "so that they will feel more comfortable returning to work sooner. It has been a very popular option."

Finally, Hewitt's other innovative approach to the rigors of working and parenting is their "Expectant Parents' Sessions and Registry," offered in most regional centers. These sessions provide information on policies and benefits affecting associates in all stages of maternity and upon return to work. Every expectant parent also receives a kit with coupons for relevant services and a complimentary book on child development. "This benefit has made a huge difference in attitude among our associates. We also send the parents a card when the child is born. They tell us it really makes them feel cared about and appreciated," explains Foster.

In a speech to the International Association of Personnel Women, CEO Friedes commented, "Now the list of things we do may create the impression that these programs may not be economically justified. I don't think that's the case. There is some real economic payoff for all this attention to work and family issues—but I'm not sure I can prove it to someone who doesn't want to believe it. The cost to recruit and train good people is enormous. (That's not news to you in the human resources field—but I don't think general managers appreciate the total cost.) Providing these work and family programs is much cheaper than having to rehire people. Our professional exempt turnover is under 10% and has been each year in the last 15 years (average 7%). The savings to get back mothers with experience versus having to hire and retrain someone else is *large*. I believe that getting back a knowledgeable person for 60% of their time is better than having a full-time *new recruit*."

"Let me try to quantify some of this," Friedes continued, "as I mentioned, our professional turnover has averaged 7% per year. The average for consulting firms is closer to 20–25%. If we use 22% as the average, that means we have a 15 percentage point *lower* turnover rate compared to the average consulting firm. At 2,800 people in the U.S., that means we save the costs associated with replacing and retraining 420 associates each year. There is also the issue of quality of work. I believe higher turnover in a professional service business means lower quality of service, lower quality means less repeat business, less repeat business means a higher cost of sales."

He concludes, "There's another economic payoff to some of these policies. I really believe that if our programs provide some relief to the normal guilt of trying to be a great worker and a great parent, we will gain in productivity in terms of less wasted time and more efficiency. We (the employer) can't make people happy—but we can help reduce some of the stresses of everyday life and we can show real support for people trying to do a good job as parents and as workers." Freides told a Chicago conference of 200 of the firm's clients exploring flexible work arrangements: "We feel having progressive work and family policies allows us to insist upon our people providing excellence in everything they do. Our work and family programs aren't to 'be nice' as much as they are to allow us to require excellent performance from our people."

PREVENTATIVE EDUCATION APPROACH

3M Corporation

The 3M Corporation in Minnesota traces its interest in work/family programs back to their employee assistance programs (EAP) in the early '70s. After becoming aware that many employees were having trouble locating appropriate child care, the EAP began listing licensed day-care programs, created a task force on women's concerns, and conducted an employee opinion survey on corporate responsibility related to child care. An in-house child-care task force studied a variety of options and shaped a thoughtful work and family program that is aimed at *prevention* of work/family conflicts—through education, information, support, and creating options for employees. The goal of all these activities is to help employees be more productive by strengthening their ability to manage both their careers and family lives by providing the information they need to make optimal choices.

The path that 3M took over the last 10 years to create this impressive array of in-house and community resources is fairly typical of the route followed by many American firms. Its work/family products are varied and comprehensive, including a full-time child-care administrator, an information/referral service, a summer day camp, parent education seminars, an adoption assistance program, part-time employment opportunities, and six to eight weeks of paid pregnancy disability leave. Their special leave program allows new mothers or fathers up to two months of additional unpaid leave with reemployment rights. Five additional family sick days or emergency leave days are an option, as well as personalized, flexible work schedules.

In line with their emphasis on prevention of problems related to work and family concerns through education and information, twice a year 65 agencies participate in a 3M Community Care Fair to inform parents of child-related resources. Employees are also encouraged to avail themselves of the St. Paul Working Parent Resource Center, supported by a 3M Foundation grant, which offers classes and a resource library on work/family issues and the Minneapolis Children's Medical Center, which operates a "warm line" providing nonmedical support and information on parenting concerns. A pilot project offering in-home care for sick children of 3M employees rounds out the list of family-friendly benefits.

All of these programs implement the work/family mission statement and operating principles adopted by the company, confirming that "male, as well as female employees increasingly have family roles and responsibilities to balance with their work. . . . 3M involvement, by design, is intended to enhance employees' confidence and ability to use their own and other available resources, rather than conveying a sense of 3M responsibility for family functioning and well-being. The 3M approach to work and family is to strengthen and utilize the expertise of community services, rather than duplicating those services ourselves at the work site."

With over 49,000 U.S. employees at varied locations, 3M has sought a variety of solutions to the child-care dilemma. At some locations, the company contracts with community agencies to provide names of child-care providers. In other areas discounts from certain child-care providers are given to 3M employees. All employees have access to an in-house information service to help locate existing community care providers.

3M continues to review the family needs of its workers, recognizing that while 78% of their employees are parents, 20% also have some responsibility for the care of an aging parent. Says Sue Osten, 3M Child Care Coordinator, "Today's working parents are not just concerned about who will care for their children while they work. Their inability to effectively handle the responsibilities of being both a parent and an employee; the time and energy demands felt by many working parents; and emerging concerns about finding appropriate care for aging parents are all aspects of the stresses employees face." It is clear that 3M has gone a long way to try to prevent as much of that stress as possible.

THE ULTIMATE WORK/FAMILY PACKAGE

Johnson & Johnson

The moment visitors enter the tower lobby at Johnson & Johnson's corporate headquarters in New Brunswick, New Jersey, they are struck by the positive energy that pervades the place. The receptionist's warm smile and polite assistance, the huge bouquet of fresh flowers, and the sight of six giggling toddlers rolling by on the J&J day-care wagon enhance that favorable impression. A sign in every wood-paneled elevator reads, "We speak the same language all over the world . . . Quality."

J&J is a model of corporate good citizenship, responsible for bricked downtown mall walkways and beautiful plantings along Johnson Drive, as well as redevelopment programs revitalizing the urban core. Internally, J&J manifests the same good citizenship, acting on a commitment to quality of products to customers, respect for employees, responsibility to the community, and return to stockholders. The company credo was recently revised to include a statement of support for work/family needs, "We must be mindful of ways to help our employees fulfill their family responsibilities."

In early 1989, to enact that commitment, the company embarked on a Work and Family Initiative, a comprehensive array of new policies, programs, and services. These were developed according to company literature, "to help employees meet the challenges of balancing work and family . . . and to attract and retain the top quality employees it needs to remain competitive." John Brown, corporate vice president for employee relations said, "We don't have a labor shortage per se, but when it comes to competing for the very best people, we want to have the benefits in place to attract them. For example, there was a woman we wanted in the compensation area, who said, 'When you have a child-care center I'll come.' We opened our first on-site child-care center in May of 1990 and she came. We've come to understand that our work force is changing and becoming increasingly diverse. We believe that these work and family accommodations are for both male and female employees and we think we've wound up with a happier and more productive work force."

With more than 35,000 employees J&J is the nation's largest health care company. Outside the U.S. it employs 81,000 people in 158 far-flung locations. To be competitive in this world-market it needs to be able to continue to deliver quality, and that requires a top-flight work force. "Perhaps no greater challenge faces working men and women today than balancing these two worlds [work and family]," states a company brochure on the Work and Family Initiative. "To strike a happy balance, however, men and women don't need to learn to walk a tightrope. They need support. At Johnson & Johnson . . . responsive company policies and programs provide employees with the flexibility and resources to address family and personal concerns while pursuing their careers." The J&J solution focuses on four goals: 1) creating supportive environments; 2) responding to changing needs; 3) caring for generations; 4) providing benefits for every individual's needs. These benefits landed J&J a spot in *The One Hundred Best Companies to Work for in America*. Components of the program include:

- *Manager/supervisor training*—designed to increase sensitivity to, and knowledge of, work and family issues and policies
- *Family care leave*—allowing up to one year of unpaid leave with benefits and assurance of employment at the leave's conclusion

- *Family care absence*—allowing an employee time off with pay to provide emergency care for a family member
- *Resource and referral program*—to help employees find child-care and eldercare resources
- *Dependent-care account*—to enable employees to pay dependent-care expenses on a pretax basis
- *Relocation services*—to assist in relocation planning, in the identification of appropriate schools, and in helping spouses to find employment
- *Alternative work arrangements*—to provide flexibility in time and place of employment
- *Adoption benefits*—providing up to $2,000 in covered expenses
- *Flexible benefits*—to allow individualized employee benefit coverage
- *On-site child-care centers*—at appropriate Johnson & Johnson facilities (first two opened in central New Jersey in 1990 and 1991)

Michael Carey, vice president for human resources at the Personal Products Company at J&J and chair of the Work/Family Task Force that developed the initiatives, explained the goals behind the series of on-site child-care centers: "We have a child *development* approach not just a child-*care* center. We strive to be the best in everything we do, so our goal was to create an excellent place for our employees' children. It is for kids aged six weeks to six years. We developed a full-day kindergarten program, so that our employees wouldn't have to struggle about where to put their child after the public schools' half-day kindergarten." John Brown added that J&J also wanted the price to be affordable to all levels of employees, so the company subsidizes a portion of the costs. "Our target is that we don't want anyone to have to pay more than 10% of net family disposable income," explained Brown. Judy Vaughn, director of the child development center at corporate headquarters in New Brunswick, attested to its popularity with J&J parents. "We opened in May 1990 and already have 130 children. By the end of 1990 we will be full at 200 children." Excellent caregiver-to-child ratios, beautiful indoor and outdoor play areas, a full-time on-site nurse and computer room are just a few of the attractions for J&J parents and their offspring.

The company's eldercare programs have also been quite popular. John Brown himself is a true believer in the Resource and Referral Program. "After my 94-year-old father had open-heart surgery, I needed to find some resources to help him in his recovery. We were able to quickly locate in-home nursing care, meals-on-wheels, free transportation, a cleaning service, everything we needed. This is going to be an increasingly utilized program given the age of our managers here at corporate," he concluded.

In summer of 1990 Ellen Galinsky and her colleagues at the Families and Work Institute in New York studied 190 Fortune 500 companies nationwide regarding family-friendly initiatives. This *Corporate Reference Guide* ranked Johnson & Johnson as the top firm in the country, citing its comprehensive and innovative work/family benefits.

The corporate description of these initiatives concludes: Johnson & Johnson recognizes, however, that this is just the beginning of a cultural change that will create a new and innovative management/employee partnership—one that will enrich the lives of its employees while at the same time strengthen Johnson & Johnson businesses. The firm's chairman, Ralph Larsen, echoes this theme: "In the intensely competitive world in which we operate, we require a great deal from our employees, and we expect our employees to give their very best. We want to free our employees from some of the burdens and worries that come with who's going to take care of the children or elderly parents that we all experience. . . . To the extent that we can help them deal with these concerns and allow them to be productive and to live up to their potential, that's what it's all about." He goes on to put the company's work/family initiatives in even a larger context: "Our heritage as a corporation, started more than 100 years ago, is of a company dedicated to caring. . . . Our work and family program is a very natural extension of that. . . . Families are the glue that keeps society together. Families are what provide stability and continuity, so we want to do everything we can to support and enhance family values."

Jim Burke, immediate past chairman of Johnson & Johnson, concluded: "I don't think there is a more important issue to the future of this corporation and what we stand for than this issue [work and family]. . . . To not be in the forefront of this issue would be morally repugnant. This commitment is for real and forever."

INTERGENERATIONAL DAY CARE

Stride-Rite and St. Francis
No overview of family-friendly companies would be complete without mentioning the Stride-Rite Corporation. The firm was cited in the October 1989 issue of *Working Mother* as being among the 60 best firms in the U.S. for working moms. The firm offers generous leaves of absence to meet family needs or the opportunity to work on flexible schedules after

employees have achieved one year of service. During maternity leave of up to eight weeks, employees are paid two-thirds salary. An unpaid leave of 18 weeks is also offered. Fifteen percent of the company's managers are women in a total work force of 4,000, with about 1,800 female employees. The oldest operating corporate child-care center in the country has been run by Stride-Rite since 1971 in Roxbury, Massachusetts. The success of the first program led to the second Stride-Rite center in Cambridge in 1982 and a third program opened in early 1990. The center in Roxbury enrolls almost 40 children, aged two to six years. Only a fourth of the youngsters are children of Stride-Rite employees, the rest are from the community. Parents can visit with their children during the day, have lunch together, administer needed medicines, meet with teachers, or breast-feed their infants at the center, thus facilitating an earlier return to work after giving birth. While child-care center workers aren't Stride-Rite employees, they are eligible for all company benefits. Stride-Rite believes that this makes for better and more committed caregivers. Center costs are shared by parents, the Stride-Rite Charitable Foundation, state and federal programs. Fees parents pay are approximately 12% of their gross household income. This a significantly lower percentage of family income than many American parents now pay. Community members pay on a sliding-fee scale based on income.

By far the most unusual aspect of Stride-Rite's work/family benefits, however, is its new intergenerational day-care center, providing eldercare for dependents of employees side by side with child care at the company's Cambridge headquarters. Day care is provided for up to 60 children, aged 15 months to six years, and 30 elderly relatives 60 and older. Stride-Rite chairman Arnold Hiatt believes that the center benefits both children and elderly more than facilities that cater exclusively to either age group. Stride-Rite hopes to create a prototype for other corporations to follow as well as provide a baseline for research on intergenerational care. Hiatt is viewed by many business leaders as a visionary. He disputes this view, however, and in comparing his firm with others he argues, "We're not visionaries. They're dumb." The 'they' he is referring to are the organizations that haven't taken work/family issues to heart, thinking that such programs may be laudatory but not very practical. "We can demonstrate the *economics* of day care," Hiatt says. He estimates that his children's centers probably save him $22,000 per employee by helping him to retain experienced high-caliber people and avoid the expensive proposition of training replacement workers. While Hiatt speaks passionately, but objectively, about the benefits of Stride-Rite's child-care programs, he doesn't harbor any illusions about a huge wave of followers. Stride-Rite is one of only about 1,000 U.S. companies that offer on-site care for children and only a handful have such programs for elders. Hiatt worries that "companies will provide care as long as the labor market is tight and they are competing for workers. But let employment fall off and business start looking for ways to trim expenses and you might have serious problems." He expresses concern about the willingness of business to take the initiative and suggests that government may need to step in. "Frankly I don't think corporate day care is the final answer. Can you imagine how many first graders would be educated if we depended upon corporate initiative? Eventually the government will have to take over," he concludes. Nevertheless, Hiatt and his colleagues continue their proselytizing and their teaching—they have participated in the development of over 50 child-care centers across the U.S.

Another firm that provides intergenerational day care at the same location is St. Francis's Extended Health Care in Bellingham, Washington, which opened its nursing home/child-care center in 1985. The theory behind the facility is as old as the family unit itself: Taking care of infants and toddlers is a full-time job and grandparents have time on their hands. The staff at St. Francis understood this natural affinity and decided to create a place where the two most often neglected and needy segments of society, children and elders, can be together, taking care of each other. Young and old bask in each other's attention in structured and unstructured activities throughout the day. While some have expressed concern that children won't accept the elderly who show physical manifestations of their age, or that older people are too frail to be with active youngsters, the St. Francis experience belies these stereotypes. Jim Hall, administrator, explained to *Washington Magazine*, "It's so obvious that the elderly should become involved with child care. . . . All these surrogate grandparents—our kids call all our residents Grandma and Grandpa. And the kids accept the disabled far better than we do. If someone's in a wheelchair or has a urinary bag hanging on a leg, it's no big deal." Hall explained that what others saw as obstacles were easily overcome. "You do have to do some child-proofing, but that's really simple. . . . If the facility is well maintained and clean, it's not as bad as going to a mall!" he explained in response to concerns about exposure to germs from children to the elders or vice-versa. Almost 50% of the children's parents work at St. Francis, the rest in the community. A waiting list signals that the concept is working well, resulting in happy children, doting elders, and pleased parents.

Other experts agree. "The focus may be on child care now, but eldercare will become the critical issue of the future," said Robert Beck, executive vice president for Corporate Human Resources at Bank of America. He and Frank Skinnic, president of Southern Bell, were commenting to *Time* magazine on the costs to employees and employers of concerns about children and elders. Older people with long life expectancies are often alone in their later years, dependent on busy middle-aged relatives for their care and support. The over-65 age group is expected to grow to 35 million by the year 2000 and the over-85 age group is the fastest growing in the country. It now numbers about 5 million, with 25,000 people having passed their 100th birthdays. Women now spend as much time caring for elders as they do children (18 years vs. 17 years), and the AARP reports that between 25–35% of the work force has eldercare responsibilities. Those employers, like Stride-Rite and St. Francis, who are responding to both needs, will have a giant leg up on the competition.

LEADERS IN WORK/FAMILY BENEFITS ALSO MOST PROFITABLE

The companies highlighted in this book are leaders in the field of work/family benefits. Many have been pioneers in other workplace innovations, such as employee stock option plans, company wellness centers, corporate resort facilities, and community redevelopment efforts. These firms are not only pleasant places to work, they are profitable business enterprises.

We believe that in some measure profitability is assisted by their work/family programs. It appears that there is more than casual connection between these firms initiatives on behalf of their employees and the bottom-line results reported on their annual financial statements. By mid-1990, Microsoft Corporation, a leader in flexible work schedules for employees, reported a 76.2% rise in net income for its fourth fiscal quarter, or a 53% gain in revenue. The Redmond, Washington, company also became the first personal computer software company to exceed $1 billion in annual revenues. Johnson & Johnson revealed earnings in the second quarter of 1990 that increased almost 19% on strong showings in its pharmaceutical and professional health care lines, while its benefit plans are among the most attractive in the nation. Proctor & Gamble ranks as the 23rd most profitable company in the United States. It has the country's oldest employee profit-sharing plan in continuous operation and it also is ranked by the U.S. Chamber of Commerce as having one of the top benefit plans. IBM makes more profit after taxes than any other company in the world, reporting record U.S. profits in 1989. The firm offers its employees extraordinary job security, high wages, generous health, pension, dental and child-care benefits, health classes and physical examinations, adoption assistance, and country clubs at several locations where employees can join for $5 per year. According to *Business Week*, they are joined at the top by AT&T, as ninth most profitable; Du Pont, as 13th most profitable; and Merck, as 18th most profitable. These are also all firms with outstanding work/family benefits.

RESULTS OF FAMILY-FRIENDLY PROGRAMS

Limited quantitative data is available on the dollar impact of providing work/family benefits. This appears to be a product of the relative newness of these offerings and an early mindset that work/family programs were good for public image and employee morale, but not business necessities. That attitude is changing for several reasons: the escalation of competition for workers due to selected labor shortages and the revelation by work/family pioneers that these benefit packages translate into bottom-line advantages.

One of the older studies, done in 1984, resulted in the collection of data on the cost savings realized by firms that provided child-care assistance to employees. Dr. Dianna Tate, chair of the Child Development and Family Living Department at Texas Women's University, studied the effects at a small textile manufacturing plant that was experiencing a 40% turnover rate. Turnover rates after the first year of their child-care programs dropped to 7% and absenteeism plummeted from 10% down to 1%. For every $1 spent, the company yielded $6 in cost containment.

A large study summarized in a 1989 report by the U.S. Department of Labor called "Employers and Child Care: Benefitting Work and Family" confirmed the value of providing child care. Fifty-eight companies that sponsor child-care centers were studied. Eighty-eight percent said their centers enhanced recruitment; 72% said they lowered absenteeism; 65% said they improved morale; and 57% said they resulted in a lower job turnover rate. It's hard to imagine any other employee benefit program that would receive such high ratings across so many gauges of effectiveness.

As we have seen, Merck & Co. credits the company's low annual turnover rate of 8% to its benefit package and flexible policies. The American average rate for employee annual turnover is 13%. One year after AEtna's family leave policy was established, retention of employees who took maternity disability had climbed from 77% to 88%. Hewlett-Packard, with 82,000 employees worldwide, has offered its workers flexible hours since the '70s, resulting in improvements in punctuality, higher employee morale, and decreased traffic congestion. Sherry Herchenroether, manager of family services for AEtna, acknowledged some resistance to its benefits from front-line supervisors but explained, "We point out to these supervisors that the cost of turnover is far more than the cost of being flexible. The cost of that employee leaving is 93% of salary, plus 100% of the salary of the person you have to hire." She concludes that, "We think the costs are well worth it."

RESULTS OF WORKPLACE FLEXIBILITY

Employers are also finding that by giving workers more control of their time everyone benefits, and flexibility in terms of hours and places of work is growing in popularity, resulting in less employee turnover and greater job satisfaction. AEtna Life and Casualty Co. cut its attrition rate from 23% to 11.5% among employees who were new mothers by introducing a six-month unpaid family leave policy. Skadden, Arps, Slate, Meagher and Flom, a New York City law firm, employs about three dozen lawyers part time, most of them are women returning from maternity leave. With this kind of flexibility on the part of their employer, these women not only feel loyal and *wish* to return to work, it becomes possible to arrange child care and time with the child to fit the family's needs. Only one lawyer on maternity leave didn't return to the firm after giving birth. Company managers at Pacific Bell say that its telecommuting program, launched in 1985, has led to increased productivity and 70% of its 1,500 telecommuters report increased job satisfaction.

Dana Friedman, in a research report from The Conference Board, summarizes the results of three studies on the benefits of flextime. Perceived improvements in productivity were reported by 48% of companies surveyed based on a 12% average increase in output per unit of input. Employees thus contributed more to the company after flextime than before it was adopted in gains estimated to be between 5 and 15%.

In another study, in 1984, researchers queried businesses about an even broader array of potential benefits of providing child care to

CORPORATE BENEFIT	% OF EMPLOYERS RESPONDING AFFIRMATIVELY
employee morale	90%
recruitment	85%
public relations	85%
employee work satisfaction	83%
publicity	80%
ability to attract new or returning workers	79%
employee commitment	73%
turnover	65%
employee motivation	63%
absenteeism	53%
scheduling flexibility	50%
productivity	49%
quality of work force	42%
equal employment opportunity	40%
quality of products or service	37%
tardiness	36%

employees. Sandra Burud, Pamela R. Aschbacker, and Jacquelyn McCroskey asked 178 businesses, "Would you say that the company-sponsored child-care service has had an effect on any of the following aspects of company operation?" Clearly, these firms experienced a positive outcome when more than 50% of employees responded affirmatively to issues of employee morale, recruitment, public relations, work satisfaction, publicity, attracting new or returning workers, employee commitment, motivation, turnover, absenteeism, and scheduling flexibility. Slightly fewer, but still more than a third, responded favorably to issues of productivity, quality of work force, equal employment opportunity, quality of products or service, and tardiness. Many managers would have a difficult time thinking of any other change they could make in the workplace that would yield such positive outcomes for both employer and employee.

Rather than showing what employers *gain* by responding to child-care concerns, on the other hand, a Portland, Oregon, study shows what companies *lose* by ignoring them. A survey of 22 firms in the city with a total of more than 8,000 employees showed that women with children under age 12 missed about 12 days of work each year. Contrast this result with the previous survey, where 53% of employers providing child-care services reported improvements in absenteeism. New trends are emerging in the society that mandate the scrutiny of business needs and employee needs in light of how to better meet both. It would appear that responding to child-care concerns must be a critical part of this examination process.

What about those who may believe that providing a family care program discriminates against those employees who don't have dependent children or elders? In the National Employer Supported Child Care Project only four companies, or 11% of the sample, found equity to be an issue with their employees. The vast majority found that childless workers or those without aged parents also benefitted when absenteeism, tardiness, and turnover are measurably reduced by the implementation of work/family programs. In addition, the less easily quantifiable results—improvements in company image, morale, and productivity can benefit every worker when translated into increased profitability.

CALCULATING THE ADVANTAGES

Ted Childs, manager of work life programs at IBM, explains that his company's flexibility and program options are "not a 'nice to do.' It costs $12,000 to $15,000 to recruit a professional employee, and training could cost another $100,000," he says. "Given that investment, isn't it important to make every effort to retain that employee?"

Some simple arithmetic based on Childs's figures and the data provided earlier in this chapter by Peter Friedes of Hewitt Associates demonstrate the financial impact of progressive policies. If recruiting a professional costs an average of $13,500 and training costs another $100,000, then how much more has Friedes's firm gained compared to his competitors'? Hewitt's turnover rate post-work/family program is now 7% per year, whereas other consulting firms experience 22% per year. Hewitt, then, would lose approximately 196 people per year while a firm of similar size would lose 616 workers. Friedes says he saves the costs of recruiting and training 420 associates each year out of his total work force of 2,800 people. If we assume that all 420 are professionals, we can multiply $113,500 (average recruiting and training costs) by 196 workers and $113,500 by 616 workers. This means Hewitt spends $22.2 million on the personnel costs of replacing professional employees while their competitor spends $69.9 million. Hewitt has $47.6 million more dollars to spend, which can go towards enhancing their profitability. While this equation is incomplete because we are not factoring in the initial costs of implementing the work and family program, it represents the type of calculations being done all over America as human resource managers seek to control labor costs so their firms can be more competitive. (In chapter 4 we summarize the results of other studies analyzing impacts of individual aspects of work/family programs.)

Of all the benefits provided, it seems clear that flexible work hours and leave policies, as well as on-site child care, are the most popular with employees and yield the greatest potential bottom-line impact. However, when we asked the managers we interviewed to calculate comprehensive bottom-line impact, taking into consideration both cost savings (via decreased absenteeism, turnover, etc.) and up-front costs of implementing family-friendly policies, the answers they gave were inconclusive. Some said it's simply too soon, as the benefits packages were just instituted or still evolving. Johnson & Johnson, Levi Strauss, and Merck, to name a few, have comprehensive studies under way. The Conference Board, source of some of our data analyzing the impacts of flexible work schedules, is also doing research on the outcomes of a comprehensive package of work/family initiatives. We look forward to the results of these analyses. In the meantime, however, we are convinced enough by current anecdotal and empirical research, despite its limitations, that work and family benefits are "worth it."

THE EDGE PROVIDED BY WORK/FAMILY PROGRAMS

Of the programs outlined above, each has been successful to some degree for that individual company and may or may not work for your firm or your family. What we can conclude, however, is that in the process of creating the family-friendly benefits we summarized, these firms are simply more attractive places to work than those firms without these benefits in place. And this is true for parents and nonparents alike, as well as for those with eldercare concerns or not. These work sites will have fewer problems attracting new employees, causing all current employees to feel motivated for top performance. Time and time again we heard anecdotes and reviewed growing statistics confirming that firms with work/family programs were more productive, positive places to work. There is less burden on all workers when fewer employees are absent due to child-care problems or turnover is reduced when adequate parental leave and new mother support programs are in place. In other words, everyone's job gets easier.

How will the companies that make it easier for people to work and be family members fare in the economically turbulent '90s? Our guess is quite well. In the '90s quality and customer service will be the hallmarks of success. The firms featured in this book are already oriented towards quality. The enhanced rates of retention/recruitment/productivity and decrease in absenteeism and turnover resulting from these family-friendly programs have the potential to translate into improvements in their products or services. While extensive empirical data is not yet available, current statistics and anecdotes from firms we studied clearly reveal that work/family initiatives enhance a company's ability to be competitive in this economy and ultimately in the world market.

In her 1989 book *When Giants Learn to Dance,*. . . Rosabeth Moss Kanter calls for a post-entrepreneurial model for management in the '90s. She postulates that those businesses that can create a marriage between entrepreneurial creativity, corporate discipline, cooperation, and team work will be those that flourish as this century ends. We believe those firms that have developed family-friendly initiatives fit this description.

FIRMS WITHOUT WORK/FAMILY PROGRAMS

What of those firms that haven't chosen to recognize the connection between work and family needs? Why have they not chosen to do so and what will be the result? We can only hypothesize about why firms have not chosen to adopt work/family programs, since we only interviewed family-friendly companies for this book. One reason for some companies' reluctance may be their relative isolation from the market-place. This isolation could be the result of the uniqueness of their service or product. If they have little competition, perhaps they haven't felt the need to operate more efficiently and reduce personnel costs. Or perhaps these companies have not yet experienced any significant shortage of skilled workers. In some segments of the country, particularly the North-east, unemployment figures are still high enough to allow employers to pick and choose in many work categories. Or perhaps the organization is still ruled by an old male guard, with stay-at-home wives, who still think it's business as usual, or business as they knew it for generations past in America. Some of the nation's universities still look at the world this way. As one university worker told us, "I looked around in the faculty club dining room the other day. All I saw was a sea of aging male faces; virtually everyone in the room was a white man over the age of 45. All of them will retire in 20 to 25 years. Who will replace them?" Many firms may decide that they aren't going to embark on family-friendly programs until there's unanimity among workers on what specific benefits are best. So, some organizations may just be short-sighted.

Others may be myopic in yet another way. Put off by the initial costs of embarking on some aspects of work/family programs they have chosen to do nothing at all. This is regrettable and not necessary as some very valuable family-friendly benefits cost little up front and in time yield significant financial rewards. Implementing a pretax dollar dependent-care account, or instituting flexible work hours or four-day work weeks are inexpensive ways to get started that have proven popular with employees. Few of the firms we interviewed launched all the aspects of their work/family programs simultaneously. A phased-in approach, analyzing costs, and popularity with workers and managers is more common.

Finally, some firms may have not initiated work/family programs because they haven't been asked. In many instances at the firms we studied, women and enlightened men in leadership positions in the company first brought up the issue of the changing work force requiring a changed workplace.

The fate of these unprogressive firms is uncertain. In areas of pronounced labor shortages, they may have difficulty competing with family-friendly firms for new workers. Or they may start to lose workers to those firms with family-sensitive benefits. Some may experience financial losses due to increases in absenteeism or lateness that seem common among parents with young children or disabled elders at home. Some may experience higher levels of attrition when new moms (or dads) find leave policies inadequate or work hours inflexible.

The savvy firms, however, will keep close track of employee wants and needs and will move forward on at least a limited basis, since virtually any benefit in this regard translates into improvements in employee morale and enhanced public image. These aware managers will continue to monitor the changes in the composition of the work force and begin to make those changes necessary to compete in the global marketplace of the next century.

6

HOW A FIRM CAN BECOME FAMILY-FRIENDLY

INFLUENCES FOR CHANGE

Throughout the course of writing this book we were asked time and again, "Specifically, how can a company come to be family-friendly?" Those questioning us wondered what had motivated some companies to adopt these progressive policies. Was it due to uprisings from the rank and file workers? Did the CEO personally experience an elder- or child-care crisis and move for action? Had these companies been sued in the past for race or sex discrimination and wanted to change their public image? Were women finally in positions of enough influence in their firms to be able to single-handedly make things happen? Were these firms experiencing major labor shortages and then were jolted into action? What we discovered in our research and interviews was that the answer to all of these questions in varying degrees is *yes*.

Rank-and-file workers through their union organizations are influencing corporate America to include family issues in their wage and benefits packages. The Service Employees International Union has issued the book *Solutions for the New Workforce*, outlining the impact of changing family demographics on America's work force and suggesting solutions. Labor organizations have also been in the forefront, pushing cafeteria benefit plans, flexible work schedules, family leaves, and wage packages that will enable workers to adequately support their families.

Women have also entered executive suites in significant enough numbers to influence corporate policies. It was a group made up predominantly of women who conceived of, gained support for, and supervised implementation of the New York area seven employer-consortium for in-home sick-child care noted in chapter 5. Women told us they believe their contributions to the workplace are becoming sufficiently recognized, so they are beginning to feel comfortable enough to speak up on behalf of their children and dependent parents. Arlene Johnson, program director for Workforce Research at The Conference Board, explained that many of the companies she's studied were motivated to initiate work/family programs because "they were losing too many of their high- performance women."

Some women have suggested that those companies that were targets of negative media attention and lawsuits in the '60s and '70s because of inequities based on race and sex decided to offer comprehensive family benefits in the '80s. The Adolph Coors Company, AT&T, a number of banks, and insurance companies have now become leaders with policies that benefit women, minorities, and those employees balancing work/family concerns. In addition, pressure on employers from a declining number of eligible, skilled workers is causing some firms to respond more creatively, to dig deeper, and to find the workers necessary to get the jobs done. A representative of U.S. West Communications told us that he sees three motivating factors for changes sweeping across corporate America: competition with other firms for workers, response to legislative mandates, and pressures from employee groups.

However, by far the most significant factor in the creation of comprehensive work/family programs, is the personal commitment of the CEO. From Frank Blethen, publisher of the *Seattle Times* newspaper, to Robert Haas, CEO at Levi Strauss, to Louis Gerstner, Jr., president of American Express, the attitudes of the person at the top are critical. Frank Blethen was a leading force in getting the Seattle Times to offer near-site child care. Robert Haas meets monthly with a diverse group of Levi Strauss employees in equal employment opportunity (EEO) forums, which go along with a variety of popular programs from a comprehensive job salary evaluation to generous family leaves. Louis Gerstner, Jr. issued a strong challenge to fellow business leaders in a March 1989 *Washington Post* editorial. Urging greater corporate commitment to children, he wrote: "We must be generous with our creativity, our attention, our enthusiasm, and our concern."

On the record, many of these men cite the labor shortage, desire to meet employee expectations, need for increased employee productivity, and community welfare. Indeed, all these reasons are valid motivators, but often the unspoken reasons are more personal. Many of these men now have wives who work full time outside the home, with young children or elderly parents to be concerned about. Often these men share child/eldercare and household tasks and are experiencing firsthand what many workers have been complaining about for years. Alan Gibbs, partner in a dual-career marriage and former executive director of METRO, Seattle's transit and water quality agency, jumped at the chance to institute a pretax dollar dependent-care account for his 4,000- person work force and utilized it for the care of his two-year-old son at a downtown child-care center.

"Some of these guys may have wives who don't work outside the home, but their grown daughters with kids do," says an East Coast entrepreneur. "It is a real eye-opening experience for them to see the struggles their daughters are going through and can cause these CEOs to sit up and listen when their Employee Assistance Program officer says, 'We've got to do something about childcare and eldercare.' "

In many firms across the country, however, there are no enlightened CEOs, powerful female managers, or assertive union leaders championing supportive work/family innovations. How then can employees encourage these changes? Linda Foster, family resource consultant at Hewitt Associates, advises employees to do their homework. "Present the facts rationally, taking into account the finances and demographics of the company. There are lots of programs besides on-site child care that can help. Look at what the competition is doing. Study turnover rates and document costs of training new workers." Ellen Bravo, associate director of 9 to 5, a national association for women workers counsels, "Negotiating for new policies doesn't always mean you'll get them, but not asking guarantees no change."

The following ideas may help start the process at your workplace:

- Talk to others.
- Establish focus groups
- Do necessary research on worker-employee needs
- Request company surveys of employee needs
- Approach your employer with specific suggestions
- Utilize data from the research
- Speak your firm's language
- Give examples of what similar companies are doing
- Set reasonable expectations
- Follow up
- Be willing to serve on a task force or employee committee

- Consider a consortium with other local firms
- Monitor benefits of the new policies for both employees and employer
- Document successes or failures and be ready to suggest needed changes
- Give your employer credit for changes in the right direction
- Keep your eye on the future; change happens incrementally

CORPORATE DECISION MAKING AND FAMILY-FRIENDLY POLICIES

In 1987, The Conference Board published the results of information gathered from more than 75 companies on the leading edge in the emerging field of work/family policy. These firms were willing to share their companies' decision-making strategies so that other firms could benefit from their experiences. What The Conference Board learned is that while any change is usually difficult in organizations, in the case of establishing family-related policies, "resistance can become passionate. Many managers do not believe that family issues are an 'appropriate' business concern." For many years when women stayed at home and men were the sole breadwinners this dichotomy was clearly established. Some managers feared being viewed as intruding into their employees' private lives if they inquired into family needs. Others were not trained to view nonwork issues as having an impact on work life.

Old habits die hard. The prevailing view of work as man's domain and family as woman's persists in many hearts and minds and indeed is still the standard for American business life in a predominance of our nation's enterprises. The fact that it has persisted in the face of so many other cataclysmic changes in the society confounds many. Man's desire for dominance, woman's acculturated submission, labor's passivity and individual workers' fear of rocking the boat all contributed to its perseverance. In reality this rift between work/home and men's and women's roles worked well for centuries. In the last several decades, however, a combination of changes in women's consciousness and the nation's economy rendered the old order obsolete. While times have certainly changed, the attitude of many supervisors has not. In recent years the resistance of business to address family issues has not only hurt the family, it has hurt business as well. Thus many firms began to put in place the internal processes necessary to weave a coherent fabric of family-sensitive policies and programs.

TAKING THE FIRST STEPS

What are some of the first steps necessary to design such a fabric? The Conference Board reports that many firms hire a consultant to do initial research, design employee- or community-needs assessments, recommend a company response, or oversee implementation actions and evaluation of appropriate programs. Other firms try to assess what the competition is doing. For instance, Johnson & Johnson surveyed 55 other companies in the pharmaceutical industry before launching its own work/family initiatives. In the public sector, while some state or local governments have been pacesetters in work/family benefits, others, including universities, have come on board more recently to establish advantages in recruiting and retraining workers. Other organizations started with a self-assessment instrument composed by senior management that became the focal point for discussions on work/family issues leading to an action plan. An example of such a worksheet is included at the end of this chapter.

Most firms seem willing to share their expertise in establishing family-sensitive programs, viewing such requests as an opportunity to enhance their public image. Wang Labs, Steelcase, Inc., and Corning Glass Works have sponsored conferences to teach others, while Stride-Rite Children's Centers sponsor meetings and tours.

FORMULATING A TASK FORCE

At the core of many firms' action plans is the formation of a work/family task force. The benefits of this approach are strengthened internal political support, shared expertise, and division of labor. The Conference Board reported that individuals in the following areas were frequently represented on task forces. Leaders in these areas stand the best chance of representing the company well and gaining overall support when plans are made.

- human resources
- community affairs
- public/government affairs
- training and development
- corporate research
- corporate libraries
- legal departments

- corporate treasury
- labor relations

Most businesses also made sure the task force was diverse with regard to sex, race, job assignments within the organization, and seniority. Representatives of the community, including those from the United Way, chambers of commerce, service organizations, and educational institutions have also been called on by representatives from businesses to augment task force expertise.

While this book highlights the successful results of many firms' work/family task forces and survey efforts, there have been some notable failures. Reasons can range from asking the wrong people to participate, low employee response to needs-assessment surveys, lack of resources, or inability to find widely acceptable solutions. The bottom line for many firms, however, is poor timing: They just were not ready to deal with the issue or there wasn't a clearly articulated employee need. The director of personnel at the *Seattle Times*, Tom Bryan, cites a dramatic change of opinion from their first child-care needs survey done in the early '80s, to one completed just three years later. AT&T was reticent to embark on child-care benefits for many years after a failed effort in the early '70s, but with increased competition for workers, they reassessed their views. Since the late '80s they have emerged as an industry leader in work/family innovations.

Melvin Benjamin, director of work and family programs for Johnson & Johnson, also recommends the creation of a company-wide task force to get a work/family program going in firms just contemplating the issue. "We had eight to nine people focusing on a four-part mission: to achieve a better understanding of the changing relationship between the organization and families; to identify objectives; to define a framework; and to make recommendations for action." He added that the group then broke into subgroups adding people from all levels and divisions of the company. They met for more than a year to design J&J's comprehensive program and continue to meet on a regular basis to evaluate and update the policies, as necessary.

SURVEYS AND PILOT PROJECTS AS TOOLS FOR CHANGE

A large number of firms utilize a written survey to assess the child/eldercare needs of their employees. It is important that the instrument be easily understood, designed to yield usable data, and distributed in such a way as to assure a significant response. Most important, it should not raise expectations that cannot be met. A human resources director for an eastern university said, "Don't ask questions about an on-site child-care center if you didn't have any intention of providing one." Most employers in The Conference Board study recommended giving anonymity to the respondents, projecting an aura of seriousness about the survey by distributing it on company letterhead with a cover memo written by the president or CEO. An all- employee or random sample survey has been a helpful tool for many firms. Some examples of good, understandable surveys are given at the end of this chapter.

Arlene Johnson of The Conference Board has studied a variety of firms in their quest to become more family-friendly. Her advice is to get managers throughout the organization on board, assessing needs, and developing guidelines. To do this, she suggests focus groups, as Home Box Office used, or surveys, or a combination of the two. Next she believes that programs should be implemented on a pilot basis. "It's less threatening to management and allows you to make changes as you learn what works and what doesn't," says Johnson. Finally, she urges that employers should communicate that flexible work schedules are a privilege, not an entitlement, urging a true partnership of both sides, with both labor and management actively striving to make it work.

Catalyst, a national research and advisory organization that works with corporations to foster the career and leadership development of women, recently completed an in-depth study of *flexible work arrangements* at the managerial and professional levels. The firms in the Catalyst study that were most successful at implementing flexible work arrangements were those that:

- appointed a coordinator—someone to see the whole process through
- studied internal demographics to assess employee needs/wants and to project participation
- built management support via use of task forces, pilot projects, focus groups, and training
- geared training toward the importance of flextime/flexplace as a business issue and how to supervise less-than-full-time or off-site workers

It is important for firms to focus their efforts. Karol Rose of Time Warner, Inc., formerly of Time, Inc. Magazine Company, said that they synthesized their needs and then identified five key goal areas for their highly acclaimed work and family program: information/support, policy changes, financial assistance, manager sensitivity, and program development. She explained that the existing networks inside the company can be sources of inspiration for program developments. For instance, out of the company's senior management women's group came the first job-sharing pilot project. Two women in advertising sales decided to maintain a single client base. They each work three days a week getting three-fifths salary but full benefits. Both women believe that it has not only improved the quality of their family life, but improved the quality of their work as well. Management at Time has wholeheartedly agreed, taking the experiment off "pilot project" status.

CHANGING THE CULTURE

For some firms, a *change of culture* is the critical next step required in those organizations that have historically embraced some variation of the "Protestant work ethic." This ethic has manifested itself in the expectation that all workers will put work first, uphold company loyalty, and agree that the work day is from 8:00 A.M. to 5:00 P.M. "Changing the culture is not something that will happen overnight," says Arlene Johnson of The Conference Board. "It's a progressive process involving training, research, and rational observation."

Time Inc. Magazine discovered that it needed buy-in from the entire organization, from the managers who will implement the new policies to the employees who will live them. To get that consensus, says Karol Rose, "We focused on achieving the three Ps: packaging, piloting, and publicizing." They packaged the plan through their work/family booklet, which was distributed to all employees, together with a special newsletter describing the work/family benefits. They piloted several of the innovations, like job-sharing, first, before making them available on a company-wide basis. Finally, they publicized the program by word-of-mouth and promoted it in an advertising campaign not unlike one they would do for a product.

Rosemarie Meschi, director of human resource projects for Ernst and Young, advises those seeking success with work/family programs to focus on fair and equal treatment. She says that in her experience, employees availing themselves of work/family benefits like flextime or job-sharing don't want to be treated differently. "They want challenging work and the top clients; they don't want to be stuck with just the routine projects," says Meschi. Second, she believes that you must articulate compensation benefits clearly and make sure they're calculated on the same basis as for other employees. She recommends a pro rata formula with regular reviews for those in part-time modes. Finally, she believes that opportunities for future advancement and access to continuing education be allocated on a fair and well-communicated basis. "We urge people to openly manage expectations on both sides, so when it comes time for performance reviews, we're doing this against the same set of expectations."

Ernst and Young now also has adopted a special career development strategy for those who opt for flexible work arrangements. Explains Meschi, "Ernst and Young doesn't allow people working part time to be partners. Both those on a traditional career path and those opting for flexible work arrangements, and there are many, are very important to the firm. Therefore, we're designing a progression system that meets the needs of the company, makes the employee feel comfortable, and makes career advancement possible." This is an example of a cultural change that still fits within the basic expectations of the company.

Diane Burrus, director of education and training for Work/Family Directions in Boston, likes to tell the story of a firm her company worked with in the early '80s, before it experienced this requisite *cultural change*. "It was the holiday season and they were trying to decide if they were going to buy four work/family seminars, or turkeys for all their employees. The turkeys won out. We've come a long way; that wouldn't have happened in the '90s. There is now an enormous array of work/family programs in U.S. companies."

OVERCOMING RESISTANCE TO CHANGE

Overcoming resistance to change by both labor and management has been a problem at many workplaces. Taking the instance of adopting flexible work schedules as an example, a number of objections are frequently voiced: "What if this is abused by participating employees? How can work be managed if employees aren't always present? How do we handle the reaction of employees who aren't eligible or whose jobs are inappropriate for flexible hours?"

The Conference Board explores responses to these concerns in the bulletin "Flexible Staffing and Scheduling in U.S. Corporations." It reports that firms that have dealt with these obstacles most successfully are those that recognize and address these concerns in an up-front fashion and then show the viability of the flexible arrangements by sharing success stories. For example, an executive at National Convenience Stores reports that his company relied on "testimonials from others who have successfully incorporated the concept." Again, The Conference Board stresses the value of focus groups and trial periods to test the practicality of such arrangements. Further, it reports that most firms move slowly with overall implementations, fine- tuning as they go. Another admonition we heard from firms adopting flexible work schedules is the need for good communication before and during implementation. A full explanation of who will or will not be eligible for inclusion in the program and why is essential to controlling resentment and avoiding destructive rumor mills.

The Conference Board acknowledges that in an assessment of management satisfaction with flexible scheduling for six different types of arrangements, the programs got high marks in terms of *how employees perform*, but all received lower marks for *ease of supervision*. While the Board postulates that these lower ratings may be the product of inexperience or corporate resistance, it suggests that companies must learn better ways of managing these employees. More effective management methods may be the key to long-term success of flexible scheduling and staffing alternatives of the future.

KEY INDICATORS FOR FAMILY FRIENDLINESS

- *Dependent care benefits* for the family members of employees including infants, children, adolescents, and elderly
- *Flexibility* in hours of work, work sites, career paths, and training opportunities
- *Validation of family issues* in company statements and manager/supervisor training

---

DEVELOPING A FAMILY-FRIENDLY MINDSET

The Conference Board is also to be commended for developing a helpful and sensible tool for thinking about the stages of a worker's life and the benefits that workers may need for themselves and their families. In the chart below, the vertical grid represents a worker's major life and work events from job entry to death. The horizontal grid represents the programs a company may wish to offer at each of the major life mile-stones. This long-range view helps put into perspective an employee's need for four years of pre-school child care or six months of divorce

LIFE-CYCLE STAGES AND COMPANY PROGRAMS

	Financial Assistance	Programs & Services	Counseling & Information	Time
New Worker	Health and Dental Insurance Disability Insurance Life Insurance Pension and/or other Retirement Programs Other Benefits	Fitness Center Employee Assistance Programs (EAP) Health Risk Appraisals	Wellness and Health Promotion Programs EAP	Holidays Vacations Sick Time Disability Leave Leave of Absence Death in Family Other
Marriage	Spouse Benefits Flexible Benefits Spouse Becomes Joint Anniutant in Pension Plan	Spouse Relocation Job Search Assistance for Spouse	EAP	Marriage Leave
Pregnancy & Adoption	Adoption Benefits Medical Coverage for Prenatal and Postnatal Care Coverage for Delivery at Hospital or Birthing Center Change in Beneficiary Coverage for Employee Benefits		Prenatal Courses Information from Benefits Manager	Parental Leave of Absence Maternal Disability Leave Use of Accumulated Sick Leave Alternative Work Schedule and Job Arrangements
Childrearing	Medical & Dental Coverage for Dependents Well-baby Care Dependent Care Assistance Plans (DCAPs) Life Insurance for Dependents Vouchers, Discounts	On-site Child Care Family Day Care School-Age Care Sick Care Breast Feeding Arrangements on site	Referrals Seminars Support Groups Handbooks EAP	Parental Leave Flexible Work Hours Use of Accumulated Sick Leave Earned Time-Off Policies Sick Leave for Family Illness

LIFE-CYCLE STAGES AND COMPANY PROGRAMS

	Financial Assistance	Programs & Services	Counseling & Information	Time
Divorce	Garnishing Wages	Pre-paid Legal	EAP	Personal Leave of Absence
	Step-children Coverage in Medical and Dental Plans	EAP		
	Divorced Spouse and Dependents can continue Medical Coverage for up to 36 months (COBRA)			
Elder Care	DCAPs	Adult Day Care	Referrals	Family Leave
	Long-term Care for Dependents	Pre-paid Legal	Seminars	Flexible Work Hours and Job Arrangements
		EAP	Support Groups	
	Respite Care		Handbooks	Use of Accumulated Sick Leave
				Earned Time-Off Policies
Retirement	Pensions		Pre-retirement Counseling	Part-time Employment for Retirees
	Retiree Health & Dental Care; Life Insurance		Newsletters for Retirees	
	Long-term Care		Telephone Hotlines	
	401K Plans and other before-tax Savings Plans			
Death	Spouse & Eligible Dependents can continue Medical Coverage for up to 36 months	EAP	Grief Counseling through EAP	Funeral Leave
	Beneficiaries receive Life Insurance and other Benefits			Personal Leave of Absence
	Spouse receives at least 60% of retiring Benefits			

Excerpted from "A Life Cycle Approach to Family Benefits and Policies." 1989.
The Conference Board

counseling in a work life that spans 30 or 40 years. This approach can help employers weigh the advantages of work/family benefits in the context of the employee's long-term contributions to the firm. It also helps employees understand more precisely what kinds of assistance is available given their particular circumstances.

WHAT QUALITIES MAKE FAMILY-FRIENDLY FIRMS?

A variety of studies provide some insights into the kinds of firms that were most innovative on work/family issues. Analyses reveal that these companies and corporations were ones that:

- Are considered to be well managed with track records in good human resource management
- Are in hi-tech or scientific industries that must respond to competition for workers
- Have relatively young work forces with more visible family stresses
- Have a high proportion of female employees who still shoulder more family burdens
- Are located in progressive communities and must remain competitive within current mores
- Are largely nonunion with more opportunities for greater flexibility
- Are close to their founders' traditions, which were often more caring and paternalistic
- Make products for, or offer services to, the consumer market and thus are expected to be more responsive to community and employee needs

STEPS TO ATTAINING A SOLUTION TO YOUR FIRM'S WORK/FAMILY NEEDS

What, then, are the steps necessary to initiate a work/family program, once the commitment has been made that change is desirable? The following outline summarizes those measures necessary for transforming your firm from one that is neutral or even hostile to work/family needs to one that can rank with the model family-friendly firms we've highlighted in this book.

1. **Assess your company's reasons for involvement, such as:**
   - Problems in recruitment, turnover or absenteeism

- Concern for employees and their families
- Desire to minimize maternity or eldercare leaves
- Commitment to being among the finest firms in employee benefits

2. **Assess the resources available to your employees:**
   - Quality, quantity, and type of child-care and eldercare facilities
   - Results of current employee benefit plans
   - Evaluation of fees and availability of community resources
   - Review of hours open and services provided

3. **Assess the demands for care in your work force:**
   - Ages of children or elders
   - Types of care used now
   - Satisfaction with current arrangements
   - Costs of care
   - Costs of missed work, unproductive uses of time, commuting to care, etc.

4. **Assess gaps between supply and demand**

5. **Analyze facts from surveys, studies and/or focus groups**

6. **Plan a course of action using a task force or committee to address:**
   - Goals and anticipated results
   - Policies and company mission statement(s)
   - Programs and benefits

7. **Communicate changes internally and externally:**
   - Document changes via company strategic plan and in memos, brochures, etc. to all employees
   - Provide training for managers, supervisors, and all employees
   - Revise plans, procedures, policies, and attitudes to be a family-friendly culture
   - Issue press releases, videos, etc. to news media

8. **Implement changes with mechanisms to monitor utilization as well as successes and pitfalls:** Communicate this information to employees

9. **Revise your programs as necessary, based on regular reviews to implement goals and achieve desired results**

PROGRAM OPTIONS

After the CEO has expressed support for family programs, the employees have been surveyed, their needs have been assessed, and a task force or planning committee is in place, the logical question is: "What do we

---

**OPTIONS FOR DELIVERING FAMILY-FRIENDLY
PROGRAMS**

Direct Services
Information Services
Financial Assistance

---

do now?" A company or consortium of firms can provide good family programs using one or a combination of the following methods: 1) direct services; 2) information services; 3) financial assistance; and 4) flexible policies. Naturally, the more methods employed, the broader the effect.

Direct Services

Direct services include company-sponsored work-site dependent day-care centers; centers for sick children, emergencies, or overnight dependent care (elderly as well as children); home-care networks; activity programs for school-age children; "warm-lines"; summer/weekend camps for dependents; health care centers with exercise areas; personal crisis counseling; apprentice training; and family-sensitive supervisors.

On- or near-site child-care centers may be costly. However, growing evidence shows that they result in long-term cost savings. Alternatives to the company's fully subsidizing the centers are to: 1) develop a consortium with other nearby firms; 2) charge at-cost fees; 3) develop co-op schedules with parents serving as staff during some part of the day; 4) initiate partnerships with local government agencies and share the cost. *On-site day care* increases worker retention and reduces

---

DIRECT SERVICES

- On- or near-work site day-care centers
- Collaborative sick/emergency/overnight care centers
- Home-care networks
- School-age day-care programs and warm-lines
- Summer and weekend camps for dependents
- Wellness activities and exercise areas
- Professional personal crisis counseling
- Apprentice training
- Family-sensitive supervisors

---

employee absenteeism. At Wake Medical Center Kidwinks, in Raleigh, North Carolina, 64% of parents surveyed said the center encouraged them to stay at their current job; 18% said they would have left had the center not been there; and 26% said the center was a factor in accepting a job. At the nearby First Environments Child Care Center, operated by the Environmental Protection Agency and the Natural Institute of Environmental Health Science in Research Triangle Park, North Carolina, 73% of parents said the center encourages them to stay at their present job; 12% said they would have left their job without the child-care center, and 19% said the center was a factor in accepting their job. In terms of reducing absenteeism, 44% of Medical Center employees and 38% of First Environment's, parents said the child-care center helped reduce their child-care related absences. Seventy-four percent of Medical Center employees and 54% of First Environment's parents said the child-care center helped them be on time for work. Finally, 51% of the Medical Center employees and 73% of First Environment's agreed that the center improved morale. While many employers fear the relatively high initial cost of establishing an on-site facility, these figures make a strong argument for cost savings after implementation.

Several firms have discovered that although their employers have regular day-care arrangements, *care for sick dependents, emergencies, and overnight care* can create crisis-proportion worries for working families. Consequently, they have established services for these situations. As this kind of service can be costly, collaborative arrangements are often made with hospitals or private caregivers who already have facilities for these needs. Lisa Albright, a veterinarian at a large animal treatment center in the Northwest can be on call day and night. She and the other vets have made arrangements to bring their children to a special wing of the hospital on nights they have to work. "It's been a life saver—and my daughter enjoys the chance to pack her bag and have what she calls a 'pajama party with the nurses'!"

It is also possible to retain a home-care nursing service to go to the homes of employees to cover emergencies and overnight or out-of-town travel. The consortium of seven major New York City employers described earlier in chapter 5 adopted this approach to meet emergency child-care needs of their employees.

Some employers are helping to find and train *home day-care* providers near their facilities or in neighborhoods where substantial numbers of their employees live. Other employers help by organizing these providers into a network and supplying support services, including toy lending or book libraries, group purchasing plans, or caregiver backup in case of illness. In exchange for such assistance the family day-care providers guarantee slots for a certain number of the assisting company's employees. Advantages to parents and children are the closer-to-home or -work location, and home-like, comfortable settings for this type of care. Other advantages include less rigid hours of operations, options of before- and after-school care, and acceptance of very young children. Many child-care centers don't offer care to infants or school-age children needing supervision before or after regular classroom hours. Some employers have chosen to supplement their on-site center with this option to avoid waiting lists or to deal with needs of parents who live very far away from the site. When St. Luke's Rush Presbyterian Medical Center in Chicago had a 225-infant waiting list for its on-site center, they established a satellite system of family day- care homes. Other firms rely exclusively on family home centers because they have too many corporate locations or have workers scattered too far away from any one facility, or because employees chose this as their first preference on the firm's child-care needs survey.

Schools are often partners in developing *school-age after-school programs* for children over six years old. Community education programs can offer crafts, recreation, storytelling, and drama opportunities from 3:00 P.M. to 6:00 P.M. every day. Organizations like the YWCA/YMCA, Boys Clubs, and Girls Clubs are set up to serve young people after school. Because they are dependent on funding from the general public, businesses can make financial arrangements with them to assure that the children of their employees are served. On-site after-school programs, an extension of the day-care programs, are also a possibility. Children in these programs usually require transportation from school to the work site.

The concept of *"warm-lines"* was developed to serve school-age children and at-home elderly. A trained person is hired by the company to answer calls coming from employees' homes during the day. This telephone counselor will talk to lonely children or elderly, answer questions, take messages, or talk through a disturbing situation with a dependent at home. The manager of a Midwest farm products company says that, "All phones in the plant were ringing off their hooks at 3:30 P.M. Little work got done until 4:30 P.M. After we established the warm-line and hired one full-time and two part-time [two-hour] 'phone counselors,' our afternoon production went up 50%. Employees tell them their dependents feel good about it too. They know they can always call and get a patient, caring answer." This solution has been adopted most frequently by the service sector, such as hospitals, but is being embraced by manufacturers as well.

Summer and weekend day camps for dependents are a method of taking care of school-age children, and sometimes ambulatory elderly, when their adult family members are at work. Because staffing, transportation, and liability for these activities can be costly, a careful needs assessment is necessary. Here, again, collaboration with community agencies already set up to provide these services can be the best approach. FelPro, a manufacturing company in Skokie, Illinois, is just one example of a pioneering firm in this area, with more than 350 children of employees enrolled in their summer camp.

In addition to health insurance benefits, many companies offer *wellness activities* in the form of exercise areas and access to company doctors, nurses, or other health professionals. Stress reduction exercises and regimens are also part of this trend. Because health care costs are a major concern now to business as well as individuals, many company-sponsored innovations are being tried. Weyerhauser is just one of many firms that has a trained health consultant who lectures on nutrition, especially in relation to heart disease, consults with employees, and directs physical activities and stress management techniques.

Professional counseling for personal crises was one of the first family-friendly benefits offered by many companies, often in response to the problem of alcoholism among white-collar male employees. Since that time, counseling and crisis programs have grown to address problems with addictions in both sexes, divorce, errant teenagers, disabilities, depression, etc. Methods range from an on-site counselor to referral of employees to outside help such as treatment centers, group and family counseling, and residential care programs.

Apprentice training is another family-centered benefit. The pressures to create a flexible workplace that requires complex skills and ingenuity to carry out a variety of tasks has led to a re-examination of apprenticeship programs. Often called "school to work programs," these approaches promote learning a trade or skill through a combination of classroom study and on-the-job training. The U.S. Department of Labor has created the Office of Work-Based Learning to support pilot projects in this regard. Elizabeth Dole, former secretary of labor, brought together labor leaders as an advisory group to suggest ways to expand apprenticeship training. "It's a market that favors employees," observes Rick Cohen of Furr's/Bishop's Cafeterias. Once they hire, "Companies will have to train people in new ways to make sure they keep learning as jobs keep changing," declares Cecilia Williams of Pacific Telesis Group.

Reacting to the labor shortage more quickly, Germany, Sweden, France, and other European countries are ahead of the United States in embracing this concept, with apprenticeship programs often financed by special taxes. Lately, however, some large American firms like Motorola, Ford, General Electric, and American Express have invested millions of dollars on this kind of training. They are making this investment in their workers to boost productivity in recognition of increased global competition, as well as to retain workers in a market where human capital is in increasingly short supply. Those most likely to benefit from this approach are single parents who can't take time off from work to go back to school and teenagers entering the labor market for the first time. Also, on-the-job learning could benefit two-wage-earner households where increased education would be a real career advantage but is not feasible in terms of family economics as these families need both paychecks each week to survive. Apprenticeship programs also provide the advantage of loyalty to the training employer, thus enhancing retention rates.

Supervisors who are sensitive to family/work problems are essential to any program. Laws and policies can be established indefinitely, but the true test of employer-employee understanding regarding workers' family needs lies in the interaction between the worker and supervisor. Supervisors who are trained and are sensitive to the critical link between retraining quality employees and dealing appropriately with their family concerns are the best ambassadors an organization can have. Sensitivity to work/family needs affects not only the employees' productivity, but also that of the supervisors and, in some cases, the entire work group. In John P. Fernandez's previously cited study on work/family productivity needs, supervisors were deemed critically important. "When my supervisor acknowledges the bind I'm in, as a single parent with two sick kids, and she helps me out in some way, I feel valued—and that makes me put out 150% for the company," claims Linda Jamison, a secretary in a small western firm. Linda's comment is typical of the many workers we interviewed. Employees are anxious to do a good job—both at work and at home.

How important is the role of the manager in implementing family-friendly policies? Some would argue that in this era of a more diverse work force, a more well-rounded manager is needed. Someone whose life is too narrowly focused may not be the best people leader. A West Coast bank executive said she thought her parenting experience

---

SENSITIVE SUPERVISORS NEEDED

- Only 25% of female managers and 39% of male managers ever dealt with the child-care problems of subordinates
- Sixty-six percent of both single and married women felt that their supervisors were somewhat supportive of their child-care needs
- An unsupportive supervisor will force parents to lie about child-care problems or miss an entire day's work rather than try to make alternative arrangements
- Almost three out of 10 women and more than one out of five men did not feel free to discuss their child-care needs with their supervisors
- There was a direct correlation between amount of stress felt in balancing work/family concerns and the amount of support for these issues expressed by the supervisor
- Lack of a uniform and fair method of dealing with child-care related absences and lateness results in lowered morale and decreased productivity of the entire work group

Source: J P. Fernandez Study

---

had taught her to be a better manager. She knows how to utilize time effectively and she believes she's more efficient at getting people moving in positive directions. She's more patient and has a better sense of humor. *Human capital has become an asset as vital to an organization's success as physical capital or financial assets. Managers who are adept at people development will be the successful leaders in the '90s.*

Information Services
Information (or indirect) services include resource and referral systems, life-skill education programs, and job change or job development training.

Resource and referral systems offer professional guidance on issues of concern to working parents and employees with aging relatives. Generally they are made available for free to employees and are designed to help clarify choices and reduce the amount of time and energy required to find appropriate care.

Employers contract with a professional service that will answer workers' questions on how to find needed child care or eldercare. They make referrals to family day-care homes, child-care or eldercare centers, preschools, school-age programs, summer day camps, and special needs

---

INFORMATION SERVICES

- Resource and referral system:
  - Child-care options
  - Eldercare options
- Life skill educational programs:
  - Health issues
  - Parenting skills
  - Financial management
  - Retirement
- Job training programs

---

programs. Most do not make referrals to individuals who provide care in an employee's home; however, they may make referrals to agencies that place such caregivers or they will assist with writing a "help wanted" advertisement.

Because finding appropriate care for an elderly relative can be especially confusing, worrisome, and time-consuming, some corporations are making a geriatric case manager available to help families with their decisions. Case managers can line up in-home care, negotiate prices, help find a nursing aide, and monitor the quality of service provided. Having objective, expert help can lessen the emotional toll of the decision maker. Unisys and 3M are but two firms that have utilized outside resources to help the firm better understand their employees' family needs.

"You can call for any reason—whether you simply want to talk something through with an expert, or you need help in finding appropriate care—or for anything else related to child care or eldercare," says Susan Geisenheimer, vice president of human resources for Time, Inc. Magazines in a brochure explaining their resource and referral program. Each resource and referral program is unique in how it is structured and what specific services are provided. Other companies merely offer objective information on child-care availability; some also provide qualitative remarks about services. Many maintain statistics only on one particular type of child- or eldercare, while others list all services within a given state or locale. Some avoid rating the quality of services, while others not only rate but train staff. Some services are highly selective, others are inclusive. Of the 415 companies surveyed by the National Employer-Supported Child Care Project, 42 indicated some type of referral services as all or part of their child-care assistance plans.

Some well-known firms that have this service are IBM, Leo Burnett, Honeywell, Exxon, and Security Pacific Bank.

Referral services may be internal, that is, staff who are regular employees of the company, or external, a separate firm hired to provide advice on child-care providers and assessment of parental needs. Some firms also provide data on quality and quantity of child-care services and counsel employers on child-care choices. IBM has hired Work/Family Directions of Watertown, Massachusetts, to establish a nationwide network of 150 local referral agencies on available forms of child care. Child Care Systems near Philadelphia is another firm that provides these services, assessing employee needs, matching employee requirements with openings, and giving parents lists of available slots near their homes or jobs. Three months later Child Care Systems gives the employer, such as Bell of Pennsylvania, a summary of data collected from employees for management to use to continue to plan for child-care needs. Child Care, Inc., a New York City–based firm, is yet another company that now provides child-care referral services, conducts needs assessments, offers consultation on options, and furnishes assistance in developing on-site child-care and parenting seminars to more than 50 corporate clients, including many of New York's largest employers.

Life skill education helps employees gain control of their own situations. As the composition of the work force changes, large corporations, small businesses, and government agencies are recognizing that the era of "leave your family problems at home" is past history. While many would agree that parenting is a rewarding endeavor, it is also one fraught with challenges. These challenges are made more complex by the demands on the job site. Thus, many firms are setting up formal or informal mechanisms to allow or encourage parents to come together to share common concerns and learn new parenting skills.

Family education programs are advantageous to both employers and employees. These are work-site programs designed to help parents know how to balance work and family life, how to discipline effectively, how to help children or elders cope with crisis in trauma, and many other topics. The assumption is the more skills you have to be effective as a family member, the more productive you will be as an employee. Employers also benefit from this visible demonstration of concern for needs of workers as family members responsible for child care or eldercare.

Among work forces with generally similar numbers of males and females, working mothers usually outnumber working fathers five to one at the seminars, explained Stephen Seal, former president of the

Philadelphia firm Resources for Parents at Work. The largest percentage of seminar participants are parents with children under seven years of age, followed by parents of teenagers. Most firms experience an initial response rate of 2.5% of the total work force. In addition to the seminars, other successful programs have incorporated a library of parenting materials. Books, magazines, and brochures provided in a comfortable on-site location or available for checkout are tangible manifestations of management's interest in well integrating work/family commitments.

In some companies, family education programs are as formal as employer-sponsored family and parenting workshops that deal not only with strategies to meet the needs of children but elders as well. In other firms, these take the form of brown bag lunch groups. While some firms subsidize the full costs of formal workshops and informal discussions, others insist that employees contribute towards expenses. In the workshops, speakers from inside or outside the organization address such topics as meeting your family's nutritional needs, toilet teaching your toddler, practicing positive discipline, or finding resources for your troubled teen. Inside speakers come from the human resource or related departments, while outside resources include the local school district, consulting firms, family practice mental health professionals, or area hospitals, to name just a few potential sources of expertise. Brown bag lunch seminars often do not feature a formal speaker but rather the company merely provides a meeting place and then parents meet on their own to share concerns and strategies for coping.

Merck & Co., Inc. offers an ongoing series of very popular Family Matters Workshops. The firm provides a box lunch for participants, about half of whom are male, according to Art Strohmer, Merck's executive director for executive staffing and development. Strohmer offers the following tips to ensure success of the seminars: Use a proven session leader to be sure employee needs are met; share costs with employees so they feel a stake in it and to assure stable attendance; obtain feedback to track developing interests; and keep the sessions small (i.e., less than 15 people), so that everyone has the opportunity to share individual experiences.

Honeywell, Inc., based in Minneapolis, is another firm with an extensive series of parenting programs. A support group for parents, The Parent Network, features facilitated twice-monthly lunchtime discussion groups, as well as workshops on timely topics that reflect how workplace changes can impact an employees' home life. One of these, "Navigating Change Together," was a result of an organizational shift at Honeywell. A hands-on approach is sought in most sessions allowing employees to gain new skills, role-play, and get support from the group. Honeywell's Kathy Barclay, health services manager, offers the following advice: Listen to employees to learn of problems; keep the workshop topics focused to better meet individual needs; develop a resource library of data presented at workshops; and seek evaluation of all programs by employees to help plan for the future.

A much smaller business that has also taken on the challenge of competing with larger firms for qualified employees is the Savings and Loan Data Corporation of Cincinnati, Ohio, a data processing service bureau with just 180 employees. To be a more attractive employer, they now offer an employee assistance program, flexible work schedules, a child-care referral network, a tax-free dependent-care spending account, and expanded short-term disability benefits. Recently, they combined

---

POSSIBLE TOPICS FOR PARENTING WORKSHOPS OR BROWN BAG LUNCHES

- Successful Step-Parenting
- Blending Work/Family Responsibilities
- Selecting Child Care for Infants and Toddlers
- Dealing with Your Child's Fears
- Selecting a Preschool for Your Child
- Positive Discipline
- Survival Strategies for New Parents
- Finding Before/After-School Care
- Helping Your Child Cope with Divorce
- Becoming a Parent
- Weaning Your Child
- Choosing Toys and Books for Your Child
- Toilet Teaching Your Toddler
- Time Management Skills for Working Families
- Providing Alternatives to TV Viewing
- Avoiding Substance Abuse by Children
- Nutrition for Kids
- Coping with Childhood Illness
- Nutrition for Elders
- Choosing Long-term Care for Elders
- Community Resources for Elders
- Parenting Teenagers
- Preventing Working Parent Burnout

the programs in a comprehensive package called Life Cycles. "We recognized that throughout a person's life, there are different ways a company can support its employees. Life Cycles ties it all together," says Leslie Kuhlman, human resources generalist for the firm. In choosing lunchtime topics, Kuhlman says that she started by conducting a survey to ascertain primary areas of workers' concerns; then she made sure to describe the topics in "parenting" terms to make the forums attractive to both male and female employees; finally, she obtained management support by giving supervisors specific training to teach them how to "assist, support, and refer employees to the company's family-related programs."

Many private services are also springing up to aid small employers in providing these benefits. The educational newsletter *Tot Memos*, written by a businesswoman in Massachusetts, is an example of the kind of printed material available by subscription.

A surprising statistic from the Fernandez study is the fact that 25% of the employees with no children under 19 were interested in these training programs. This perhaps means that they recognize their role in assisting others in their work group to deal with work/family problems, or that they want information that might be helpful in the future, such as advice on investing, financial management, and retirement planning. Although it is difficult to assess the impact of educational programs such as these, their popularity indicates they are seen as good benefits.

Job development or training programs are also important to the new workers of the '90s because many will be unfamiliar with highly technical workplaces and the changing work ethic. It will be equally important to older workers who need training in new technological advancements. It is estimated that business will far exceed universities in the amount of training and education it will provide in the next decade.

Financial Assistance

Financial Assistance as a method of meeting family/work needs may take the form of the company providing fully paid or reimbursed benefits, partial subsidies, tax-exempt programs, purchase of care "spaces," flexible spending accounts, or contributions to community care centers. Special needs also arise when one or both spouses must relocate.

For years, health care insurance has been a *fully paid benefit* of most large companies. Other common fully paid benefits might include term insurance or membership in an exercise facility. Some companies are now offering fully paid child-care or eldercare centers. These fees might be paid directly through the firm's treasurer, or reimbursed to

---

FINANCIAL ASSISTANCE

- Fully paid or reimbursed benefits
- Partial subsidies
- Tax-exempt care programs
- Purchase of care "spaces"
- Flexible spending accounts
- Contributions to community care centers
- Relocation assistance

---

employees after they pay the fee and submit receipts. Long-term health care insurance is another benefit that will be expected in the '90s, which employers will need to include in existing insurance plans at an added cost, offer to employees at a group rate, or entreat the federal government to provide via some type of national coverage.

Another benefit option for many working parents is a *partial subsidy for child-care or eldercare costs* where the firm pays a portion of the cost. The payment may be a fixed dollar amount or be determined by a sliding scale based on need. "The child day-care program at my company is a big plus for the corporation and its employees," said one single parent at Control Data Corporation in Minneapolis. "It is such a relief to be able to go to work knowing my child is right on the grounds if she needs me, just footsteps away. And I enjoy that she's learning and working in a structured environment all day." As a worker earning between $10,000 and $18,000 per year, she expressed one critical note, however. "I have to take her out of the day-care this summer for financial reasons. It would be nice if the company could pick up more than 10%; maybe a sliding fee-schedule based on salaries," she suggested. Another parent expressed gratitude at her employer's subsidy of the off-site day- care center's fees. "Our employer provides excellent fringe benefits in rates for all employees. I could not provide care for him anywhere for the amount I pay daily."

The Internal Revenue Code Sections 89, 125, 129, 162, 168, 170, 195, 419a, and 501 outline the *tax-exempt care incentives* that help working parents and their employers afford dependent care. These regulations allow certain costs of child-care to be deductible. They also allow tax exemptions and use of pretax dollars on some kinds of employees' child-care arrangements. Capital expenditures for construction and furnishing day-care centers can also become an amortized deduction. Some of these deductions apply even when companies form a consortium to provide services or create partnerships with public institutions. (See the end of chapter 7 for a listing of tax information sources.)

Purchasing care "spaces" from existing child-care or eldercare facilities has merit for small companies or firms where few employees have dependent-care needs. In this case, XYZ Company would reserve and pay for 10 children at the local child-care center, which is operated as a private business. Up to 10 employees' children would then be served at this center. The same could be true for adult day care or elderly home care. Some of the purchase cost is a tax-deductible cost to the firm buying the "spaces." Other firms provide cost subsidies. The Seattle Times uses a disinterested third party, a consumer credit counseling firm, to assess eligibility for tuition financial aid for their near-site child-care center. This is a benefit much appreciated by lower-income workers and it assures them of impartiality in making the decision as to who is eligible.

Many employers who do not believe that they have the financial resources to establish an on-site child-care center or employ a resource and referral service, or even offer direct tuition reimbursement, are taking a first step by offering employees a *flexible spending account*. Funds from this account are available to cover costs or care for children, elders, or other dependent family members. It may also be used for medical expenses. The account entails a reduction in the employee's annual pretax salary by as much as $5,000. These funds are placed in a separate account that is managed by the employer. The employee pays his or her dependent-care expenses and then is reimbursed for these costs from the account. The employee pays no income tax on this money and the employer pays no social security or unemployment taxes. Because a pretax-dollar account costs little and is useful to many employees, it is becoming a very popular benefit.

Contributions made to community care centers can provide a company with a tax break and ensure its use by company employees when the need arises. Much like purchasing spaces, but considered a true contribution, this method helps when care is needed on an informal, irregular, or perhaps emergency basis. As in all financial arrangements, responsibility on the part of both partners needs to be spelled out and in a contractual form.

The stress and logistical problems encountered in relocating when a family is transferred to another community are especially difficult for two-paycheck families. Families need *relocation assistance* when selling one home and buying another, regardless of the market. Finding the "trailing" spouse a new job, acclimating children to new schools and the family to new medical and service professions can be very costly, both financially and emotionally. Employees need considerable help in making these adjustments. Recent worker trends indicate many upwardly mobile young professionals are dropping out or refusing promotions if they involve relocating. Some couples are settling for a "commuter marriage" with spouses living in different towns and visiting each other as frequently as possible. This arrangement often results in counterproductive workaholism, where employees work to relieve the loneliness of not being with spouses or families. International transfers can be especially stressful. Executives eligible for international transfers are often likely to be part of a dual-career partnership. Immigration laws often make it very difficult, if not impossible, for spouses to find work. Cultural differences can also take their toll on adolescent children who need to identify with their peers. A company that provides assistance with the relocation process is supplying a much-needed benefit.

Flexible Work Policies

A recent national survey of corporate executives by the Olsten Corporation revealed that 75% of the respondents said they would consider hiring workers who wanted special flex schedules.; only 33% answered this question affirmatively just five years earlier. The U.S. labor market now includes almost 20 million part-timers of whom 3 million are on the professional level. This is a trend likely to continue to grow rapidly throughout the '90s in this tight labor market.

FLEXIBLE WORK POLICIES

- Flexible time scheduling:
  - Flextime
  - Compressed work weeks
  - Job-sharing
  - Part-time
- Flexible workplaces:
  - Home/telecommuting
  - Alternative work sites
- Parental/medical leave
- Cafeteria benefit plans
- Phased retirement

Flextime, as defined by a Conference Board survey, is "a work schedule that permits flexible starting and quitting times but requires a standard number of hours to be worked within a given time period. "Shift work is a precursor of flextime, where an individual chooses the particular eight hours to be worked within the 24-hour day. Both options can be helpful to family members or students at different times during their careers or life cycles. 3M instituted its flexible-hours program in response to a national opinion poll of employees, more than half of whom said flextime would be helpful. When tested on a trial basis, both employee morale and productivity increased.

Compressed work weeks are full-time weeks completed in fewer than five days per week. General Mill's *American Family Report* revealed that as early as 1980, nearly 2 million workers chose to gain free time by working four 10-hour days (the 4/40 approach) or three 12-hour days instead of the "normal" five-day week.

Two people voluntarily sharing the responsibilities of one full-time position is called *job-sharing*. Salary and benefits are prorated according to the percent of time each party contracts. Research indicates that these arrangements have been most popular in those fields such as sales or client-centered services where employees can work on a more individualistic basis. It is a tremendous help to professionals who are trying to cope with heavy family demands for a few years but want to remain fully active in their fields.

Part-time work is considered any work schedule of less than 40 hours a week, predetermined most often on a regular basis. Benefits may be provided, but often are not available for half-time or less. New parents and those caring for elderly relatives are not the only workers who seek flexibility in work sites and hours. The growing number or people over age 55, many of whom don't want or can't afford to retire early, may seek reductions in hours of work or the ability to work from home, reducing burdensome commutes.

Working at home or in a *flexplace* and communicating by telephone and computer is becoming a popular method of increasing productivity, by eliminating time lost in traffic, and the stress and expense of commuting. Jill Styles, a promotion executive for a textiles company, works at home three days a week. "My productivity has increased 100%. Creativity requires quiet time and no distractions. The office is full of nonstop distractions. I have finally found my quickstone!"

It is also important that companies be flexible with regard to *parental/medical leave*, including time off for the illness of a child, spouse, or elderly family member. The amount of leave varies widely from employer to employer. IBM provides full pay for medical leave of up to 52 weeks and Campbell Soup Co. offers three months' paid leave for the serious illness of a dependent child, parent, or spouse. While these companies may be the exception rather than the rule, clearly some type of adequate leave time is in order.

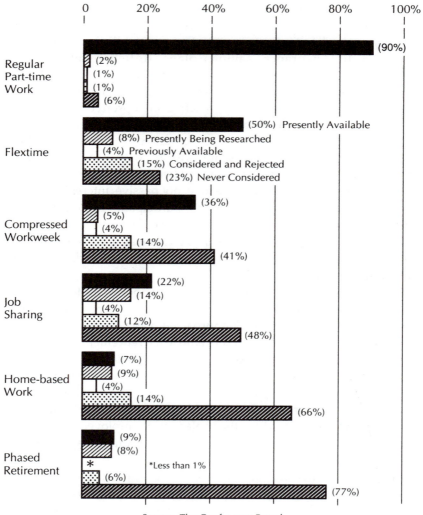

PREVALENCE OF FLEXIBLE SCHEDULING ARRANGEMENTS
Total responces for each arrangement = 100%

Source: The Conference Board
Work and Family Center

Some may argue that providing elder- or child-care benefits, flextime, job-sharing, and other family-friendly options is inherently unfair to those employees without family concerns. Some issues can be resolved by utilizing *cafeteria-type benefit plans.* One approach gives all employees a specific dollar amount and a list of benefits with their respective costs. Employees then choose, based on their needs and preferences, up to that dollar limit. Another plan provides certain basics for all employees and then optional choices, again up to a set dollar amount. A third option allows one of the first two approaches listed above within a cash amount with which the employee may purchase benefits not offered by the company. Thus, a complete cafeteria benefit plan would allow employees to select among vacation time, medical/dental/vision coverage, life insurance, savings plans, tuition reimbursement, child-care or eldercare assistance, and pretax dollar accounts. United Hospitals of Cheltenham, Pennsylvania, is just one employer experiencing the pluses of this approach. United projects a $2.5 million annual savings in employee benefits costs since adopting a cafeteria or flexible benefits plan. These plans recognize that employees have different needs and provide alternatives to deal with them. It also results in highlighting to employees the costs of benefits. Being more aware of benefits and their costs creates an active, not passive, interest in crafting the plan and makes employees aware participants in holding down costs. While cafeteria plans can greatly benefit both businesses and workers, only 8% of the 374 firms in the Catalyst study said they had such plans, though this number is predicted to grow rapidly before the end of this century.

Phased retirement gives older workers the opportunity to reduce the number of hours worked for a specified period of time prior to retirement. This part-time work approach is being offered by firms that don't want to lose seasoned workers who reach retirement age. Creating schedules that meet the needs of the organization and the individual can be a challenge, but the result is less traumatic to the worker and smooths the transition at the workplace as well. Thus, the firm can be assured of the retiree's talent for a longer period of time, assuring work quality and perhaps a training period for the replacement employee. At the same time the retiree's income needs and request for time away during the regular work week can be honored. One variation might be the introduction of emeritus status, where valued employees are contracted back, after retirement, to consult on special projects or lend their expertise in other ways. Surprisingly, business has been slow to institute this benefit. The Yankelovich Group conducted a poll for the American

Association of Retired Persons in 1989, to update a study completed in 1985. "While personnel executives, or 'gatekeepers' have grown to recognize the need to fully use long-time employees, that view is not reflected in a commitment by senior management to skill training for older workers. Only 25% of the companies surveyed have formal programs focused on the use of employees over 50 years old, down from 33% in 1985. "Although 45% of the companies surveyed viewed phased retirement as an effective way to use older workers, only 18% have such programs. The labor shortages of the '90s may change that picture.

DEBUNKING MYTHS

A Catalyst study debunked several persistent myths about the problems of innovative workplaces, specifically focusing on alternate work schedules. Myth #1 states: Flexible schedules only work for routine or project-based jobs. Christine Scordato of Catalyst demurred: "We found many instances of success in line positions with significant bottom-line responsibility as well as those with supervisory responsibility, direct client contact, and with travel requirements." Myth #2 is that people who utilize flextime are less dedicated to the company or their careers. The Catalyst study found that three-quarters of those utilizing flexible work arrangements had significant tenure and many cited flexibility of working hours as an alternative to quitting their jobs. Myth #3 is that changing head counts deters managers from approving flexible work arrangements. "We found in reality that there was no real concern here once people utilized an FTE (full-time equivalent) system," said Scordato in which two job sharers are counted as one employee. She added that professional firms, like law or accounting practices, were particularly good at being innovative, trying flexible schedules based on work load according to slowest times of the year.

Another myth debunked in several studies is the "slippery slide" or as one manager put it, "once I do this for one employee, everyone will want it." The reality is that many workers don't want flexible work arrangements because they can't afford them. Part-time work, job-sharing, and phased retirement call for reductions in salary and, in some firms, reductions in benefits. The exceptions are flextime, flexplace, and the compressed work week, which generally do not call for reductions in salary or benefits. However, each of these approaches has drawbacks that make it somewhat less attractive for workers, as well. Flextime may or may not play havoc with child-care or eldercare arrangements, which generally require same time drop-offs and pick-ups throughout the year. Flexplace, which allows employees to work from home or a small satellite office, may result in feelings of isolation for the worker involved. It also requires extra effort on the part of the employees to communicate with co-workers and supervisors. Compressed work weeks, like the 4/40, can result in employees exhausted from working such a long day or in problems with child-care or eldercare scheduling. Overall, relatively small numbers of workers request flexible schedules for relatively limited periods of time.

Despite these drawbacks, those workers at all levels who do avail themselves of these options are surprisingly satisfied with these arrangements, as are their managers. A 1989 Conference Board study documents these results as the graphs below and following illustrate.

The other reality managers need to remind themselves of is the generally short time period during which employees seek flexibility. As the new mother's child gets older she will probably want to work more hours. When the single father of a troubled pre-teen finds the before- and after-school care he needs, he will probably want to go back to a regular work schedule. When the parent of an ill elder finds appropriate in-home

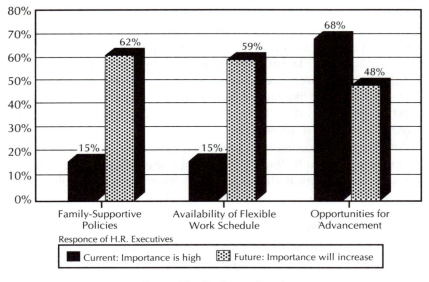

WHAT INCENTIVES ARE IMPORTANT FOR RECRUITING AND RETAINING EMPLOYEES?

Responce of H.R. Executives

■ Current: Importance is high   ▦ Future: Importance will increase

Source: The Conference Board
Research Bulletin

OCCUPATIONAL DISTRIBUTION OF
EMPLOYEES USING FLEXIBLE SCHEDULES

Source: The Conference Board
Work and Family Center

care or the elder's health improves, he or she will no longer need to work flexible hours. These and many other family situations are short-term and require some options that generally will be utilized for a finite period.

Rosabeth Moss Kanter, in her 1989 book When Giants Learn to Dance, writes extensively about the growing time expectations of corporate America and their employees' eagerness to keep up. "In a world in which anything is possible, but nothing is guaranteed, and the failure to pursue opportunity may be a worse sin than making a mistake, how much work, how much activity, how much is enough? In a post-entrepreneurial workplace 'enough' is defined not by some pre-existing standard like the length of the work day but by the limits of human endurance."

Perhaps family endurance must also be a measure of the amount of time family members can stay away, or otherwise be engaged "at work." What measure of flexibility an employer can provide to help employees deal with these varying endurance limits will be a hallmark of the successful firm in the '90s. Enough has been said recently about

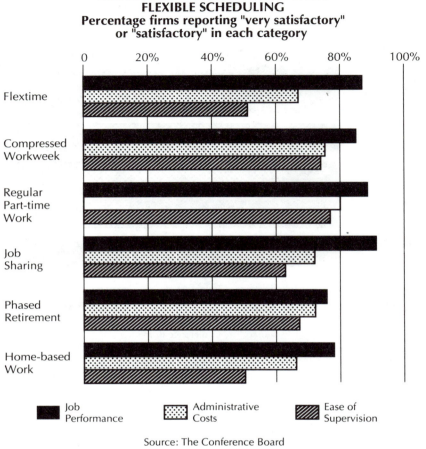

**MANAGEMENT SATISFACTION WITH
FLEXIBLE SCHEDULING**
Percentage firms reporting "very satisfactory"
or "satisfactory" in each category

Source: The Conference Board
Work and Family Center

parental/medical leave, both here and in the national media. Now is the time to do something about it. If nothing else, families need time to integrate new members into the circle and time to take care of one another when a crisis occurs. Human life is based on those simple, caring gestures. Employers need to provide the opportunities. Some states are now mandating that they do, and many of us believe they will become part of a national family policy as well.

To summarize, then, the first steps companies that desire to become family-friendly must take involve acknowledging the need for balance in the nonwork and work responsibilities people bear. At the first level, this awareness can be symbolic: changes in the company's mission statement, rewriting the credo, or modifying the personnel and benefits handbooks.

The second step focuses on *skills*. Employees need to help workers achieve better personal time management techniques and also assist these workers in identifying the particular needs dictated by their nonwork/family situation. Skills should also be shared in *prioritizing*, *delegating*, and *simplifying* so that the worker is fully creative, knows how/when to seek help, and is less bureaucratic/hierarchical in making decisions. Remember: The goal is not the employer's becoming a substitute for the family, rather we want workers to have the tools necessary to identify and then meet their own unique family needs.

The third and perhaps most critical step is to *provide institutional supports*. These can take many forms from child-care and eldercare assistance to flexible work schedules. A broad enough array to meet the many situations workers face over the course of their work lives is most desirable. To achieve these changes in *symbols, skills, and supports* requires greater cooperation between employers and employees than has existed in many organizations. It will hinge in many instances on less adversarial relationships with labor unions and a willingness to move beyond historic internal structures and divisions. It will also be dependent on prodigious amounts of internal communication. There must be meetings to explain the new goals and objectives, memos on how everyone can benefit from the change, and follow-up to make sure all workers understand how work/family policies contribute to the economic vitality of the firm.

Finally, a word to those managers who launch work/family programs or who draft changes to the corporate mission statement: You must "walk the walk and talk the talk." In other words, you must be a living model of the values your words embrace. No more working 60-hour weeks, if you're preaching more time with children for your workers. And if your elderly parent becomes ill, sign up for the company's program offering assistance in finding at-home eldercare. Attend the brown bag seminars on dealing with troubled teens or ill toddlers if you have children in those age groups. In other words, let your workers see that it's OK to acknowledge their family's needs, that you have them too, and we're all trying to be the best we can be as family members and employees.

CREATING YOUR OWN PLAN OF ACTION
A SELF-ASSESSMENT AND WORKSHEET

HELPING YOUR EMPLOYER BE FAMILY-FRIENDLY

1. What kinds of benefits does your firm already have in place to meet the needs of employees with child/eldercare concerns?
2. What additional kinds of benefits would you like to see your firm offer?
3. Has there been a survey done in the last year regarding employees' work and family needs?
4. Has anyone in the firm set up a formal or informal group to talk about work/family concerns?
5. Are there other avenues available to employees to make these needs known to the firm (i.e., employee forums, union contract, suggestion boxes, surveys, focus groups, etc.)?
6. Are there other firms located close to or affiliated with your company with whom you could establish a consortium to reduce costs for certain benefits?
7. Has your company begun to feel the effects of the labor shortage?
8. Briefly state your goal as to what changes specifically you are going to work to achieve with your firm resulting in a more family-friendly work environment.
9. List three steps you will take to help your firm address these issues and note the time frame for accomplishing these. . .
    * _____
    * _____
    * _____
10. List three people or firms you can call on to be a resource to you or your firm in creating a family-friendly work environment. . .
    * _____
    * _____
    * _____

Source: BV&A, Inc., Seattle and Princeton © 1989

SURVEY EXAMPLES

September 1986

CHILDCARE SURVEY

We need to determine if there is enough employee interest and/or need in establishing a childcare facility (age 6 months and above) in proximity to the *Seattle Times*.

1. Indicate the days and hours you use or would use childcare. This should include any unusual job-related hours or overtime you may work for which you would use childcare.

    Sunday_____ Hours_____
    Monday_____ Hours_____
    Tuesday_____ Hours_____
    Wednesday_____ Hours_____
    Thursday_____ Hours_____
    Friday_____ Hours_____
    Saturday_____ Hours_____
    Example: Monday_X_____ Hours_8:00 A.M.–1:00 P.M._____
    or Saturday_X_____ Hours_10:00 P.M.–Sunday, 4:00 A.M._____

2. If the following forms of childcare services were available to you, which would be your first and second choice: (Indicate by number 1 and 2)

    Childcare center (year round)   _____
    Summer program only   _____
    Information and Referral Service   _____
    Other (please specify)   _____
                                         _____

3. Would you enroll a dependent child(ren) in a daycare center governed by participating parents and located in proximity to the *Seattle Times* and comparable to your present facilities in terms of price and quality?

    Yes_____   If yes, number of children_____

    Age(s) of child(ren) you would enroll:

    Child #1 ____ Child #2 ____ Child #3 ____ Child #4 ____

    No_____

4. Would you serve on a committee to establish and/or govern a childcare facility?

    Yes _____   No _____

Thank you for your input. We will provide details of the survey and any anticipated action to each respondent.

Name_____   Department_____

Source: The Seattle Times Company, Seattle

UNIVERSITY OF MEDICINE & DENTISTRY
OF NEW JERSEY CHILDCARE SURVEY

NAME_____ Campus Address
Home Address: _____ Camden/Stratford   _____
_____ Newark   _____
_____ Piscataway/New Brunswick _____
Job Title: _____ Department: _____

1. What are your regular working hours?_____to_____
   Full time _____? Part time _____?

2. How many children do you have?_____
   Please indicate age and number of children in each group:
   ____6 wks. to 12 mos.   ____2 ½ yrs. to 5 yrs.
   ____12 mos. to 30 mos.   ____6 yrs. to 12 yrs.

3. What hours do you require care for your pre-school child?_____to_____

4. What type of childcare are you using now?
   ____ Friend or neighbor   ____ Family member
   ____ Childcare Center   ____ Other (Specify)

5. What types of childcare problems interfere with your job or job performance?
   ____ Sitter illness   ____ Inflexible hours
   ____ Worry about safety   ____ Inconvenient location
   ____ Poor program   ____ Expense

6. What do you presently pay weekly for childcare per child?
   _____ Below $50_____$51–$75_____$76–$100_____Over $100

7. What aspects of childcare seem most important to you in a childcare
   environment? Please rate from 1-10 with 1 being most important and 10 being
   least important.
   ____ EDUCATIONAL PROGRAM   ____BALANCED MEALS
   ____ QUALIFIED STAFF   ____REASONABLE TUITION
   ____ FIELD TRIPS   ____PARENT INVOLVEMENT
   ____ SAFE & CLEAN ENVIRONMENT   ____TOYS & MATERIALS
   ____ NICE PLAYGROUND   ____LOCATION CONVENIENCE

8. Are you interested in after-school care for your school-aged child(ren)?
   Yes_____No_____   If yes, please indicate age and number of children:
   _____

9. What school does your school-aged child attend?
   Name and Address of School:_____

10. Who currently cares for your school-aged child after school?
    ____ Friend____ Family member____ Other (Please Specify)_____

11. My current childcare arrangement/location is inconvenient because (please
    check if applicable):
    ____ My office is too far from the caregiver's location
    ____ My home is too far from the caregiver's location
    ____ The caregiver's location is out of my way to work
    ____ The caregiver's location is hard to reach during peak traffic hours

Other (Please specify)_____

12. What is your current driving distance/time to work?
    ____ miles/____ minutes.
    Are you in a car pool? Yes____ No____ How many members?____
    Major route to work? (i.e., NJ Turnpike, G.S. Parkway, Rt. 280, Rt. 78, etc.)

13. Are you interested in any of the following?
    ____ Accredited Kindergarten Program
    ____ Special Classes (gymnastics, ballet, foreign language, etc.)
    Other (Please specify)_____

14. As a working parent do <u>YOU</u> have special needs associated with your job?
    Yes_____No_____
    If so, please specify_____

15. IN COMPLETING THE REMAINDER OF THIS SURVEY, PLEASE
    ASSUME THE FOLLOWING: Within the next year, a childcare center will
    be located near your work site; the center will open at 6:30 A.M. Monday
    through Friday and be open until at least 6:30 P.M.; additional hours and days
    will be considered; an after-school program will be available for children up
    to age 12; and weekly fees would be competitive with prices charged locally.

    A. If such a childcare center were available now, would you enroll your
       child(ren)?
       Yes:_____ Probably_____ Possibly_____ Undecided
       No: _____ Definitely_____ Probably

    B. If you answered "No" to Question A, would you please tell us why. We
       will appreciate your comments and there is no need to answer any further
       questions on this Survey.

    C. Would you use the center: _____Regularly? _____Occasionally?
    D. What days of the week would you use the center?
       (Circle all that apply)
            Mon.   Tues.   Wed.   Thurs.   Fri.   Sat.   Sun.
    E. What hours would you like to use the center?
       ____ Workdays, between 6:30 A.M. and 6:30 P.M.
       ____ Evening, until midnight
       ____ Other, special times_____

16. We are interested in your comments.

RETURN THIS SURVEY TO MS. KIM D. OSTERHOUDT, DIRECTOR OF
BUSINESS SERVICES AND CONTRACT PERFORMANCE, 123 ADMC,
NEWARK, NEW JERSEY.

Source: University of Medicine & Dentistry of New Jersey

EMPLOYEE QUESTIONNAIRE

Thank you very much for spending
the time to fill in this questionnaire.
These answers will provide valuable
information on daycare arrangements
used by working parents. Your
individual answers will remain
confidential.

Part 1: Your Family and Household

1. ____(10-11) Number of adults
   (persons 18 and older) in your
   household.

2. Check the statement below which
   most nearly describes your family
   structure.

   ____(12) Single parent living alone
   with child(ren).

   ____(13) Single parent living alone
   with child(ren) and other
   adult(s).

   ____(14) Married parent living
   with spouse, child(ren).

   ____(15) Married parent living
   with spouse, child(ren), and
   other adult(s).

   ____(16) Other: (specify)_____
   _____

3. Please indicate below the number
   of children you have in each age
   group:

   ____(17) Less than 1 year old

   ____(18) 1 to less than 2 years
   old

   ____(19) 2 to less than 5 years old

____(20) 5–6 years old

____(21) 7–13 years old

____(22) 14–18 years old

4. How many children do you have
   who are regularly cared for by a
   friend or relative while you
   work?____(23)

   Please give their ages:

   ____(24)   ____(27)
   ____(25)   ____(28)
   ____(26)   ____(29)

5. How many children do you have
   who are regularly cared for in a
   daycare center while you work?
   ____(30)

   Please give their ages.

   ____(38)   ____(41)
   ____(39)   ____(42)
   ____(40)   ____(43)

7. The childcare I use is (check all
   that apply):

   ____(44) In my home

   ____(45) In my neighborhood

   ____(46) On my way to work

   ____(48) Out of the way to home
   or work

   ____(48) At my work site

8. All of my out of home childcare
   is:

   ____(49) In the same place

____(50) In several places near each other

____(51) In several places far from each other

Part 2: The Childcare Service Provided by Your Employer

A daycare center is provided for children of employees where you work. The questions in Part 2 relate to this service.

9. Were you informed of the availability of this childcare service when you first began your employment here?

____(52) Yes

____(53) No, not informed

____(54) No, service not available when first employed

10. If yes, did the availability of this service influence your decision to accept this employment?

____(55) Yes

____(56) No

11. Are you now using this service?

____(57) Yes

____(58) No

12. If yes, have you used this service?

____(59) Less than 12 monoths

____(60) 12–24 months

____(61) More than 24 months

13. Please indicate below the number of children you have who use the childcare services provided by your employer.

____(62) Less than 1 year

____(63) 1 to less than 2 years old

____(64) 2 to less than 5 years old

____(65) 5–6 years old

____(66) Older than 6 years

14. Does the availability of this childcare service influence your decision to continue your present employment?

____(67) Yes

____(68) No

15. Did the availability of this childcare service enable you to shorten your maternity leave?

____(69) Yes

____(70) No

____(71) Not Applicable

Is there anything else you'd like to add?

Thank you very much for spending the time to fill in this questionnaire. These answers will provide valuable information on daycare arrangements used by working parents. Your individual answers will remain confidential.

SOURCE: Foundation for Human Service Studies, Inc. and CSR, Inc., "An Experimental Study of the Effects of Employer-Sponsored Childcare Services on Selected Employee Behaviors," Appendix C, Ann Gilman Dawson, Principal Investigator, Chicago, 1984.

7

HOW GOVERNMENT CAN HELP

THE PRESENT REALITY

The policies and practices of the U.S. government in relation to family needs are often contradictory. In 1989, the Act for Better Child Care, which would have increased the earned income tax credit for parents with children in child-care programs, created a new credit for children's health insurance, and set up a national advisory body on child-care standards, was defeated. The Family and Medical Leave Act, which would have required employers with 50 or more employees to provide up to 12 weeks of unpaid family or medical leave, was vetoed by President Bush in 1990. These defeats would lead one to believe that the federal government is strongly resisting involvement in policy for working families.

The defeat of these bills occurred shortly after a national survey, conducted by 21 U.S. magazines, revealed that 75% of the respondents felt that family issues should be a top priority for the president and Congress. Eighty-one percent of the respondents thought the federal government did not pay enough attention to family concerns, and 65% felt that government should help make good, affordable child care available. The most significant majority, 93%, claimed that parents should have the right, without fear of job loss, to take a leave from work to care for a newborn, newly adopted child, a seriously ill child, or parent. Thus, there appears to be a wide disparity between what families think and lawmakers enact.

It is at this juncture that the contradictory nature of federal policy and practice becomes most apparent. While Congress is refusing to act, administrators and managers of public agencies are opting to implement family-friendly programs for their workers. Departments in the federal bureaucracy have some of the most sophisticated and well-funded child-care centers in the nation. The Central Intelligence Agency, Department of Defense, U.S. Congress, and Housing and Urban Development, all in Washington, D.C., provide care centers for employees' children. More federal employees are also being offered flexible workplace opportunities. The General Services Administration claims that advantages from allowing employees to work at home or in satellite offices has already produced beneficial results. Agencies can retain trained employees who have special family needs, and can eliminate the loss of time and stress of commuting. Legislation was introduced in 1989 to encourage all federal agencies to experiment with more flexibility in working conditions.

So although the federal government is, as an employer, trying to meet some of the family needs of its employees, Congress and the executive branch appear loath to create national policies that could benefit all workers. The reluctance of the federal government to become involved in family issues is most often credited to three reasons: cost, invasion of privacy, and excessive governmental control. The cost of such programs both to government and the private sector is paramount. However, the history of public spending makes it clear that we have and do spend money on those things that are valued. Robert McCord, director of the Congressional Clearinghouse on the Future, a research arm of Congress, remarked recently that the $1.6 billion requested for air-conditioned hangars for Stealth Bombers is almost equal to 20% of the national subsidies for low-income housing. "Maybe we should move homeless families into Stealth hangars!" he quipped.

There is no doubt that the federal budget deficit continues to constrain action on social problems. But the cost of programs should not be the only criterion—or even the most important consideration—in national policy planning. Gail Fosler, chief economist of The Conference Board and former chief economist for the U.S. Senate Budget Committee, acknowledges that using the budget as the tool for change is "government by hindsight—and merely reacting to past mistakes."

The same is true of the private sector, even though it has always been willing to compete for quality workers and do so in a more entrepreneurial way than public institutions. Parking lots are an example of this—one often used by Congresswoman Pat Schroeder. When business learned that workers needed places to park, they created parking lots near the factory or store. Now workers need quality "parking," i.e., good care for their children and the elderly in their families. What will be the response? Will cars prove to be more highly valued than people?

Fear of invading the private domain of the family is the second reason given by members of Congress who resist legislating on family-related matters. Private issues become public issues when the majority of citizens are troubled by the same problem. This has become increasingly evident in the case of long-term care for the elderly. Because more family members are living longer and needing medical care over several years, the lack of such care has become a national public dilemma. It is doubtful that many families would object on the basis of loss of privacy, if much-needed health care services were made available to their elderly family members. Historically, government has not been reluctant to set policies regarding the education of children and the welfare of the poor. So it's particularly mystifying to witness the federal government's failure to act on these issues of critical importance to so many American families.

The private sector's fear of excessive governmental control is a longstanding one in American history. Consequently, American business, along with professional medical associations, have on their payrolls some of the most effective lobbyists in Washington to stave off government intervention—especially in the areas of social programs and business regulation. Pressures on Congress through PACs (political action committees) and individual lobbying efforts make it very difficult to get bills in either of these areas passed. However, the near future may present a surprising schism that could break through these power blocks. The issue of "who will pay for health care" may be the blockbuster. The American Medical Association has historically resisted the notion of a nationalized health care program, but seems to be changing its attitude, as the nation's health care crisis deepens. Business is finding that health insurance costs in benefits packages are almost unaffordable. The next 10 years may see business lobbying for a national basic health care plan simply because they can no longer afford the insurance costs and desperately need the coverage to compete for employees. But, even if that does occur, most businesses are likely to hold to the original stance against governmental interference in other areas. Consequently there is likely to be no great surge of mandated federal family policies.

PITFALLS OF A DE FACTO POLICY

The lack of a tangible federal policy on work/family issues leaves the U.S. with "a hidden family policy," according to Urie Bronfenbrenner, professor of human development and family studies at Cornell. This hidden or de facto policy has several pitfalls.

This hidden policy 1) is being made not by legislation, but by administrative actions taken by individual government officials; 2) has transferred major responsibility for funding and action to state and local levels; and 3) is carried out by many local governments that must depend on volunteer staffing and ad hoc arrangements. In addition to the three pitfalls that Dr. Bronfenbrenner points out, we see a fourth—one that directly affects business. The de facto policy also results in fragmentation of programs, with some areas of the country being much better for families than others. National corporations then have difficulties making personnel transfers and have to deal with fairness-of-treatment issues.

There is always danger in replacing legislative decision making with the actions of a single government administrator. Inherent in the democratic ideal of legislation is the opportunity for many different views to be heard, and as much information as possible brought to bear on the subject. Acting on his/her own, the administrator may or may not have access to good information. And, without the backing of the law, that individual's actions are often challenged or overruled.

When concerns that affect the majority of the society's population are not addressed on a national level, they are delegated down to smaller, more local governmental units with no system for monitoring results. On the positive side, programs that truly meet the needs of clientele may result, because the answer is designed in close proximity to the problem, and, people locally can be energized to care about issues they would not deal with if they were not given the responsibility directly. On the negative side, nothing may be done on the local level and many needy working families may fall through the cracks.

Many state and most local governments are currently stretched very thin. The lack of adequate funding, effective leadership, and enough people to do the job are hardships faced by most communities today. Since the beginning of the Reagan Administration, the job of dealing with most human problems was left on local government's doorsteps. Necessity has sent them scurrying to the volunteer sector, or in search of soft-money grants in order to meet the needs of their people. Citizen participation is the plus side of this situation. Instability and inconsistency are the negatives.

President Bush's "1000 Points of Light" notion—that individuals can themselves effectively respond to social ills—illustrates beautifully the value of volunteer efforts. However, those who direct volunteer-intensive programs will be the first to tell you that volunteerism, by its very nature, is erratic. In order to sustain a program carried out by volunteers, money must be found to pay a staff that can give continuity to the program, and to train and coordinate those volunteer services.

The economy is adversely affected by fragmentation of services, and will be even more so into the '90s. Areas of the country that have family policies will be favored by workers. Firms in areas that resist dependent care, flexible hours and workplaces, health care benefits, and good wages will suffer from the inability to recruit workers and maintain productivity—and will lose tax revenues. National corporations will have to deal with new equity issues if some employees are located in family- friendly areas while others are not. Relocations will also become more difficult and may require "hardship area" financial compensation when workers must move to the less desirable areas.

So, America's hidden family policy has created a Catch-22 for local governments, and has put many working families, whose needs may be small at first—but grow as they are neglected—in jeopardy. As a result, one of the major political issues of the '90s will be to determine the federal government's role in shaping family policy, something other industrialized nations have already done. Following are some of the choices these governments have made in favor of families.

WHAT OTHER COUNTRIES ARE DOING

Most countries, both the industrialized and the third-world nations, value their children and the elderly, and take great pains to keep families strong and intact. They do so primarily through national policies and governmental support.

In Norway, Dr. Trand Torgersen is the Barneombudet, or government official, who is an advocate for children. His office represents true innovation in national government. The mission of this office is to ensure that "children are seen as people, with their own needs and their own rights—rights equal, but not identical, to those of adults." For instance, the Barneombudet has worked with the energy minister to move high-tension wires from areas where children play, to decrease the potential risk of leukemia. It has also lobbied Parliament for a law against parents' striking their children. The office does not become involved in private matters, but works to set the national tone in attitudes toward children's rights.

The Nordic countries (Norway, Sweden, Denmark, Finland, and Iceland) all guarantee some form of child support, furnished by the government when the "other parent," or the one with whom the child is not living, fails to share adequately in the child's support. A government agency then collects payment from the noncustodial parent. This system, unlike the one in the U.S., guarantees that the child will receive aid.

In Sweden, 85% of women with preschool children work outside the home. They are helped by a policy that provides generous parental leave—nine months for the mother and three for the father. And Swedish parents do avail themselves of this benefit, with women taking an average of 258 days leave and men taking an average of 44 days. These combined 12 months are at full pay; mothers may take an additional six-month leave at 70% pay. Funding for day-care programs available for all ages comes from local taxes, parents' fees, and state subsidies financed by employer payroll taxes.

Europe is ahead of the U.S. in providing both child-care and training programs. The first crèches (day nurseries) for infants of workers were set up in France in the '30s. French women receive 90% of their regular pay during 16 weeks of maternity leave. When they return to work, they can leave their children in publicly supervised family nurseries with licensed "mothers' assistants." The French and Germans developed an aggressive and comprehensive approach to child care because of a shortage of workers. Public policies in France offer all mothers of children under age three a choice of whether to work or remain at home to nurture the family. During the period of unpaid leave, jobs are protected. Corporate leaders do not appear to be concerned over any possible negative effect in productivity or profits from their generous paid and unpaid leaves. By contrast, the lobbying efforts by American business interests against the legislation that would have provided 12 weeks of solely unpaid leave led to President Bush's veto.

PERCENTAGE OF WOMEN AGES 15–61 EMPLOYEE OUTSIDE THE HOME

France	48%
West Germany	52%
Sweden	69%
U.S.	56%

Many European nations, including Spain, France, and Germany, also provide maternity grants at the time of child bearing, to assist with the cost of supplies and equipment for the new baby. Single mothers often receive additional assistance. France, Austria, and Germany all supplement family allowances for single mothers. In Norway, single mothers receive extra pay for living expenses, education, and child-care; loans; priority in day-care centers; and one year's leave from work. Although some of these choices may never be available to American mothers or fathers because the national economy and family welfare philosophy here is very different from that abroad, some of these ideas could be modified to make child-rearing more compatible with work schedules and personal ambitions.

In several areas, the U.S. trails significantly in the amount of help—or perhaps it is value—granted to workers who are also new mothers. *The U.S. and South Africa are the only major industrialized nations that do not guarantee some form of job-protected maternity leave.* Of 135 industrialized and non-industrialized countries providing leave, 125 mandate *paid* leave. All European nations, and 81% of nations in Central America, the Caribbean and South America provide statutory cash benefits during maternity leave. But in the U.S. only 5% of all employers offer paid parental leave, with unpaid parental leave provided by only 44%.

The status of children in the U.S. has reached a new low in modern history. Hunger, medical problems, abuse, and early death are rampant. Of eight Western countries studied between 1979 and 1982, the U.S. and Australia claim the most families with children at the poverty level before taxes and transfers. (Transfers are payments made through the U.S. welfare system, such as Aid to Families with Dependent Children [AFDC] payments, food stamps, commodity distribution programs, etc.) While taxes and transfers reduced poverty in every country, these two countries continued to have more poor families with children after the impact of benefits was taken into account. Compared to other nations, the U.S. spends less per poor family with children than any other county except Switzerland. U.S. needs-tested benefits, although presumably better targeted than social insurance, are too low to lift the average family with children out of poverty.

According to Kamerman and Kahn, family sociologists writing on European policies that affect families, in many other countries divorce is being defined as a "social rather than individual risk." This means that the entire community takes on the obligation for the women and children of divorce. In the U.S. the women and children are expected to manage their own lives even though the family income plummets almost 40% after the marriage is dissolved. Sixty-seven industrialized nations, excluding the

U.S., provide a monthly or weekly cash benefit to families for every child, regardless of income and work status of parents. Among European nations, family allowance benefits range between 5% and 10% of median wage and may be higher for larger families.

GOVERNMENTS WITH MINIMUM STANDARDS FOR PARENTAL OR MATERNITY LEAVE		
Country	Duration of leave (weeks)	Number of paid weeks and percent of normal pay (paid by government and/or employer)
AUSTRIA	16–42	20 weeks/100%
CANADA	17–41	15 weeks/60%
FRANCE	18	16 weeks/90%
FINLAND	35	35 weeks/100%
GERMANY	14–26	14–19 weeks/100%
ITALY	22–48	22 weeks/80%
JAPAN	12	12 weeks/60%
SWEDEN	12–52	38 weeks/90%

Source: *Women at Work*, International Labour Office, Geneva, Global Survey.

Since Israel became a nation, the kibbutz has been an integral part of Israeli society. All able-bodied individuals were expected to work at establishing the new country. Thus the presence of women in the work force has been a cultural norm from the beginning. At the same time, the Jewish tradition values children highly. Consequently, Israelis were eager to create the best possible care situation for children while parents worked. In the kibbutzm, where children were taught and cared for by trained workers, then slept and ate with their families, children thrived. They were able to interact with older people, have lunch with their parents, and visit different parts of the neighborhood during the day. The Israeli government has had a hand in the development and maintenance of quality care in these centers since they were established.

In 1988, the Conservative Canadian government passed a bill with a $4 billion commitment to provide tax relief for parents with young children, to give operating and start-up grants for child-care centers and to establish a special needs fund to examine child-care problems. An important aspect of the bill was a $100 million fund to research and develop solutions for unique child-care problems. As a result, a "Strategy for Child Care" was recently announced by the Canadian government. It is intended to enrich and upgrade programs more than a dozen years old being run by the provinces with support from the federal government. In the next seven years, $5.4 billion will be available for matching by the provinces on a one-to-three basis. By providing child care, Canada is expecting to create 40,000 new jobs, thereby giving more people the opportunity to enter the work force (and pay taxes!).

Tradition-minded Japan even offers a bit of support to working mothers who are entitled to 14 weeks of maternity leave. Japan's National Children's Castle child-care program seeks to be the basis for a national child center network in touch with other such centers throughout the world. Companies in Japan also provide applied learning programs for employees, while European countries have long provided sophisticated apprenticeship programs.

It is easy to see from these examples that the attitude toward meeting and nurturing the needs of workers is, in most countries outside the U.S., a taken-for-granted objective of national public policies. At the same time, the "hidden" or de facto policy of the United States has relegated the responsibility for families, and related social problems, to state, county, and city governments, and the private sector.

STATE GOVERNMENTS ARE RESPONDING

Although this deferral of responsibility, which began primarily during the Reagan years, created a very unrealistic financial burden for states and local communities, there is evidence that the programs are more relevant than they have been in the past. Involvement of local people in solving local problems is effective and empowering. The most important outcome is that local governments are paying attention to what families are saying, and many are taking as proactive a stance as their strained budgets allow.

By summer of 1990 more than ten states had laws mandating maternity leave for the birth of a child. Several others, like New Jersey and Connecticut, have laws extending such leave to care for a disabled or seriously ill child or other relative or for the adoption of a child.

New Jersey's Family Leave Act, which became effective on May 4, 1990, may be viewed by many as a model for other states. It stipulates that:

- Employers with 100 or more employees must comply. By 1994, firms with 50 or more employees must comply
- Leave shall be up to 12 weeks within any 24-month period
- Leave is for birth or adoption of a child, or "serious health condition of a child, spouse, parent, or parent of a spouse"
- Family leave is separate from and in addition to any disability leave
- The law affects both public- and private-sector employers
- The only exemptions are for employees whose base salary ranks within the highest paid 5%, or whose base salary is one of the seven highest in the firm (whichever number of employees is greater), or if the employer can prove economic injury by granting such leave *and* the employer notifies the employee of such injury

The New Jersey law further guarantees job security and continuation of health benefits during this leave. In the preamble to the act the legislature "finds that it is necessary to promote the economic security of families by guaranteeing jobs to wage earners who choose to take a period of leave. . . . The Legislature therefore declares that it is the policy of the state to protect and promote the stability and economic security of family units."

Washington state has had such a law since early 1989, and Vermont has recently passed a 12-week maternity leave law. Connecticut enacted a parental leave mandate that makes it possible for employees to take up to 16 weeks of unpaid family and/or medical leave within any two-year period without losing their jobs. Employees are required to give two weeks' advance notice, if possible, provide physicians' statements, or birth/adoption notices as far in advance of the event as possible. They must also give two weeks' notice before the date they plan to return. The act went into effect for companies with 250 or more employees in July of 1990.

A bill allowing pregnant workers to request transfers to less hazardous jobs or take medical leaves of absence was passed in Oregon in 1989. The bill was sponsored by the Oregon AFL-CIO and requires an independent physician's opinion. After delivery and up to 12 weeks of unpaid leave, the woman may return to her former, or an equivalent, job under the state's parental leave law.

California lawmakers were recently considering a bill that would offer personal and business income tax credits to employees or employers to encourage more telecommuting. The tax credit would be $2,000 or less annually per employee who telecommuted three days per week or 15 days per month. Michigan established and administers tax-free dependent-care spending accounts for state employees and employees of small businesses. The partnership action makes it possible for small businesses to provide family- friendly services. The governor's and the treasury departments' theory is that a worker shouldn't have to be in a big company to get a federal tax break. The program for the 60,000 state employees is called "Family Care Accounts," while the one for small businesses is labeled "Care Plus Accounts."

Care for aging family members is also an area finally getting attention from state leaders. Eldercare provisions, which include adult day-care and respite care services were added to Idaho's Senior Services Act in 1989. Governor Cecil Andrus signed the bill which calls for six one-year demonstration grants costing $100,000. Organizations receiving these grants will "demonstrate" how programs and systems can be developed locally to meet the needs of the elderly. Delaware is also concerned about elderly family members. "We live in a society where people are often juggling their careers and their commitments to aging parents," explained Governor Michael Castle when he signed a bill establishing the state's Eldercare Information and Support System in mid-1990. "This situation adds stress to their lives and can also take a toll on their effectiveness as employees," he concluded. A toll-free number to provide counseling information and referral services for the elderly is being established by Indiana's Area Agencies on Aging. In Kansas, the state secretary on aging's office screens applicants and sets the sliding fee schedule for in-home support services for Kansans who are 60 years or older and have functional limitations.

A great deal of momentum has been created by the legislative activity on behalf of families in these states and others. The '90s may see a flood of new state laws requiring both benefits from employers as well as state funding, especially for child care, eldercare, family leave, and health care benefits.

PARTNERSHIPS AT THE LOCAL LEVEL ARE EFFECTIVE

Progressive thinking and planning on behalf of many cities is also championing family needs. And, it is at this level that some of the most effective partnering of government and business is taking place to help solve work/family dilemmas.

San Francisco has taken the lead in establishing and implementing policies that assist families and allow businesses to partner with government to do so. The city has established a Family Policy Task Force, which has recently issued a report with several recommendations that, if enacted, will ease the health care scare. It recommends that businesses:

• Extend health care benefits to 19- to 24-year-olds who are living at home
• Allow grandparents, or other nonlegal guardians who are raising children, to add these children to their policy coverage
• Provide unpaid family care leave of up to one year
• Extend health care benefits to unmarried partners

"Carrot and stick" strategies are working well in most local partnerships. For instance, a small but growing number of developers are incorporating child-care centers in their projects in an effort to attract tenants. In New York, the city council has proposed several incentives to encourage developers to join efforts to expand child-care options. In one proposal the New York City administrative code would be expanded to exempt from some real estate taxes most existing office and hotel buildings that add child-care centers. While some envision their centers as only for children, the intergenerational day-care experiences of Stride Rite and St. Francis outlined in chapter 5 certainly make clear that eldercare could be incorporated as well. Another bill pending would require builders of new hotels and office space to provide day care or pay the city a fee.

The Real Estate Board of New York took yet a different approach, proposing that private builders be allowed to construct six extra feet of commercial space above current zoning limits for each foot they set aside for a child-care center. The City of Seattle has adopted this approach and now has several excellent examples of downtown child-care centers in new high-rises. These developers were able to add extra floors of prime-view office space in exchange for indoor and outdoor play space realizing higher rental revenues while working parents gain a convenient child-care resource.

A landmark child-care ordinance established in San Francisco in 1985 requires developers of major projects to provide space for child-care centers or give money to existing facilities. This resulted in the contribution of $153,000 by a developer, to the city's Affordable Child Care Fund. Another developer will soon construct an on-site child-care center in a new downtown office building. Developers must comply with the city's Office-Hotel Child Care Program to receive occupancy permits. Proponents of downtown child care cite not only benefits to parents and children but also the city in general. "Child-care centers in often sterile downtown offices help humanize the environment," said one hotel sales executive. Portland, Cincinnati, and Hartford are other cities using this type of bonus law, while 14 other municipalities are currently debating it. The Child Care Action Campaign, a national nonprofit organization that lobbies on behalf of children, has identified a number of these successful public/private accommodations. Across the nation public requirements or rewards have led private developers to build 35 day-care centers with space for a total of about 1,335 children.

Not surprisingly the carrot approach—tax breaks, or building-size bonuses—are more popular with developers than the stick approach—such as mandatory contributions to a day-care fund or space set-aside requirements. Some city officials and downtown businesspeople express initial skepticism about parents' willingness to bring their children downtown with them. This notion dissipates, however, when parents enthusiastically flock to sign up. As one Seattle secretary with a child in a high-rise center told us, "I thought it might be a hassle to bring my son downtown with me, but actually we both enjoy having the commuting time together, and if he becomes ill, it makes me feel better to know I'm just two blocks away. It also makes me feel good to know that the tuition money we pay goes to the teachers, since the rest of the costs are mostly picked up by the developers." Downtown business leaders in several cities using the bonus approach have been delighted with the advantages from both marketing and public relations perspectives. As Steven Trainer, a senior vice president of Wright Runstad Development Company in Seattle told the New York Times, "I think most resistance is dissolving." His firm put a day-care center in the base of one of its office buildings in the heart of the city. They paid to build the center and also cover costs of maintenance, thus reducing fees to parents and maximizing teacher salaries.

In Milwaukee, Wisconsin, the county government adopted flextime, job-sharing, tuition reimbursements, pretax dollar vouchers for child-care, and incentive pay programs. Four years ago the county opened a child-care center that appears to be benefiting both parents and government. A spot check of five county employees revealed that three reported improved work attendance, two said they returned to work sooner after giving birth, and two considered resigning had it not been for the center. County officials say they have seen a marked decline in the utilization of sick leave, which is a partial gauge of job satisfaction. The county lost 514,600 work hours to sick leave in 1982 and 477,400 in 1988 after implementation of these workplace innovations. Annual job turnover is beginning to also show a downward trend: in 1986 it was 8.6% and in 1987 it was 2.2% lower, at 6.4%. The children of city employees in St. Paul, Minnesota, now have the opportunity to attend a city day-care center. An old YWCA was recently renovated, with the help of $30,000 provided by a vote of the city council.

Some cities are experimenting with yet other policies to promote private-sector family responsiveness. In Los Angeles contractors bidding for city jobs will be given preference if they have a stated child-care policy. Those wanting to contract with the city must complete a checklist of child-care options they provide. The policy serves as an educational tool, as well as providing an incentive to help employees care for their children. Washington, D.C., now requires employers with 50 or more workers to give workers up to 16 weeks of unpaid leave on the advent of a new child or to care for a sick family member. The leave also applies to nontraditional families, including homosexual partners and common law spouses. The act will cover employers with 20 or more employees in 1993.

DO TAX INCENTIVES REALLY HELP?

One benefit the federal government provides is help to employers through financial incentives. Firms may deduct expenses for dependent-care programs that impact absenteeism and turnover. If a company sets up a Dependent Care Assistance Program (DCAP) employees will not be taxed on any monies the company provides for child care. When a set-aside salary plan is created within the company, employers can eliminate payroll taxes on the set-aside portion of workers' salaries and employees can pay for dependent services with pretax dollars.

Some companies have chosen to create a Voluntary Employee's Beneficiary Association (VEBA), or a tax-exempt entity that provides child-care. Capital expenditures on a child-care center, under this IRS stipulation, can be amortized over 60 months. The Accelerated Cost Recovery System (ACRS) may be used to amortize costs. If an employer makes a gift to dependent-care information and referral agencies qualified as tax-exempt organizations, these gifts may be deducted as charitable contributions. Although these tax laws require professional interpretation, and are not intended to assist all families, especially those with middle to high incomes, they are an encouraging start. Sources for obtaining information regarding these IRS regulations are listed at the end of this chapter.

Perhaps not so surprisingly, far fewer individuals and businesses are taking advantage of these motivators than was expected when the incentives were designed. The reasons for this lack of utilization are not clear, but one might assume the complexity and need for interpretation of the law, and the cost of managing the outlined benefits might be prohibitive for medium-to-smaller firms. Also, employee pressure for use of the incentives may not yet be adequate in some cases to generate lower-level participation. In other businesses, higher salaries may make the paperwork outweight the potential benefits.

There are, however, widely utilized tax incentives for individuals and couples that saved almost $4 billion in taxes for the 9 million couples and individuals claiming them on returns filed with the IRS in 1989. Others benefited from tax-free child- care assistance provided by employers. For example, up to $5,000 worth of day-care services provided by an employer are tax free, if documented by a written plan that does not discriminate in favor of higher paid employees. Or a tax credit can be used by individuals or families that reduces taxes dollar for dollar up to $720 for one child, or up to $1,440 for two or more children of working families. The credit is calculated on a maximum of $2,400 in eligible expenses for one child or $4,800 for two or more. One important caveat is that any employer-paid assistance must be subtracted from eligible expenses before the credit is calculated. IRS publications 503 and 926 outline these provisions in greater detail.

Given that the costs of child care an American household average from $2,500 to $10,000 per year, the first of these two options—up to $5,000 of care from an employer tax free—is clearly more desirable for most working parents. One broadcast executive said she and her husband saved $1,650 in taxes last year under the payroll deduction plan. Had they used the standard IRS child-care tax credit, they would have saved only $480, barely putting a dent in their yearly child-care bill.

ENCOURAGING MAY BE THE
BEST STRATEGY

Several factors are coming together to indicate that the most appropriate role the federal government can play is to encourage, rather than mandate, supportive family/work policies. It is apparent that in the 20 years that these needs have been put forth, primarily through the women's movement, little has been done to create national policies: Lawmakers are not prone to take action. Business lobbyists are part of the reason. Congress shows little propensity toward establishing national family policy, due to the fear most business has of government regulation. Secondly, the effectiveness of local policies supersedes what might be expected of nationally administered programs. The big drawback here is the lack of funding at local levels to keep good programs viable and stable. This is compounded by the lack of consistency and quality across local or state boundaries.

Given these factors, partnerships between business and government, undergirded by significant economic incentives in the form of accessible block grants and easy-to-get, across-the-board tax incentives, may be the most effective way to keep working families healthy and businesses solvent. This approach does not advocate mandatory family-support statutes, but rather promotes further changes in the Internal Revenue Services tax codes in the form of dependent-care tax credits. Providing grants and tax credits as incentives to starting new home- or company-based child-care or eldercare services, should yield more positive results than fighting in state legislatures and the Congress. Clashes between pro- and anti-government mandate advocates waste precious time and money in their legal battles. This is money that could be better spent on renovating buildings for child/eldercare programs and buying essential services for working families.

Some experts have suggested additional government incentives by guaranteeing school districts higher per capita state and federal funding if district buildings and buses can be used for before- and after-school care programs. We advocate both of these approaches because they hold promise of more immediate results. Both needs, for infant/preschool care and before/after-school care, are extremely pressing and require swift action. Another type of motivation could be structured in terms of preferential treatment to potential contractors who provide family supportive benefits to their workers. Because the federal government is one of the biggest users of private contractual services, this action would impact a large number of families. Finally, other government initiatives that could help include boosts to the minimum wage, more support for job-training programs, universal health care coverage, and increased funding for programs such as Headstart, to aid all children. All of the above would serve to diminish the reliance of this generation and the next on welfare, as well as help increase the pool of skilled, healthy, available workers.

The reticence of the federal government in the last decade, however, to tackle head-on in any meaningful way the family-work problems that plague the U.S. makes their role in innovation or even encouragement seem unlikely. Perhaps understanding this will bring public and private sectors together in a more realistic way—both to lobby for helpful federal incentives and to go about creating partnerships that will really do the job of supporting families at work in their own local areas.

The other possibility—one that we favor most highly—is for business to begin pushing the federal government to develop national policies that truly encourage public/private-sector partnerships. These must be national in scope, well-funded, and monitored, so all working families have adequate support for staying healthy and productive in their jobs.

SOURCES FOR GAINING INFORMATION ON
DEPENDENT-CARE TAX CREDITS

<u>Summary of Tax Provisions for Employer-Supported Child Care with Model Dependent-Care Assistance Plans</u>

Write to: Child Care Law Center
                             22 Second Street, 5th Floor
                             San Francisco, California 94105

                             (Fee: $10.00)

<u>RIA Section 89 Compliance Manual #20994</u>

Write to: Research Institute of America, Inc.
                             Subscriber Services
                             111 Radio Circle
                             Mount Kisco, New York 10549-9983

                             (Fee: $75.00)

<u>Other Sources for Information on Family Care Resources</u>

Child Care Action Campaign   Children's Defense Fund
99 Hudson Street   12 C Street NW
New York, New York 10013   Washington, D.C. 20001
(212) 334-9595   (202) 628-8787

Clearinghouse on Implementation   Families and Work Institute
of Childcare and Eldercare Services 330 7th Avenue
[CHOICES]   New York, New York 10001
U.S. Dept. of Labor Women's Bureau (212) 465-2044
200 Constitution Avenue NW S-3306
Washington, D.C. 20101
1-800-827-5335

Family Resource Coalition
200 South Michigan Avenue, Suite 1520
Chicago, Illinois 60604-9753

8

ADVICE FOR THE NEXT DECADE

In the recessionist '90s the challenge for all companies is how to do more with less. Thus, retaining workers and helping them become more productive are critical components of a firm's success. At the same time, the startling demographics of the new work force make it clear to management that meeting work/family needs is the key to competing successfully throughout the decade. And according to figures from The Conference Board, the largest potential source of workers to meet the burgeoning labor shortage is the estimated 14 million women who are not now working outside the home. Since a vast majority of these women are in the home caring for young children, aged relatives, or disabled spouses, employers will have to lure them into the workplace with benefits such as flextime, job-sharing, telecommuting, child/eldercare, and the like.

The traditional corporate culture is based on a linear, mostly white male prototype. Often this culture is not flexible enough to assimilate the changing attitudes, flexibility, and diversity needed to become family-friendly. Consequently, major adjustments will have to be made beginning at the management level and radiating throughout the organization. These modifications need to be made quickly and must carry the weight of the CEO's blessing. In the companies we studied, a commitment to change at the very top levels of the organization proved to be a major component of success in meeting worker needs and thus company goals.

There are eight areas of adjustment we believe companies must make to be successful. They are to: (1) take care of basic family needs; (2) become "double-jointedly" flexible, as flexibility is the primary characteristic of good family-oriented programs; (3) "think female" (this might well be the new company bumper sticker)—women need to be

172

shown that they are understood and valued, or firms will lose out; (4) reframe policies and practices to reflect the new personal values of the '90s work force; (5) welcome diversity—this will bring exciting new understandings and openness to everyone in the organization as well as increasing competitive ability in the world market. Because many of the qualities of industrial age leaders are no longer relevant to today's needs, it will be important to (6) redefine the characteristics of a leader in the '90s workplace to ensure that these adjustments can be made and the firms will continue to have a visionary future. (7) Abandon isolationism and form partnerships with public and volunteer organizations; this is necessary in a time of shrinking fiscal and physical resources. This posture can also put a firm in a visible leadership position in the community. Lastly, business and government must (8) reward right actions in regard to family, female, and cultural diversity issues; this is the most potent step management can take in the '90s to increase morale and secure loyalty and success.

TAKE CARE OF BASIC NEEDS

Peters and Waterman in their 1982 best-selling business management book, *In Search of Excellence*, introduced the phrase, "productivity through people" to describe those companies that were classified as excellent firms. ". . . If you want productivity and the financial reward that goes with it, you must treat workers as your most important asset," these authors counseled. Advice from this corner is the same. Taking care of basic needs of employees and their families in a consistent and conscientious manner is the best insurance for productivity.

While there are still great differences in how work/family programs are implemented based on the firm's culture, history, resources, and current situation, there was not one firm among those researched that did not benefit overall as a result of work/family programs. Time and time again we received reports of decreased employee absenteeism, and increased retention, recruitment, and productivity. Simultaneously, just as there are degrees of success for the employer's bottom line, there are degrees of satisfaction by the employees. The option to work part time or job-share doesn't mean much to a minimum-wage single parent struggling to keep his or her child fed, clothed, and schooled. A half-time work option may not be much of a benefit to a professional who now works 50 plus hours a week but who would like the flexibility to occasionally leave early to see her child's ball game or come in late to take him to the doctor. Brown bag seminars on choosing eldercare may not do much good if there are no quality eldercare programs in the community. Paid parental leave won't be utilized if that means the employee is permanently derailed from an upward career path or comments are made that he/she just isn't serious about work anymore. There are no easy, piecemeal solutions to the work/family dilemma. A delicate balance in this equation is best assured in those firms with a comprehensive approach, company-wide family/work training programs, and enough flexibility to deal with needs as they arise on a case-by-case basis. Most of all there must be a pervasive sense of respect for the individual and practices that treat people with dignity, trust, and regard for them as individuals.

When a firm begins building its family program, we recommend starting with the two areas that seem most vital: dependent care and health protection. Without good substitute care for dependents, workers are constantly stressed, absenteeism increases, and loss in good personnel is probable—especially among women, as they are prone to quit if good arrangements cannot be made for dependent family members.

The federal government could require a combination of employee-employer contributions toward an insurance fund, covering short-term disability and infant-care leave. This approach is not entirely novel. Canada does it and the states of New York, New Jersey, California, and Rhode Island have state short-term disability insurance funds. The state of Hawaii requires employers to obtain disability coverage through private carriers. According to some child-care experts, 60% of America's working women are not covered by disability insurance during pregnancy. We believe this method could do much to meet the interests of both employees and employers and would help create the stable work force needed to compete globally in the '90s.

Further, we agree with the Yale University Bush Center in Child Development and Social Policy's insight that until there is a cogent national policy requiring infant-care leave, employers must be the ones to provide this to their employees. And we would go a step further, recommending that employers take the leadership to provide child care for those workers who desire it for their young offspring. This could take the form of building on or near site centers or could take the form of subsidization and training of community care-givers. Employers also should be encouraged to provide flextime, flexplace, job-sharing, part-time work, and resources to help employees meet the needs, not only of children but also other dependents, such as elders or disabled spouses.

The problems of health care coverage and costs grow more insidious every day. Business will have to choose a best path. Will it be to bite the bullet and pay more so all workers are adequately covered? Or, will they choose, in large numbers, to avoid this need and assume workers must pay for this benefit themselves? The third choice is perhaps the most foreign, but the one we feel to be the best: that of linking with government to create a national health care system. The mistakes of the welfare system and socialized medicine can be avoided if the private sector gives the government guidance. The benefits can be great for all.

To further recognize the changing nature of employee needs in the benefits area, we recommend adoption of flexible benefits plans, giving an employee the opportunity to custom-tailor a benefits package to his or her own needs. In general terms, employers would allocate a specific amount of money beyond regular earnings to each employee to choose benefits from among a list of options. These options, often called "cafeteria plans" (described in Chapter 6), should range from health care and life insurance programs, to long-term disability insurance, retirement savings plans, dependent care, and long-term care insurance.

In summary, an ideal work/family program would have as its basis: adequate parental leave for birth or adoption of a child of at least six months with job protection, full pay, and benefits; provision of excellent child care and eldercare on or near-site at nominal cost (not to exceed 10% of net family income) or comparable reimbursement for parents' choice of caregivers; provision for care of ill children or elders; comprehensive family health and retirement plans, with prenatal and well-baby coverages; access to quality after-school, before-school, and summer vacation care for children at nominal costs; a family education program during work hours; and flexible arrangements affecting both hours and places of work.

Government could assist by giving more tax breaks to firms that provide comprehensive health care, child-care, or eldercare benefits. Also, tax incentives should be provided for those firms offering training programs for new immigrants or workers returning after many years' absence from the work force due to family caretaking responsibilities.

School districts should be encouraged to provide before-, after-, and summer-school programs, as well as preschool programs for children age three and up. Helen Marieskind, chief executive of a health product technology firm, expressed it well: "We're wasting a tremendous resource. Schools both public and private should be turned into community centers for before- and after-school care." Not only would such programs assist working parents, the society as a whole would benefit from more academically adept children.

Finally, and perhaps most critical, is an attitude, from top management to supervisors, to support and production workers, that *family is important.* This attitude goes hand in hand with the requirement that top management communicate a sense of respect for all workers. A recognition of the interconnectedness of family life and corporate success is a key thought to communicate to each worker and his/her family.

BE FLEXIBLE

Many human resource professionals have identified flexible work hours and locations as *the key benefit issue of the '90s.* "We are at the beginning of a decade that is going to explore the limits of flexibility; how far can flexible work arrangements go and still meet the needs of business? The answer, I think, will be a lot further than many believe." So said Arlene Johnson of the Conference Board at a New York City Chamber of Commerce and Industry Conference in August of 1990. She and seven other panelists gave example after example of firms utilizing flexible work arrangements for management, professional, support, and production workers who wanted to create a better balance between work and family needs. The benefits these firms are experiencing as a result of these arrangements are impressive. Believe it or not, American workers now put in about 95 more hours on the job each year than they did in 1979. When both parents work during business hours, there is no time to take care of family business. Just a little flexibility, in times people can come in and leave for the day, or places they can do their work, eases the tension considerably.

Other flexible work arrangements can have a positive impact as well. The provision of nursing mothers' rooms at the work site as Hewitt Associates in Illinois has done, is an important step. In addition, longer standard maternity leaves, greater part-time and telecommuting work opportunities for new moms would also help prolong nursing for infants and young toddlers. We talked to one executive mother who nursed her child until he was two and a half and took him on more than a dozen business trips throughout the world. She said, "While it was hard on me physically, it helped me assuage my guilt about going back to work a few months after he was born. Nursing was really good for him emotionally and nutritionally, so I felt that it was really worth it." She admitted that she knew it raised some eyebrows from clients when her child, and her babysitter or spouse, showed up, but she reported general support and understanding. "It helped that I had good long-term working relationships with most of my clients. The only time it became a real issue is when I had to cancel a speech at the last minute when my child became too ill to travel with me. I agonized over the decision but finally realized that there was this very short time in both of our lives when he would ever need me that much and in that way, versus a 45 year work life. Unfortunately, the client was angry and disappointed." The concept of putting children first, for their own sakes, for the sake of the next generation and the health of the global economy, is still, regrettably, an alien concept to many businesspeople.

The impact of business travel on families also mitigates in favor of flexibility and accommodation on the part of employers. Again, Hewitt Associates is a leader in providing reimbursement for the cost of babysitters when late-night or overnight travel is required of their employees. Firms might also consider bearing the costs for travel and hotel accommodations so that nursing mothers could have their child and babysitter or spouse accompany them on business trips.

Flexibility has perhaps had the greatest positive impact on male workers in some firms. In the past few years the number of men opting to take advantage of parental leave policies has grown significantly. AT&T reports a jump in the ratios of men taking family leave from 400 to 1 a decade ago to 50 to 1 in 1990. Similar gains have been reported at AEtna Life and Casualty Company, Eastman Kodak, and DuPont. Some of the men who choose to reduce their time at work are responding to the pressures of dual- career marriages. Others are second-time-around fathers who feel nostalgia or guilt over time missed with their first families. One such dad told us that he took two unpaid weeks off when his second wife gave birth to their son and felt real pangs when he went back to work. "I love my job but this puts things into perspective. What's happening at home is simply more important." The director of the Fatherhood Project at the Families and Work Institute in New York, James A. Levine, calls this trend, "the new fatherhood." Many feel secure enough in their jobs to take advantage of company policies that are still quite new and somewhat controversial. A survey by Catalyst, a New York–based research group, revealed that while 114 companies offer unpaid leave to fathers for birth or adoption of a child, 41% of the companies said new fathers shouldn't take any time off in response to a question about men and paternity leave. It appears that a double standard exists in some firms: It's OK for a woman to take leave to care for a child or elder but not for a man. Even worse, at other firms the entire issue is ignored, as if somehow the next generation is supposed to raise itself, as neither sex is offered family leave; or if it's offered, there's the not-so-subtle pressure to not actually utilize the leave. This must change if America is to remain a great nation. The next generation won't raise itself and the seniors in our society deserve attention to their needs by today's working families. Let's hope that men who avail themselves of family leave policies won't be relegated to a "daddy track," that becomes a euphemism for sidetracked career, as the "mommy track" has for some women. We believe that both sexes should have access to corporate policies that help them to be loving family members *and* effective workers.

The *National Report on Work and Family*, published by the Bureau of National Affairs, Inc., in 1989, recently revealed that any benefit termed "paternity leave" is not often used by fathers, because they perceive a negative attitude by their employers. Joseph Pleck, a professor at Wheaton College, Massachusetts, said that "in the U.S. there is. . . some indication that fathers more often take leave when it is called something other than paternity or parental leave. Instead of applying for paternity or parental leave these new dads piece together unused vacation days, sick leave, and coverage from co-workers in order to spend a week or two with their offspring." Most firms we interviewed confirmed that parental leave was rarely used by male employees, reflecting both concerns about employer perceptions and a social view that bonding need only occur between mother and child. Most other cultures in the world dispute this view. T. Berry Brazelton, a leading light in the U.S. child development field, also contends in his book *Working and Caring* that both parents need time in those early critical weeks to develop an appropriate attachment to the child. This results in more secure parents and children.

Somehow managers must communicate to their employees that such leaves are *not only permissible but necessary*, if we are to have the kind of loving, stable, family relationships that lead to a more productive society. Whatever forms flexibility will take in the workplace from now on, there is assurance that families can benefit. And, because it is so important to both working partners, it will continue to be an excellent recruiting tool.

THINK FEMALE

The old Chinese saying, "Women hold up half the sky" has never been translated in the United States to mean that they have equal value with men in the workplace. Perhaps times are changing.

"If women enter the work force in smaller numbers, labor could become a scarcer commodity, one that can't be thrown away or underpriced so easily," said Frank Levy, a University of Maryland labor economist who specializes in income trends. Levy was commenting to the *New York Times* in late 1990 on a small but growing trend of women choosing not to enter the labor force as rapidly as they did in the '70s and '80s. The U.S. Department of Labor is beginning to see a diminution in the numbers of women working or seeking jobs. This development appears to be a product of a weakening economy and an increase in the number of births. While many of these new mothers are temporarily at home, some with greater family income flexibility may well stay there, if adequate child care is not available. Or, they may wind up staying out of the work force for a longer period than they would have preferred, if their employers don't provide incentives for a quick return to the work force. Such options as four-day work weeks, flextime, part-time positions, job-sharing, and assistance with finding and financing child care all serve to motivate new moms to return to work. They also statistically return to work sooner than those workers in firms without such benefits.

But if employers don't take the initiative to provide these incentives, the result may be not only a loss of workers but also higher labor costs, as firms compete against each other for scarce workers. Indeed, for the last 25 years, the median incomes of all workers have failed to keep up with inflation. Some argue that this was a direct result of a dramatic flood of women workers into the work force since 1971. This theory seems to be reinforced by the fact that women still earn only 67 cents for every dollar a man earns. Women have been forced to work for less because that's all the market will pay them. "In our hearts, we all know that what we pay women is not fair," wrote John Naisbitt and Patricia Aburdene in *Reinventing the Corporation*, several years ago. "Even the most hardened free-market businessman knows that it is unfair to pay women less than they are worth, less than they contribute to the enterprise." It seems obvious that no supplication to moral or ethical standards is going to change the pay inequity felt by women, but perhaps supply and demand will.

While some men and greater numbers of women have demanded more flexibility, most men continue to work in the same old ways and most women have adapted to the draining work schedules of men. In many organizations it seems accepted as a given that men and women will work long and hard for the company and then women will go home and work just as hard for the family. What recent surveys indicate, however, is that all Americans are suffering from this approach. Women are becoming exhausted and resentful, some dropping out of the work force, others compromising their home lives or career success. Firms are experiencing the ill effects of "brain drain" or productivity decline at a time when America needs to be at its most competitive. Our children are being undereducated and neglected in record numbers, just when we need a new generation at its healthiest and best prepared.

The working women we interviewed expressed a desire for employers to provide opportunities for advancement as well as family-supportive benefits, and a chance to achieve their career objectives as well as a flexible benefits package. If companies want to attract and retain female employees, they must be open to their employees' needs, both personal and professional. It would be useful for visionary leaders to step into a woman's shoes for a while, and spend some time "thinking female."

One result, in addition to including women in the planning process, creating fair pay scales, and instituting dependent care, flexibility, and health coverage benefits, would be to give women more leadership opportunities, especially in areas where negotiation is important. According to a study conducted by the Dartmouth School of Business, women were judged to be "superior deal makers." They were seen as more flexible, less deceptive, more emphatic, and more likely to reach an agreement than the men studied. The researchers agreed that men tend to see a negotiation as a one-shot deal that will either be won or lost. Women most frequently see it as a long-term relationship. Since long-term relationships with clients and vendors are what most businesses want, this "female approach" is more productive.

An inescapable fact of life is that since its inception the world of business has been predominantly male. For most of its history business could be home to assorted male bonding rituals without fear of intervention by, or causing offense to, the female sex. But those days are no more. While some women can ignore or view male-only office routines with the bemused detachment of a sociologist, others feel left out and angry. The annual office exec's deep-sea fishing trip caused one of our colleagues no real feelings of envy until she realized that future years' sales goals were somehow always set during these excursions. This year she plans to insist on an invitation, even though she has nightmares about getting seasick and humiliating herself in front of "the guys." Another colleague thought the factory football pools were just innocent fun, until she discovered that by not chipping in she was viewed as not being a team player. She feared that this might hurt her chances of being promoted to supervisor. Other women expressed dismay that so much work time is lost to "schmoozing over last

Saturday's basketball game." Some of these little rituals are harmless fun, others serve to make women feel like "odd person out." What are the signals to an employer that these "games" have gone too far? A company needs to become concerned if it can't keep women employed in a particular unit or can't successfully recruit women to work there. Such male bonding activities may make women feel unwelcome on the job.

Some progressive firms have started to rethink how they structure company leisure time events and company planning retreats. Softball leagues are becoming co-ed. Avon Products, Inc. changed its annual "President's Golf Day" to include swimming and tennis. Now this informal gathering for socializing and sharing a good time includes more women executives. Other companies, like Johnson Wax, sponsor family-oriented company events where spouses and children can participate. Some firms have decided that any off-site retreats are structured to appeal equally to male and female workers. The most successful employers have decided that fun, creativity, and relaxation shouldn't be viewed as single-sex activities.

Companies with strong family benefit policies have a better chance of retaining talented women. However, many women comment that even if the formal culture acknowledges the dual roles women hold, often the informal culture ignores or rejects them. Limited career opportunities, a good old boys' club atmosphere, pay disparities, and being left out of company social events send women a not-so-subtle message: You are not really wanted here. Catalyst, Inc., an organization promoting women's leadership, noted in 1990 that in 60% of large corporations, fewer than 5% of senior managers are female. Women will leave if they are made to feel that they do not fit in. It is a surprising anomaly that some of the firms surveyed with good family-oriented benefits still had few women in top management or board positions. Conversely, Kelly Service's top management is 30% female but they have only standard work and family benefits. A people-oriented manager at the top of the company can be the catalyst for change.

David Stanley, CEO of Payless Cashways, Inc., told *Business Week* on August 6, 1990, that he was influenced to change his thinking by his wife, a high-ranking health care executive. His firm now has a large number of female managers. At Avon Company, women hold 27% of 41 officer positions and they have instituted on-site child care. Du Pont, where less than 3% of top professionals and managers are women, has started a required program for managers to increase sensitivity to issues affecting women in the work force. Strategies are discussed to assure that women are in the information loop and have access to the networks that can lead to upward mobility. Du Pont already has two women on the board and a very strong program of family benefits. Pitney Bowes CEO George Harvey has issued a directive that women now get 35% of all new management jobs and promotions. Harvey told *Business Week* in its August 6, 1990, issue, "Women were putting in more time than the men—and more consistently beating their sales quotas. If I'm going to get the best talent, I've got to look at the entire population."

Because some CEOs have discovered that their managers have been a bit slow in promoting women, they have begun to tie compensation to goals of promoting women and minorities. Gannett Co., a media conglomerate, and Baxter International are two firms that link bonuses to these promotions. And, at U.S. West, women hold 21% of the jobs in the company's top 1% salary level. They have a firm goal of raising that percentage to 35% in this decade!

It is also time to shed notions of the traditional up or out career path. The '90s are a time for flexible career paths for both women and men, resembling more of a spiral or gently sloping horizontal than a straight, vertical line. Renee Magid, project director of work/family initiatives at Beaver College in Glenside, Pennsylvania, explained at a Bureau of National Affairs roundtable discussion, "Everyone was expected to progress straight up in rocket-like fashion. We never discuss those paths that may come in between, or instead of, like a spiral path, or a plateauing path—paths that allow individuals to have options." We must recognize that there are times in a person's working life when he or she won't be willing to relocate, or travel, or take on extra projects due to family responsibilities, but at other times these same employees may not only agree to these things but aggressively seek them out to get onto the fast track to the top. The danger for today's employers is to assume that all male employees want to be on a fast track and all female employees don't.

Faith Wohl, director of work force partnering for the Du Pont Company, amplified this point at this same roundtable discussion, "We're finding increasing reluctance to relocate," she revealed, "which is a prime hurdle that you have to get over to move to the top, both among men and among women. We're finding people who don't want to travel. We're finding men and women in the corporation, the younger people who have young children, unwilling to do some of the things that drove today's CEOs to the top. So if a business is facing that in both men and women, aren't we ultimately going to have to step back and say, 'We have to redesign the workplace. We have to rethink the model that has been followed for all these years because it may not be possible anymore.' " Nor may it be desirable, if the old rigidity causes a firm to lose employees to an organization that has created flexible career paths for all workers. The traditional career development system has clearly become dysfunctional for women and men with dependents.

Women currently climbing the corporate ladder represent the first generation of American women who grew up dreaming of having a perfect marriage and a perfect career simultaneously. Women now are more than half of all U.S. undergraduates, a third of all M.B.A. students, half of law and accounting students, and comprise rapidly growing percentages of medical students. This is also the first generation of men married to these women—men who are now expected to not only pay for the diapers but change them, while also earning a living and doing housework. It is an exhilarating and frustrating time—one that has taxed our personal energies to the limit but has spawned creative solutions across the nation.

REFRAME POLICIES TO REFLECT NEW VALUES

Workaholism is passé. At least that's what workers across the country told us in our interviews. We're beginning to see this manifested in not-so-subtle ways. "I no longer bring work home every weekend; that's a time to spend with our child and each other," said one entrepreneur. "Both my husband and I plan to be home by six o'clock or we'd never see our daughter—she goes to bed early, so no more takeout Chinese at our desks 'til 9:00 or 10:00 P.M. Our values have changed and with that so has our life-style." She is not alone. Rampant no-holds-barred career-ism is on the wane. Overachievement symbolized in 60+-hour work weeks, car telephones, 24-hour fax transmissions, and Federal Express's tracking workers down on vacation beaches is going by the wayside. On the upswing are family photos on the desks of both male and female workers and a workplace melting pot or conversational common ground in discussing child-rearing strategies.

Experts suggest that much of the change is merely a reflection of baby boomers' aging—they are settling down and having children—about 4 million of them last year. This baby boomlet is the biggest number since 1964, the last year of the 18-year baby boom. With these children comes a shift in priorities, a fact expressed by virtually all the working parents we interviewed. "Watching our baby learn to smile, crawl, walk, and talk is just so much more fascinating than negotiating a new contract to me right now," said a West Coast development consultant. "It's not that my business is unimportant; it's just not all-encompassing like it used to be. I think my life has more balance now," she concluded.

Finding some balance is a juggling act some women workers cannot easily master. As one Michigan lawyer said, "I 'balance' by losing myself, my free time. I have no hobbies, little time to assess who I am and where I want to go. I 'balance' by foregoing social opportunities and chit-chat with my peers." We think that all work and no play makes Jill a dull woman. Even worse, it bodes ill for her mental health, self-image, and, ultimately, work performance. American women, while experiencing more career mobility than many of their European or Asian counterparts, experience many fewer supports for family obligations. From prenatal checkups to after-school care, Europe and Japan make it much easier to be a good parent, worker, and mentally healthy person. Florence Chauveau, a young Parisian mother, who worked for a government agency, told us that her reduced work week and excellent neighborhood child-care center allowed her time to unwind by herself in the afternoons by reading or taking in a movie. Consequently, she wouldn't think of leaving her employer and said that she was glad to come back from maternity leave knowing that she had these supports in place. She also said she is working more productively since coming back from leave because she isn't preoccupied by child-care worries.

One would have hoped that in the United States attitudes about family and work would have changed more rapidly, since women have been in the work force in significant numbers for most of the last two decades. During the '70s, women who in earlier generations might have remained at home entered professions, factories, and service positions in large numbers. Many believed that this transformation of the workplace into a two-gender domain also would have led to a fundamental restructuring of the concept of work. Some of us thought that everyone would work shorter hours with flexible career paths so that all workers could have richer and more rewarding family and career lives. Of course, for the most part, that has not happened. Instead, some organizations have responded by creating the infamous "mommy track," treating their female employees differently than their male workers purely on the basis of reproductive organs. A reporter for a West Coast television station responded succinctly to this development: "I'm offended by the 'mommy track' concept of employment. It presumes the only valued employees are those who spend too much time working and devote no time to contributing to the community or raising functional families. I don't think as a society we can afford to divide people into such narrow groups. We need whole citizens. Work has its place, but the workplace should not be worshiped."

Some family-dedicated workers tell us that they are working more efficiently than in their old stay-at-the-office-'til-midnight workaholism days. Perhaps many inadvertently got involved in "make work" activities or perhaps standards have changed. "I'm less perfectionistic," said one new dad. "I have to be or I'd go crazy. There's no such thing as being able to do it all or have it all. Right now my wife and I are involved in a constantly shifting set of compromises, each day trying to balance what we can accomplish at work and at home. We're still dedicated to our jobs, but we're not obsessed like we were before our son was born."

Instead of compartmentalizing their lives—worker, parent, spouse, caregiver—the '90s are a time to seek integration in various life roles. To fail to do this guarantees for many a debilitating sense of guilt that undermines sense of self and ultimately one's success as workers, caregivers, and spouses. For some this means recognizing that life is a continuum—we may be able to have it all, but perhaps not all at the same time. "After my first child was born," said one mother who also had been described in the local paper as a compulsive activist, donating much of her time to others, "I realized that I wasn't going to be able to continue all my roles simultaneously: worker, mother, activist. So I gave up most of my volunteer work. It just dawned on me that raising a healthy, well-adjusted child was the best contribution to the community that I could make." She admitted that while her decision was made calmly and rationally, response to it often was not. "Some people got angry when I backed out of some community commitments and said no to some new work assignments. Initially they neither understood nor supported me. I think that's changing now as more people realize that the myth of Superwoman is just that—a myth." On the other hand, there are work endeavors that will require 70-hour work weeks and an all-out effort—to take a case to trial, finish a manuscript, or win a design competition. Fortunately none of these projects lasts forever. Schedules can be adjusted to deal with big work efforts or big issues at home—the sick child or the aging parent in crisis.

In fact we think it's time to stop using the phrase "juggling work and family demands" as it implies a precariousness without a sense of balance. We prefer the expression "composing a life," coined by Mary Catharine Bateson in her 1990 book of the same name. "Composing" connotes a more graceful, balanced approach to working out these sometimes conflicting demands. Bateson describes this approach as "discovering the shape of our creation along the way, rather than pursuing a vision already defined." This attitude strikes us as much healthier, less stressful, and more in tune with the '90s.

Many may ask what impact these changes in attitude and cutbacks in hours are having on corporate productivity. Well, these new values certainly fly in the face of the "organization man" and his way of showing allegiance to his employer. To many who still adhere to the industrial age paradigm, they may appear to be in opposition to corporate productivity. Nothing could be further from the truth.

What these employees are expressing is the willingness to give a new kind of loyalty and provide a more vital work contribution, in exchange for respect shown for their family and personal responsibilities. They want their employers to recognize that they are full human beings with lives and activities outside the workplace. They believe that their obligations to family and community do not oppose their work—but with a little creativity and flexibility, can blend with it to the advantage of all.

Others suggest that a commitment to family is not the only motivation for more balance. There is also a hint of disillusionment expressed by some of these career-dedicated baby boomers as they talk about new priorities. They made it to the top only to feel, like Peggy Lee's old ballad, "Is That All There Is?" Others appear to be shell-shocked from the downsizings and layoffs in the aftermath of the leveraged buyouts, mergers, and acquisitions of the mid '80s. Their values changed because they sought new, more secure avenues for satisfaction.

How, then, will visionary company leaders capitalize on these new values? The most obvious payback to acknowledging a worker's humanity is *loyalty*. Loyalty translates into productivity, high morale, and retention. Because these new values are also part of clients' and customers' way of looking at the world, understanding these new values guarantees being closer to customers and serving them better. It appears that the corporate cultures most sensitive to employees' needs are also closest to their customers or clients. For example, Security Pacific Bank extended its banking hours to benefit its customers; employees benefited also by more opportunities for part-time work and more flexible hours. Johnson & Johnson's work and family amendment to their corporate credo not only boosted employee morale, it also elevated the company's credibility in the eyes of the millions of parents who buy their baby-care products. Microsoft's humanistic approach to work hours and assignments is also reflected in its commitment to the development of user-friendly software. St. Francis's long-term care program also takes its customer orientation a step further than the competition. It provides a day-care facility for children and elders, resulting in happier clients and employees and a higher standard of care than most "traditional" nursing homes. These are but a few examples of other possible outcomes beyond those envisioned by the work/family advocates who lobbied for these innovations. And the stakes have never been higher. Not only does America need companies that are top business performers in this next decade, they need firms that will contribute to the greater societal good as well.

In the last year or two much has been written about the decline in quality of many American products and services. Consumers have moved beyond moaning about it to being assertive: They are simply refusing to buy from certain vendors and they are going public with their gripes. This is all part of the new '90s values system. Recent research suggests that customers who have bad experiences tell approximately 11 people about it; but those with good experiences tell only six. Not only do unhappy customers not come back, they'll tell anyone who will listen not to also. Companies who want to be successful must take steps to assure that everyone in the organization has the skill, motivation, and authority to make top-quality customer service the rule rather than the exception. Training employees to act and take responsibility for good customer service and quality products is more likely to occur in those firms that communicate respect for employees.

W. Edwards Deming, an award-winning management guru, has developed a 14-point "path to quality," resulting in a well-trained work force to assure the motivation necessary for excellent customer service. Key among Deming's points are exhortations to:

- Drive out fear
- Institute leadership
- Institute training on the job
- Promote education and self-improvement

He advocates a company-wide commitment to constant improvement. He warns managers to remember to stay focused on what the company is about and on the value of the workers. Deming sees as the primary obligations of management anticipating the desires of customers, enlisting the cooperation of employees, and improving processes and products constantly. Further, he urges business executives to evaluate every component of the system not as a profit center in and of itself, but rather for its contribution to the system as a whole.

For example, he questions, "What should be the aim of a company travel department, to save money or make the arrangements necessary to send employees out on assignment fit to carry out their jobs?" In the former instance, the department could send a West Coast worker to a New York meeting on the overnight plane or "red eye," generally a much cheaper fare. But in the latter instance, the firm would pay for an overnight hotel room and send the employee out on a flight the day before. This worker then arrives for the meeting rested and able to focus on performing well the business at hand. Many firms we featured in chapter 5, like Hewitt Associates in Illinois, understand this, paying for after-hours babysitters and late-night taxi rides. They know that spending a little can get you a lot. Associates at Hewitt are loyal, quality performers who deliver what their clients want.

This investment in workers yielding increases in sales from loyal customers is also what helps motivate IBM, AT&T, American Express, and others to offer extensive training programs that embrace customer satisfaction as a primary goal of business. E. B. White once wrote, "The only sense that is common in the long run is the sense of change," and we all instinctively avoid it. To try to avoid the powerful changes brought on by new worker and customer values would be a serious mistake. To embrace these changes and make them work for the bottom line is the smartest move a business leader can make.

WELCOME DIVERSITY

Corporations are known for their conformist ways. Workers at each level dress in a similar manner, often have the same color or style office furniture, and adhere to prescribed protocols when dealing with other workers and officials. One new hire said of the environment in the company she was entering, "I felt like I was back in parochial school. I immediately went shopping for a wardrobe of blue blazers and ribbon ties." Sometimes this conformity is forced—to regulate behavior—and sometimes it happens for a more collegial reason—simply as an expression of similar values; other times it occurs out of habit—people are locked into their own comfort zones responding to others who look or act just like themselves. Whatever the cause, conformity can hamper the birth of new ideas and the free flow of valuable information. It can also cause an organization to overlook an important potential labor source—ethnic minorities and new immigrants of both sexes, as well as people with disabilities. It can also cause a firm to overlook a great potential market—people of color.

Facing competition for this labor pool made up of nontraditional workers, many of them from immigrant families and the entire spectrum of ethnic groups now living in the U.S., business leaders need to adopt new attitudes and practices toward diversity. It is surprising that while many school districts have embraced multiculturalism, most businesses have not. The up and coming generation of workers will have some experience and appreciation for working with others from diverse backgrounds and abilities. Savvy managers will capitalize on this.

At the Xerox Corporation, minorities held 16% of managerial jobs and 10% of professional posts in 1987, closely reflecting the overall percentage of minorities in the work force that year (21%). Since that time both numbers are increasing. Xerox is achieving success by encouraging minority networks that provide advice and support to black, Asian, and Hispanic employees of both sexes and to white females.

Taking full advantage of this new work force may require a manager to suspend old judgments and acquire new skills. A person's comfort level may be challenged by a person of a different culture, if that culture espouses values alien to those of the manager. Managers may feel inadequate because they don't know or understand these values and may not feel able to predict consequent behaviors. These managers may need training to increase cross-cultural understanding, and to improve listening skills, key to understanding all workers' needs. They also need to focus on performance. "My workers may act different from me in terms of style and approach," explained one manager we spoke to, "but the bottom line is—do they produce? Once I was able to focus on getting the job done and not on the language or personality variations, I became a better boss."

Acknowledging the global economy and seeking to compete in a world market is another reason for opening up the vision of the workplace to include diverse cultural influences. How can this be done? Much will happen automatically if an attitude of acceptance is there when workers from various cultural viewpoints come on the scene. Planned changes can coincide with the introduction of family/work programs if the firm makes a conscious decision to reach out and *embrace* diversity, not reject it. Examples of this embracing attitude include sponsoring workshops in cross-cultural communication techniques and eliminating bias in the workplace, holding seminars on antidiscrimination laws, creating internship programs that reach out to potential workers of minority cultures, celebrating Hispanic, African-American, Asian, or Native American heritages in special events, scheduling English as a second language classes, and promoting image-enhancing symbols.

REDEFINE LEADERSHIP

Collaboration, participation, and viewing leadership as a process rather than a person are the appropriate leadership approaches for the '90s. Gone is the image of the man on the white horse who singlehandedly rallies the troops, knows all the right answers, and is willing to take the final bullet in defending his turf. A new kind of leadership is essential to make work/family programs successful. Leadership activities are needed at all levels of an organization, with vision being the primary quality needed at the top. While the ability to effectuate plans predominates at the vice presidential levels, project managers or supervisors have the most direct influence on worker productivity and loyalty. It is there that the new definition of leadership is most crucial. Some leadership gurus make a strong case that managers are not necessarily leaders. We concur. However, in this new world of the '90s, managers and supervisors, because of their influence on employees, will need leadership skills to carry out the company's mission and reflect its new values.

Diane Burrus, director of the education and training program at Work/Family Directions, says that through her firm's experiences in implementing family-friendly policies and benefits, she has learned how important managers are as "transmitters of culture." Unless managers are firmly committed, the goals of work/family programs won't be taken seriously and then not implemented consistently or used by those who need them. To achieve management support, consistent implementation, and appropriate level of employee utilization, she explained how IBM sought to help its managers:

- Learn about changes in the labor force
- Understand the environment in which the business operates
- Work in partnership with employees
- Understand the company's programs/practices and how to apply them effectively
- Utilize management tools to develop appropriate responses analyzing options
- Assist employees in long-range career planning taking into account the generally short-term need for flexibility

We recommend four to eight hours of training for managers to work through their concerns, analyze real work problems, and design appropriate solutions. IBM does this and also utilizes a pre-program and post-program attitude and knowledge survey designed to evaluate the effectiveness of the training. Johnson & Johnson not only trains all managers in a similar program, it provides one hour of training to all employees on how to avail themselves of benefits, as well as the company's expectations of this partnership. One of these expectations is that women will be trained, recruited, and promoted to management positions.

Another quality of leadership is the ability to convey an attitude of caring and flexibility. Workers need policies that allow for phone calls during the workday from children, spouses, or elders. Indeed, when the worker is out of town on assignment, reimbursement for at least one daily phone call home should be provided. Said one top-level manager, "I know my employees see overnight travel as necessary but detrimental to their family lives. We should take steps to encourage them to stay in touch with home. A worried worker is not a productive one."

In looking at younger workers' needs and priorities, the smart manager/leader realizes that the 20-something staffer values family and leisure as much as work. The worker in the '90s has redefined his/her notions of success. Thus, when it comes time to pass out rewards for top performance, this group would often prefer time off or more vacation days. This can be preferable to additional responsibilities or a promotion, if either means additional hours on the job or more overnight travel. The '90s manager thus must not only seek new ways to recruit and train his/her employees, but also innovations in how to reward and retain this new generation.

In *Megatrends 2000*, John Naisbitt and Patricia Aburdene claim that much of the business leadership that will give the U.S. an edge in the global economy will come from women. Given that, firms would do well to begin looking to women as emerging leaders by offering special training and upward mobility strategies. In her landmark research regarding the moral development of children, Carol Gilligan of Harvard University discovered that young females make decisions based on a holistic appraisal of the situation, taking into account human dilemmas and feelings as well as objective data. Young males, on the other hand, made moral judgements using a linear thinking model where objective data and win-lose paradigms hold sway. The complexity of the business world today requires holistic and divergent methods of thinking. Enter the female leader, who is geared to creating win/win opportunities for her workers.

The recognition of leadership qualities in everyone who works for the organization is another '90s mandate. The expectation that everyone has the potential for self-leadership can create a sharing of goals, responsibilities, and expectations between employee and management. The sense that "we are all in this together—hence we all have a responsibility to make it work" is strong medicine. It can create a powerful esprit de corps—and assure the success of the business. Supporting self- leadership, however, requires supervisors without oversized egos. Only those who truly have respect for the employees they supervise can make it work.

What does the redefining of leadership have to do with work/family programs and business success in the '90s? Everything. In this redefinition there is an acknowledgment of the humanity of the employee, a faith in his/her ability to contribute to the company's success through leadership, and a method for accommodating the new values of employees and customers.

FORM PARTNERSHIPS

Chapter 7 describes the successes created when government partners with the private sector to make work/family programs available to their communities. *Partnering* is a smart move in the resource diminishing '90s. Many companies have perpetuated an isolationist stance through-out the years. The tangle of government regulations, the red tape, and multiple copy requirements of many potential partnership opportuni-ties made them less than desirable in the past. However, the advantages of collaborations are now beginning to outweigh the disadvantages. In the arena of family/work needs, partnerships and coalitions have made many programs possible, from use of zoning incentives that encourage builders to provide downtown child-care centers to tax changes favoring flexible spending accounts for dependent-care needs. For small busi-nesses particularly, joining together to meet dependent or health care needs appears to be the only reasonable alternative to defray both start-up and operating costs.

Business leaders of the '90s also have to view their employees and their customers as partners. Old labor/management antipathies must fall by the wayside. Employees need to feel empowered to take some control over their workplaces, so that they will feel responsibility for the outcomes. The market will also be driven by customer demands taking the form of concerns for quality, environmentally sensitive products, and services produced by companies with a reputation for caring about employees and their families. American business has become a real power in terms of the quality of life of U.S. citizens. With this power comes a responsibility to address a broad range of societal needs that can be converted into profitable business opportunities. Companies that invest in urban revitalization, like Control Data, or invest in turning around the lives of welfare mothers, like Security Pacific Bank, or create dependent care benefits, like the firms highlighted in chapter 5, are making these management-worker- customer partnerships realities.

REWARD RIGHT ACTION

"If we went around blaming our own people for the recession, advertising wouldn't be up in nine out of ten of our magazines," claims James Autry, president of the highly successful Meredith Corporation and recent author of *Love and Profit: The Art of Caring Leadership*. He heartily supports the notions of "catching" an employee doing well and rewarding that action. Because so many U.S. workers have grown up with puritanical beliefs that whatever one does, at least part of it will be wrong, a subtle sense of guilt and self-disappointment exists in the minds of most. The resulting anxiety spills over into work and family life. Reinforcing right action with consistent praise or rewards can change that. It matters in the workplace and it also counts on the home front.

The parents we spoke with not only talked about changing corporate and government policies, they also expressed a sense of longing for a "good family life." A recent Gallup Poll of Americans reported that 81% believe that "raising children today is more difficult than when my parents were raising me," and a recent Harris Poll found that most adults also believe it's harder to be a child today than when they were growing up. Questions about how to parent well came up as frequently in our discussions as how to set up a company child-care or eldercare center. Issues as diverse as dealing with a two-year-old's temper tantrums to talking to adult siblings about an elderly mother's financial woes dominated many discussions. Our rapid demographic and societal changes have led many to believe that today's families are in uncharted waters. Concerns were also frequently expressed about how to transmit appropriate values to children in an average day with so few precious minutes allocated exclusively to children. One dad, an owner of a small computer services company, said, "My job as a parent has several critical parts: making sure my kids are fed, loved, clothed, and teaching them right from wrong."

These kinds of concerns aren't going to be alleviated just by official guidelines and mandates. We have to create a culture, a society where children, elders, and parents are all valued. As Lynnette Friedrich Coffer of the Institute for American Values said, "We need to infuse research and policy discussions with a consideration of the human values involved . . . and to use the language of families as we craft both public policies and scientific research." This goal has to be reinforced daily in the news media and in the day-to-day actions of each person.

It also means that parents will have to give themselves and each other permission to take action to create balance in their own lives and to self-nurture. Workers must determine their own level of commitment to work/family balance. They need to become advocates inside their companies for flexible work hours, dependent-care programs, and performance-based pay programs. They must act consistently to demonstrate their commitment to family and personal priorities, including scheduling non-work time in advance and saying no to requests that take away from family time. Dr. Barbara Mackoff argues forcefully in *Leaving The Office Behind* (1984) that, when you're away from work, let go of work concerns and really focus on your family and yourself. Not only will you feel less guilty, studies show you'll actually be healthier, happier, and a better-performing worker.

We recommend that families struggling to do it all ask for help—help from other family members, friends, and employers. None of the work/family programs featured in this book is a panacea. But they do help create balance. None was created in a vacuum—all were the products of people who recognized and sought assistance in the daily struggle most Americans face. It will be interesting to see how these delicate balancing acts impact our businesses, homes, and children over the long run.

FIRST AND LAST: SUPPORTING THE NEW AMERICAN FAMILY IS GOOD BUSINESS

Twenty-five to thirty percent of students who enter high school drop out. This high number of high school dropouts now costs the U.S. $240 billion in lost wages and taxes. Half the children born in the U.S. this year will be on welfare by the time they are 20 years old. Our elders are feeling betrayed and shunted aside. "Quite simply, our society suffers from a family deficit—one that is probably more dangerous for our culture than either our trade or financial deficit," says David Blankenhorn, president of the Institute for American Values. Children are the poorest group in society, with more than one in five living in a household whose income is below the poverty level. Despite medical advances, the U.S. has an infant mortality rate higher than some third world countries and more than 1 million teenagers become pregnant each year. We need to act on our convictions that every child has the right to grow up healthy, literate, and loved so that the next generation can be economically and socially productive. Society is now exposed to a great threat from the breakdown of families spurred by poverty, drugs, and the growing alienation between children and our institutions. A concerted effort must be made among workers, lawmakers, and business leaders to strengthen the family and thus strengthen our entire society. The time has come for a new American agenda that makes it easier for people to work, give care, and be active in the community.

A recent survey asked high school students how important it is to them to have a good marriage and family life. Ninety-three percent of senior girls and 86% of boys answered "extremely important" or "quite important." These statistics reinforce the shift that is already occurring in the '90s away from the "me generation" to a time when a new set of family values will dominate the society. In some instances this will be a product of children raised by "me generation" parents who experienced the sorrows of abuse, neglect, or drug/alcohol addiction firsthand. They are determined to make things better for their kids. But in many other instances the offspring of the working families profiled in this book will continue to insist on changes throughout the society that reinforce fulfillment of family obligations. Often, that young person's first exposures to supportive influences outside the immediate family were the ones provided by the workplace. The company child-care center, elder day-care program, or the opportunity for her/his mom or dad to be home when needed are the early experiences that these children will remember. Thus the company as a nurturing role model is both the progenitor and perpetuator in the cultural rebirth of new American values. As a nation, we have great challenges to meet in this area.

The family structure is a foundation for our country. Yet somehow we have forgotten that families in America are under siege. And nowhere is that more obvious than at the workplace. We must change public policy and private actions to accommodate the needs of the changing modern family. Our governments and American businesses large and small must act to encourage families to stay together and have time to spend together to cement that bond. Those bonds depend on fostering a sound atmosphere for child rearing, which will yield a more stable society and a stronger American economy. To make the needed changes happen, these issues must be higher on the agenda in boardrooms and voting booths than they have been up to this point in our history.

Donald Kanter and Philip H. Mirvis, authors of *The Cynical Americans: Living and Working in an Age of Discontent and Disillusion* (1989), discovered that behind the pessimism there is a strong commitment to "traditional values that encourage self-reliance, promote productivity and accomplishment, and sustain our economy and society." The challenge they see is to tap into these latent ideals. They suggest that it can be done by giving employees more control over their time (by flexible work hours and arrangements), allowing workers more control over their jobs, by decentralizing and creating smaller work units, and encouraging closer contact with customers.

The essential theme of this book has been the interdependence of family and work, the undeniable reliance of profitability on good workers, and the need for big picture thinking as problems of congruence are ironed out between home and the workplace. No longer are family issues private matters or community problems the sole responsibility of volunteers, nor is the economic recession in which the country now finds itself, a challenge only to large corporations. We are all in this together. Not until the United States as a nation takes a holistic approach to creating family-community-business systems can we expect to succeed as families, businesses, or as a nation.

This is both an exciting and unsettling time in American business, ripe with chances to succeed globally or fail miserably by not responding to these warning signals. The '90s are a time marked by a more diverse and skeptical work force with significant family responsibilities, competing against countries with extensive track records of dealing effectively with diversity, changing attitudes, and the needs of children and the elderly. Can we learn to nurture the family unit so as to stabilize the society while increasing our productivity? Perhaps Woody Allen has the answer: "It is clear that the future holds great opportunities. It also holds pitfalls. The trick will be to avoid the pitfalls, seize the opportunities, and get back home by six o'clock."

REFERENCES

Adolf, Barbara, and Rose, Karol. *The Employers Guide to Child Care: Developing Programs for Working Parents*. New York: Praeger, 1985.

Anderson, B. "Seeking Child Care in the Middle of the Night." *The New York Times*, January 3, 1991.

Autrey, James. *Love & Profit: The Art of Caring Leadership*. New York: Morrow Publishing Co., 1990.

Axel, Helen. "Corporations and Families: Changing Practices and Perspectives." New York: The Conference Board, Report No. 868, 1985.

Ball, Karen. "Will the 90s Be Kind to Labor?" Associated Press. The Conference Board, September 1,2, 1990.

Belsie, Laurent. "Telecommuting Catches On in U.S." *Christian Science Monitor*, January 3, 1991.

Birnbach, Lisa. *Going to Work*. New York: Villard Books, 1988.

Blankenhorn, David. "Does Grandmother Know Best?" In *Family Affairs*. Institute for American Values. Vol. 3, No. 1–2, Spring/Summer, 1990. New York.

Bohen, H. H. and Long, A. V. "Balancing Job and Family Life." In *Work and Family*, edited by P. Voydanoff. Palo Alto: Mayfield Publishing Co., 1984.

Bowen, G. "Corporate Support Mechanisms for Families: An Exploratory Study and Agenda for Research and Evaluation," *Evaluation and Program Planning*. Vol. 8, 1985.

Brazelton, T. Berry, M.D. "Why Is America Failing Its Children?" *New York Times Magazine*, September 9, 1990.

Bronfenbrenner, Urie. "A Generation in Jeopardy: America's Hidden Family Policy." Testimony to the Senate Committee on Rules and Administration on a Resolution to Establish a Select Committee on Families, Youth, and Children. Washington D.C., 1986.

Bureau of National Affairs. *National Report on Work and Family*. Washington D.C.: Buraff Publications, Inc.

————. "Alternative Work Schedules: Changing Times for a Changing Workforce." *National Report on Work and Family*, Special Report #5. Washington D.C.: Buraff Publications, May 1988.

————. "American Child Care: Problems and Solutions." *National Report on Work and Family*, Special Report # 12. Washington D.C.: Buraff Publications, December 1988.

————. "Bank's Child Care Center Saves Money Due to Less Turnover and Absenteeism." *National Report on Work and Family*, Vol. 1, No. 12, November 15, 1988.

————. "Child Day Care in the 101st Congress: Early Initiatives, *National Report on Work and Family*," Special Report # 17, May 1989.

————. "Companies Discover Benefits in Job Sharing." *National Report on Work and Family*, Vol. 2, No. 21. October 13, 1989.

————. "Corning Finds Absenteeism Due to Child Care Problems." *National Report on Work and Family*, Vol. 2, No. 19. September 15, 1989.

————. "Corporate Work and Family Programs for the 1990's: Five Case Studies," *National Report on Work and Family*, Special Report # 13. Washington D.C.: Buraff Publications, January 1989.

————. "Delaware Residents Get New Elder Care Resource System." *National Report on Work and Family*, Vol. 3, No. 17. August 3, 1990.

————. "Employee Assistance Programs: Focusing on the Family." *National Report on Work and Family*, Special Report #6. Washington, D.C.: Buraff Publications, June 1988.

————. "Employee Housing Assistance Helps Retention, Experts Say." *National Report on Work and Family*, Vol. 2, No. 22. October 27, 1989.

————. "Employers and Child Care: Tax and Liability Considerations." *National Report on Work and Family*, Special Report #7. Washington, D.C.: Buraff Publications, 1988.

————. "Firms Reports on Parental Leave Laws in Four States," *National Report on Work and Family*, Vol. 3, No. 13. August 17, 1990.

————. "Michigan to Begin Family Care Accounts for State Workers and Small Businesses." *National Report on Work and Family*, Vol. 2, No. 6. March 3, 1989.

————. "Pregnant Workers May Switch to New Jobs Under Oregon Bill." *National Report on Work and Family*, Vol. 2, No. 15. July 7, 1989.

————. "Report Finds Telecommuting Boosts Worker's Productivity." *National Report on Work and Family*, Vol. 2, No. 18. August 18, 1989.

————. "Research: Male Employees Take Leaves If It's Not Labeled Paternal." *National Report on Work and Family*, Vol. 3, No. 1. December 8, 1989.

————. "Research: Survey Shows On-Site Day Care Increases Worker Retention." *National Report on Work and Family*, Vol. 2, No. 6. March 3, 1989.

————. "Results of AEtna's Family Leave Program Yield Dramatic Increase in Retention." *National Report on Work and Family*, Vol. 2, No. 22. October 27, 1989.

————. "St. Paul City Council Votes $30,000 for Day Care."*National Report on Work and Family*, Vol. 3, No. 13. June 8, 1990.

————. "The Bottom Line on Benefits: New Way to Gauge Productivity." Vol. 1, No. 7. June 15, 1988.

————. "The 'Mommy Track' Debate and Beyond: Public Policy? Corporate Reality?" *National Report on Work and Family*, Special Report #16, Washington, D.C.: Buroff Publications, April 1989.

Burge, Penny. "Preparing for the Personal Side of Work." *Vocational Education Journal*. Vol. 64, No. 6. September 1989.

Burke, J. E., and Larsen, R. S.: Address to the Council of Personnel Directors on Balancing Work and Family, May 17, 1989.

Burlingham, Bo. "This Woman Has Changed Business Forever." *Inc.*, Vol. 12, No. 6. June, 1990.

Burud, S., Collins, R. C., Hawkins, P. D. "Employer Supported Child Care: Everybody Benefits," *Children Today*. Vol. 12, No. 3. May-June, 1983.

Burud, Sandra; Aschbacker, Pamela R.; McCrosky, Jacquelyn. *Employer Supported Child Care: Investing in Human Resources*. Boston, Mass.: Auburn House, 1984.

Castro, Janice. "Economy and Business: Home Is Where the Heart Is," *Time*, October 3, 1988.

Catalyst. "Corporations and Two-Career Families: Directions for the Future." New York: Catalyst, 1984.

————. "Flexible Work Arrangements: Establishing Options for Managers and Professionals." New York: Catalyst, 1990.

"Child Care Fact Sheet—National Outlook: Who Supports Child Care." Washington D.C.: National Commission on Working Women, 1987.

Christensen, Kathleen. *Flexible Staffing and Scheduling in U.S. Corporations*. New York: The Conference Board, Research Bulletin No. 240, 1989.

Cohen, Sharon. "Companies Turn to Rank and File." *The Trenton Times*, December 2, 1990.

Conference Board. "The New Corporate Family: What You Don't See Is What You Get." *Across the Board Journal*, July/August, 1990.

The Conference Board Work & Family Information Center, New York, June, 1989.

Deutsch, Claudia H. "Saying No to the 'MOMMY TRACK'." *New York Times*, January 28, 1990.

"Doing the Right Thing," *Newsweek*, January 7, 1991.

Dole, Elizabeth. "Resources: Where Employees Can Get Help." *Business and Health*, January 1990.

Drucker, Peter. *The New Realities in Government and Politics, Economics, and Business in Society and World View*. New York: Harper & Row, 1989.

Dusky, Lorraine. "Companies That Care: What the Best Employers Offer Families." *Family Circle*, April 25, 1989.

———. "Top Companies for Working Mothers." *Good Housekeeping*, August, 1990.

———. *The Best Companies for Women*. New York: Pocket Books, 1989.

Eimno, David. "Daycare from the Employer's Perspective." *Seattle-Sound Business*, April 1990.

Emlen, A. C., Koren, P. E. *Hard to Find and Difficult to Manage: The Effects of Childcare on the Workplace*. Portland, Oregon: The Workplace Partnership, 1984.

Erlich, E. "The Mommy Track." *Business Week*, March 20, 1989.

"Executive Memo," Marriott Health Care Services. Vol. 12, Number 10, 1990, Washington D.C.

"Expert Predicts Explosion in Employee Housing Aid," *Daily Labor Reporter*, Bureau of National Affairs Current Developments (No. 248), December 26, 1990.

"Family Supportive Policies: The Corporate Decision-Making Process." Report No. 897. New York: The Conference Board, 1989.

"Family Survey II." Louis Harria and Associates, Inc. for the Philip Morris Companies, Inc., April, 1989.

Fenn, Donna. "The Kids Are All Right." *Inc.*, January 1985.

Fernandez, John P. *Child Care and Corporate Productivity, Resolving Family/Work Conflicts*. New York, N.Y.: Lexington Books, D.C. Heath & Co., 1986.

Fields, D. M. "Governace with Foresight." *The Futurist*. Vol. 24, No. 4. July-August, 1990.

"Finding the Guts to Go." *Working Woman*, May 1990.

Ford Foundation. *The Common Good: Social Welfare and the American Future*. New York: Ford Foundation Office of Communications, 1990.

Friedes, Peter E. "Work and Family Issues at Hewitt Associates: One Employer's Initiatives." Remarks to the International Association of Personnel Women. July, 1989.

Friedman, Dana. "Family Supportive Policies: The Corporate Decision-Making Process." The Conference Board Report No. 897, 1987.

———. "Childcare for Employees' Kids." *Harvard Business Review*, Vol. 64, No. 2. March-April, 1986.

Friedman, Dana and Hernandez, Carol. "The Family as a Bottom-Line Issue." *Metro Connection* (a publication of the University of New Orleans). Volume 5, Number 2, Fall, 1990.

Friedman, Howard. "Special Report: Child Care for Employees' Kids." *Harvard Business Review*. Volume 64, No. 2. March-April, 1986.

Fuchsberg, Gilbert. "Many Businesses Responding Too Slowly to Rapid Work Force Shifts, Study Says." *Wall Street Journal*, July 20, 1990.

Gabor, Andrea. "Deming's Quality Manifesto." *Best of Business Quarterly*, Winter, 1990–91.

Gardner, M. "Family-Friendly Corporations." *The Christian Science Monitor*, June 30, 1988.

General Mills American Family at Work Report: "Families Strengths and Strains." Minneapolis: General Mills, 1988.

Gerwig, K. "Tailor Work Policies to Workers." *Washington Report*, February 2, 1981.

"The Global 1000." *Business Week*, July 16, 1990.

Gordon, Susan. "America's Day Care Crises." *Entrepreneur Magazine*, March, 1989.

Grass, R. J. "How State Governments Are Looking Ahead." *The Futurist*, September-October, 1990.

Gray, Wendy B. "A Life Cycle Approach to Family Benefits and Policies." In *Perspectives*, No. 19. New York: The Conference Board, 1990.

Greer, Kate. "Dear President Bush." *Better Homes and Gardens*, August, 1989.

"Hang Up the Help-Wanted Sign." *Newsweek*, July 16, 1990.

Harris, Marlys, "What's Wrong With This Picture?" *Working Woman*, December, 1990.

Hart, W. L., Heskett, James L., and Sasser, W. Earl, Jr., "Soothing the Savage Customer." *Best of Business Quarterly*, Winter, 1990–91.

Herr, Martha. "Policy Directions for Child Care in 1989." *Future Choices Toward a National Youth Policy*. Premier Edition. Spring, 1989.

———. "Child Care: An Ad Hoc Update." *American Family*, Vol. 11, No. 11. Washington D.C.: Youth Policy Institute. December, 1988.

Hudson Institute. *Work Force 2000—Work and Workers for the 21st Century*. Indianapolis: Hudson Institute, 1987.

"Human Capital: The Decline of America's Work Force." *Business Week*, September 19, 1988.

Hymowitz, Carol "As AEtna Adds Flextime, Bosses Learn to Cope." *Wall Street Journal*, June 18, 1990.

Josefowitz, Natasha. *You're the Boss*. New York: Warner Books, 1985.

Kamerman, S., and Kahn, A. "What Europe Does for Single-Parent Families." *The Public Interest*. Number 97. Spring 1988.

Kanter, Donald L., and Mirvis, Philip H. *The Cynical Americans: Living and Working in an Age of Discontent and Disillusion*. San Francisco: Jossey-Bass, 1989.

Kanter, Rosabeth. *Men and Women of the Corporation*. New York: Basic Books, Inc., 1977.

————. *The Change Masters*. New York: Simon and Schuster, 1983.

Kanter, Rosabeth Moss. *When Giants Learn To Dance*. New York: Simon & Schuster, 1989.

Kaplan, Amy. "How Not to Survive in America—Be a Mom." *The Christian Science Monitor*, October 23, 1990.

Kennedy, Robert D. "Inroads that Go Beyond Affirmative Action: Manager's Journal." *Wall Street Journal*, September 10, 1990.

Kennedy, Shawn G. "Drawing Developers Into Day Care." *New York Times*, August 26, 1990.

"Kids and Companies: The Employees' Guide to Child Care Solutions." Carson, CA: Lakeshore Curriculum Materials Company, 1988.

Kiplinger, Austin and Kiplinger,Knight. *America in the Global 90s*. Washington D.C.: Kiplinger Books, 1989.

Konrad, Welecia. "Welcome to the Woman Friendly Company." *Business Week*, August 6, 1990.

Kovar, Grace, and Harris, Tamara. "Who Will Care for the Old?" *American Demographics*. May, 1988.

Krantz, Paul. "Day Care—Are We Shortchanging our Kids?" *Better Homes and Gardens*, June, 1988.

Lawson, Carol. "With Job Sharing, Time for the Family," *New York Times*, 1989.

————. "7 Employers Join to Provide Child Care at Home in a Crisis." *New York Times*, September 7, 1989.

Levering, Robert; Moskowitz, Milton; Katz, Michael. *The 100 Best Companies to Work for in America*. New York, NY: Addison-Wesley Publishing Co., 1984.

Levine, Karen. "Flextime—It Works!" *Parents Magazine*, September, 1990.

Lewis, Robert, "Firms Reshape Policies for Families." *Trenton Times*, November 19, 1990.

Mackoff, Dr. Barbara. *Leaving the Office Behind*. New York: Dell Publishing Company, 1984.

Magid, R. Y. *Child Care Initiatives for Working Parents: Why Employers Get Involved*. Washington D.C.:American Management Association, 1983.

Markowich, M. Michael, DPA. "United Hospitals Makes Flex Fly," *Personnel Journal*, December, 1989.

Martel, Leon. *Mastering Change*. New York: Simon and Schuster (Mentor Books), 1986.

Mastabich, Raymond. "Help for the Working Caregiver." *Consumer Notes*, Washington D.C.: American Council of Life Insurance and Health Insurance Association of America, 1988.

Maxwell, Jessica. "Family Tree: A Bellingham Nursing Home Doubles as a Day Care Center." *Washington Magazine*, March, 1990.

Meszaros, Peggy. "Family Realities in the 21st Century: Policy Options and Directions." In *Increasing Understanding of Public Problems and Policies—1989*. Oak Brook, Illinois: Farm Foundation, 1989.

Milkovich, George and Gomez, Luis. "Day Care & Selected Employee Work Behaviors." Academy of Management Journal, March, 1976.

Monkman, Carol-Smith. "Businesses Must Address Needs of Working Parents." *Seattle Post Intelligencer*, September 29, 1989.

Moskowitz, Milton and Townsend, Carol. "The 60 Best Companies for Working Mothers." *Working Mother*, October 1989.

Naisbitt, John, "Trend Toward Flexibility Reshapes the Workplace," *Trend Letter*. Vol. 9, No. 23. November 22, 1990.

————. "Higher Salaries, Other Incentives on Tap for Labor Shortage in 1989." *Trend Letter*. Vol. 8, No. 3. February 9, 1989.

————. "Spurring Productivity: A Huge Managerial Challenge for the 90's." *Trend Letter*. Vo. 9, No. 2. January 18, 1990.

————. "Trend Update." *Trend Letter*. May 12, 1988.

————. *Trend Letter*. Volume 9, Number 23, November 22, 1990.

Naisbitt, John and Aburdene, Patricia. *Megatrends 2000*. New York: William Morrow & Co. 1990.

————. *Reinventing the Corporation*. New York: Warner Books, Inc., 1985.

Nickels, Elizabeth, with Ashcroft, Laura. *The Coming Matriarchy*. New York: Berkley Books, 1982.

Nika, Susan. "The Child Care Predicament." *Rotarian Magazine*, December, 1989.

"N.J. Supermarket Chain Wins Praise," *The Trenton Times*, January 9, 1991.

"Non-Traditional Benefits for the Workforce of 2000," International Foundation of Employee Benefit Plans, Brookfield, Wisconsin, 1990.

Perham, John. "Eldercare: New Company Headache" *Dun's Business Month*, January, 1987.

Peters, Tom and Austin, Nancy, *A Passion for Excellence: The Leadership Difference*. New York: Warner Books Inc., 1985.

Pogrebin, L. C. *Family Politics—Love and Power on an Intimate Frontier*. New York: McGraw-Hill, 1983.

Popenoe, David. "New Hope For The Family?" *Family Affairs*, Spring/Summer, 1990. New York: Institute for American Values.

Pulliam, Elizabeth. "Juggling the Children." *The Seattle Times/Post-Intelligences*, May 11, 1986.

"Resource and Referral Services: The Child Care Solution and the Elder Care Connection." The Partnership Group, 1988.

Roberts, Sam. "Note to the U.N.: Talk to Jonas and Jonathan." *New York Times*, October 1, 1990.

Rodgers, Fran Susner, Rodgers, Charles. "Business and the Facts of Family Life." *Harvard Business Review*, November-December, 1989.

Roosevelt Center for American Policy Studies. *Balancing Work and Family*, (Briefing and Workbook). Washington D.C., 1989.

Rosow, J. "Quality of Working Life and Productivity—The Double Pay-Off." *Vital Speeches of the Day*, Vol. XXXXIII, No. 16. June 1, 1977.

Rubin, Karen. "Whose Job is Childcare?" *Ms.*, March, 1987.

Ryan, M. "Who Speaks for Children?" *Parade*, July 8, 1990.

Senate Bill Number 2035, State of New Jersey, Introduced February 18, 1988. *The Family Leave Act*.

Silverman, Elizabeth S. "The Child-Care Revolution Entering the Workplace." *New Jersey Business*, March 5, 1990.

Skrzycki, Cindy. "He's Washing Dishes and Baby Clothes." *The Washington Post Weekly Edition*, November 26–December 2, 1990.

Solomon, Jolie. "Firms Grapple with Language Barriers." *Wall Street Journal*, November 7, 1990.

Solomon, Robert C., Hanson, Kristine R. *It's Good Business*. New York: Athenaeum, 1985.

Stephens, R. "New Hurdles at Work." *American Association of Retired Persons Bulletin*. Vol. 30, No. 11. 1989.

"Studies in Marriage and the Family." Census Bureau. Washington D.C., August, 1989.

"Successful Ways to Manage 20something Staff." *Working Smart*. National Institute of Business Management, Inc., Vol. 17, No. 17, September 15, 1990.

Sullivan, Elizabeth Ryan. "Employers Will Have to Adapt." *The Trenton Times*, April 25, 1990.

Sweeney, J., Nussbaum, K. *Solutions for the New Work Force: Policies for a New Social Contract*. Washington D.C.: Seven Locks Press, 1989.

"The Family Business: Workplace Programs Offer Support to Parents," *Health Action Managers*, Vol. 4, No. 21. November 10, 1990.

Thomas, Edward G. "Flextime Doubles in a Decade." *Management World*, May, 1987.

"3M Corporation Addresses Needs of Working Parents." People & Programs, Family Information Services. November, 1989.

Toffler, Alvin. *Power Shift*. New York: Bantam Books, 1990.

Townsend, Bickley, and O'Neill, Kathleen. "Women Get Mad." *American Demographics*, August, 1990.

"Trading Places." *Newsweek*, July 16, 1990.

"Training in Business." *Human Resources Newsletter*, New Jersey State Chamber of Commerce, Trenton, N.J., November, 1990.

Trost, Cathy and Hymowitz, Carol, "Careers Start Giving in to Family Needs." *Wall Street Journal*, June 18, 1990.

U.S. Department of Labor. *Child Care: A Workforce Issue Report of the Secretary's Task Force*. Washington D.C.: U.S. Department of Labor. April, 1988.

U.S. House of Representatives Select Committee on Children, Youth and Families. Hearing Summary: *Double Duty: Caring for Children and the Elderly*. Washington D.C.: U.S. Government Printing Office. May 3, 1988.

Uchitelle, Louis, "Women's Push Into Work Force Seems to Have Reached Plateau." *The New York Times*, November 24, 1990.

United Way of America's Strategic Institute. *What Lies Ahead: Countdown to the 21st Century*. Alexandria, Virginia: United Way of America, 1989.

United Way of America. *The Future World of Work: Looking Toward the Year 2000*. Alexandria, Virginia: United Way of America, 1988.

Wallo, Terri J. "Corporate America Prepares for Eldercare." *Compass Readings*. Vol. 21, No. 9. September, 1990.

"Welcome To The Woman-Friendly Company." *Business Week*, August 6, 1990.

White, E. B. quoted in *Forbes*, August 20, 1982.

Whitehead, Barbara Dafoe. "The Family in an Unfriendly Culture." *Family Affairs*. New York: The Institute for American Values. Vol. 3, No. 1-2, Spring/Summer, 1990.

"Who's Minding the Children?" *Solutions for the New Workforce*. Service Employees International Union AFL-CIO, CLC, 1988.

Whyte, William H., Jr. *The Organization Man*. New York: Simon & Schuster, 1956.

Wingert, Pat and Kantrowitz, Barbara. "The Day Care Generation." *Newsweek Special Edition*, Winter/Spring, 1990.

"Women and Work." *Christian Science Monitor*, Friday, December 7, 1990.

"Wooing Workers in the 90's." *New York Times*, July 20, 1988.

"Work and Family Booklet." Time, Inc. Magazine Human Resources, 1988.

"Work and Family Issues in the 90s." Remarks before Hewitt Associates Flex Forum. Chicago, Illinois, May 18, 1990.

"Work and Family Life: Balancing Job and Professional Responsibilities." Bank Street College, New York, November, 1989.

Wynter, Leone and Solomon, Jolie. "A New Push to Break the Glass Ceiling." *Wall Street Journal*, November 15, 1989.

Yogman, M., Brazelton, T. (eds.). *In Support of Families*. Cambridge, Mass.: Harvard University Press, 1986.

Yote, Martin. *Keeping the Best*. Holbrook, Mass.: Bob Adams, Inc., 1991.

Youngblood, S. A. and Chambers-Cook, K. "Child Care Assistance Can Improve Employee Attitudes and Behaviors." *Personnel Administration*, February, 1984.

Zigler, Edward and Frank, Meryl (editors). *The Parental Leave Crisis: Toward a National Policy*. Hartford, CT: Yale University Press. 1988.

Zeitz, Baila, Ph.D., Dusky, Lorraine. *The Best Companies For Women*. New York: Pocket Books. 1988.

INDEX

A

Absenteeism
family needs and, 60–62
Aburdene, Patricia, 8, 179, 191
Accelerated Cost Recovery
System (ACRS), 168
Act for Better Child Care, 154
Adolph Coors Company,
25–26, 113
AEtna Life and Casualty
Company, 62, 91–93, 106, 177
After-school child care, 27
AIDS, 57, 80
Albright, Lisa, 127
Alcoholism, 4
American Affordable Housing
Institute, 63
American Association of
Retired Persons, 29, 142–143
American Can Co., 31
American Express Co., 35, 83,
113, 130, 188
American Family Report, 140
American Hospital
Association, 10
American Medical
Association, 156
American Telephone and
Telegraph Co.—*See AT&T*
American Values and Lifestyles
(annual survey), 8
America West Airlines, 27
Andrus, Cecil, 164
Apprentice training, 129–130
ARCO (Atlantic Richfield
Co.), 57
Arizona Bancwest
Corporation, 59
Aschbacker, Pamela R., 107
Atkins, Diane Keel, 61
Atlantic Richfield Co.—*See*
ARCO
AT&T (American Telephone
& Telegraph Co.)
child-care, 117
customer loyalty, 188
flexible schedules, 16
parental leave, 177
profitability, 105
women, 113
AT&T Credit Corp., 69
Austin, Nancy, 68
Autry, James, 193

Avon Products, 181

B

Baby boomers, 183–184
Barclay, Kathy, 135
Basic needs, 173–176
Bateson, Mary Catharine,
185–186
Baxter International, 182
Baxter Travenol Laboratories,
40
Beaver College, 182
Beck, Robert, 104
Bell of Pennsylvania, 133
Benjamin, Melvin, 117
Bennis, Warren, 67
Big M, Inc., 68
Black, Bim, 67
Black women, 51–53
Blankenhorn, David, 195
Blethen, Frank, 113
Body Shop, 56
Boeing Co., 69
Bravo, Ellen, 114
Brazelton, T. Berry, 178
Breast-feeding, 20–21
Broadcaster's Child
Development Center, 72
Bronfenbrenner, Urie, 156–157
Brown, John, 99, 100–101
Brown, Sydney T., 84–85
Bryan, Tom, 117
Budget deficit, U.S., 155
Burbank California Unified
School District, 72
Bureau of Labor Statistics
family composition and
structure, vii–viii
flexible work schedules
and child care, 33
growth in labor force, 2
Bureau of National Affairs, 65,
178, 182
Burke, Jim, 101
Burrus, Diane, 120, 190
Burud, Sandra, 107
Bush, George, 154, 157, 159
Bush Center in Child
Development and Social
Policy (Yale University), 174
Business, needs of, 9–10, 54–74
employee benefits in the
year 2000, 73–74
family friendliness, 63–66

image, 55–57
increasing worker
participation, 68–71
low absenteeism, 60–62
on-the-job training, 66–68
productivity, 59–60
profitability, 54–55
recruitment, 57–59
retention of employees,
62–63
small firms, 71–73
Business Week, 105, 181, 182
Butler, Barbara, 73

C

Cafeteria plans, 142, 175
California, 31, 60, 164, 174
California State University at
Long Beach, 34
Campbell Soup Company, 27,
141
Canada, 162, 174
Caplan, Barbara, 8
Career choices
dedication to family and,
18–19
women and future,
181–183
Carey, Michael, 100
Carver Corporation, 88–89
Castle, Michael, 164
Catalyst, Inc., 118, 142–143,
177, 181
Cederholm, Lynn, 88–89
Central Intelligence Agency
(CIA), 155
Chamber of Commerce, U.S.,
63
Chambers-Cook, K., 61–62
Changing the workplace,
112–153
corporate decision
making, 115
cultural attitudes, 119–120
developing mindset, 121,
124
myths, 143–147
particular needs, 124–125
personal influences,
112–115
pilot projects, 118–119
program options, 125–143
task force, 116–117
Chaparral Steel Co., 69, 70

Chauveau, Florence, 184
Child care
  absenteeism and, 61–62
  after-school, 27
  Carver Corporation, 88–89
  Department of Labor
    report, 105
  employee retention and, 62
  estimated annual cost, 50
  Europe, 159
  government agencies, 155
  IBM, 83–84
  local governments,
    165–167
  Merck & Company, 77–78
  Microsoft Corporation, 87
  National Council of
    Jewish Women study
    on, 65
  numbers of companies
    offering, 24–25
  options, 126–128
  parents' concerns about
    quality of, 25–26
  preschool, 23–27
  purchasing spaces for, 138
  St. Francis's Extended
    Health Care, 103
  and sickness, 28
  small firms, 71–72
  stress and, 59–60
  Stride-Rite Corporation,
    102
  subsidies for, 137–138
  survey, 149–150
  tax credits, 168
  3M Corporation, 98
  Time Warner, Inc., 78
  Union Bank, 63–64
  women in labor market
    and increased need for, 3
Child Care, Inc., 90, 133
Child Care Action Campaign,
  24
Child Care and Corporate
  Productivity, 33, 46
Child Care Systems, 133
Children's Castle child-care
  program (Japan), 162
Children's Defense Fund, 50
Childs, J. T., Jr., 83
Childs, Ted, 108
Chubb & Sons, Inc., 65
Church and Dwight
  Company, 63
Cigna Corporation, 27
Cincinnati (Ohio), 166
Civil rights movement, 6
Coffer, Lynnette Friedrich, 194
Cohen, Rick, 129
Colgate-Palmolive Company,
  56, 63, 90
Columbia Pictures, 72
Comerica Incorporated, 31
Community care centers, 138

Compressed work weeks, 33,
  140
Con Edison—See Consolidated
  Edison Co. of New York, Inc.
Conference Board, The, 118,
  119, 155, 176
  child-care, 24–25
  corporate decision
    making, 115–116
  flexible scheduling, 33–34,
    106, 120–121, 144
  women in labor force, 172
Conformity, 188–189
Congress, U.S., 154–155
Congressional Clearinghouse
  on the Future, 155
Connecticut, 163
Consolidated Edison Co. of
  New York, Inc., 90
Control Data Corporation, 57,
  137
  employee advisory
    resource, 39
Corning Glass Works, 116
Corporate decision making,
  115
Corporate Reference Guide
  (Families and Work
  Institute), 101
Cost benefits of family-friendly
  programs, 105–106
Council on Economic
  Priorities, 55–56
Counseling, 129
Counterculture of 1960s, 6
Crowe-Innes, Jenny, 81–82
Cultural change, 119–120
Cynical Americans, The: Living
  and Working in an Age of
  Discontent and Disillusion
  (Donald Kanter and Philip
  H. Mirvis), 196
Czerniak, Mike, 68

D

Dartmouth School of Business,
  180
Day camps, 129
Day care—See Child care
DCAP—See Dependent Care
  Assistance Program
Decker, Stephanie, 35
Defense, U.S. Dept. of, 155
Delaware, 164
Deming, W. Edwards, 187
Denmark, 159
Dependent-care
  Hewitt Associates, 94–95
Dependent Care Assistance
  Program (DCAP), 167
Dependent-care tax credits
  (list of sources), 171
Digital Equipment
  Corporation, 69
Direct services, 126–131
Discrimination, 11

Disney World, 27
Diversity, value of, 188–190
Dole, Elizabeth, 129
Dominion Bankshares, 61
Down-payment loans, 63
Drucker, Peter, 1
Duke Power Company, 83–84
Du Pont de Nemours & Co.,
  E. I., 76
  mission statement of, 11
  parental leave, 177
  profitability, 105
  women in labor force,
    181–182

E

Eastman Kodak Company, 15,
  76, 177
Economic Policy Institute, 23
Educational Testing Service, 31
Eldercare
  family needs and, 28–29
  future of, 104
  resource services for, 132
  St. Francis's Extended
    Health Care, 103
  state governments, 164
  Stride-Rite Corporation,
    102
  subsidies for, 137
  women in labor market
    and increased need for, 3
Emergency child care, 78,
  90–91, 127
Emlin, A. C., 60
Employee advisory resource
  (EAR), 39
Employee assistance
  programs (EAPs), 38–39
  3M Corporation, 97
Employee questionnaire,
  152–153
Employee recruitment, 57–59
Employee retention, 62–63
  SAS Institute, Inc., 65–66
  small firms, 72–73
Employee satisfaction, 173–174
Employee services network
  (ESN), 39
"Employers and Child Care:
  Benefitting Work and
  Family" (U.S. Department of
  Labor report), 105
Employment in Perspective:
  Women in the Labor Force
  (Bureau of Labor Statistics),
  61
Entrepreneur Magazine, 71
Equal Opportunities
  Commission, U.S., 46–47
Ernst and Young, 89–91,
  119–120
Esty, Katherine, 62
Europe
  family programs, 158–161

Extended Personal Leave Plan (IBM), 83
Exxon Corporation, 76, 133

F

Families and Work Institute (New York), 101, 177
Family
  balancing work and, 18–23
  basic needs, 23–40
    after-school child care, 27
    benefits to companies responsive to, 63–66
    eldercare, 28–29
    family leave with job security, 31–32
    flexible workplaces, 38
    flexible work schedules, 32–37
    health insurance, 30–31
    inappropriate corporate responses, 40–41
    living wage, 23
    overnight dependent care, 28
    preschool child care, 23–27
    sick child care, 28
    special problem help, 38–40
  changing composition and structure of, vii–viii
  decline of traditional, 3, 195
  industrialization and, 19–20
  new definition of success and, 7–9
Family and Medical Leave Act, 154
Family education programs, 133–136
Family Independence Program, The (Security Pacific Bank), 85
Family leave, 31–32
Family Leave Act (New Jersey), 163
Family support seminars
  AEtna Life and Casualty Company, 91–93
Federal Employees Part-Time Career Employment Act (1978), 35
Fel-Pro, 27, 129
Fernandez, John P., 33, 46, 59–61, 130, 136
Financial assistance, 136–139
Finland, 159
First Environments Child Care Center, 127
First Fidelity Savings and Loan, 63
Flexible benefit plans, 175

Arizona Bancwest Corporation, 59
  health insurance, 31
  Time Warner, Inc., 78–79
Flexible spending account, 138
"Flexible Staffing and Scheduling in U.S. Corporations" (Conference Board), 120–121
Flexible workplaces—See Flexplace
Flexible work policies, 139–143
  Catalyst study of, 118
Flexible work schedules—See Flextime
Flexplace, 144
  employer benefits from, 106–108
  family needs and, 38
  as option, 140
Flextime, 33
  Eastman Kodak, 15
  family needs and, 32–37
  future of, 176–178
  Merck & Company, 78
  Microsoft Corporation, 87–88
  myths about, 143–144
  as option, 140
  and women, 179
Focus groups, 118, 121
Ford Motor Company, 130
Foreign countries
  family benefits in, 13–14
  government family programs in, 158–162
  productivity and competition from, 2
Fortune (magazine), 8–9, 77
Fosler, Gail, 155
Foster, Linda, 94–95, 114
4/40 week, 34
France, 130
  child care, 159
  maternity benefits, 160
Friedes, Peter, 93–94, 96, 108
Friedman, Dana, 106
Fully paid benefits, 136–137
Furr's/Bishop's Cafeterias, 129
Future of family/work policies, 172–196
  business interests and, 194–196
  diversification, 188–190
  new values, 183–188
  partnerships, 192–193
  redefinition of leadership, 190–192
  women's needs implementation, 178–183

G

Gadbury, Sharon, 40
Galinsky, Ellen, 101
Gallup Poll, 193
Gannett Co., 182

Geisenheimer, Susan, 132
General Electric Co. (GE), 69, 130
General Mills, Inc., 56, 57, 69, 70, 140
General Motors Corp. (GM), 69
Germany, 130, 160
Gerstner, Louis, Jr., 113
Getzelman, John, 84–86
Gibbs, Alan, 114
Gilligan, Carol, 191
Goodyear Tire & Rubber Co., 69
Googins, Bradley, 5, 22
Government, role of, 154–171
  de facto policy, 156–158
  encouragement of voluntary approaches, 169–170
  in foreign countries, 158–162
  at local level, 165–167
  present reality, 154–156
  at state level, 162–164
  tax incentives, 167–168
Goya, Donna, 81
Green, Jim, 30

H

Haas, Robert, 80, 113
Harbor Hospital Center, 28
Harris Poll, 193
Hartford (Connecticut), 166
Harvey, George, 182
Health insurance
  family needs and, 30–31
  future of, 175
Healthy Expectations program, 30–31
Herchenroether, Sherry, 62, 92–93, 106
Hewitt, Ted, 93
Hewitt Associates, 114, 188
  babysitters, 177
  financial benefits, 108–109
  health care, 31
  as innovator, 93–96
  nursing mothers' rooms, 176
Hewlett-Packard Co., 35, 106
Hiatt, Arnold, 102–103
Hoffmann-LaRoche Inc., 61
Home Box Office, Inc., 90, 118
Home day-care, 27
Honeywell, Inc., 133, 134–135
Hottle, Logan, 56
Housework
  working women and, 45–46
Housing and Urban Development, U.S. Department of (HUD), 155
Housing assistance, 63
Houston Committee on Private Sector Initiatives, 27

Hudson Institute, 9, 10, 58

I

Ibis Consulting, 62
IBM—*See International Business Machines Corporation*
Iceland, 159
Idaho, 164
Image, corporate, 55–57
Immigrants in labor force, 3
Indiana, 164
Infant mortality, 195
Influences, personal, 112–115
Information services, 131–136
In Search of Excellence (Peters and Waterman), 173
Institute for American Values, 66, 194, 195
Institutional supports, 147
Intergenerational day care
   St. Francis's Extended Health Care, 103
   Stride-Rite Corporation, 102
Intermedic, Inc., 62
Internal Revenue Code, 137
Internal Revenue Service, 168, 169
International Business Machines Corporation (IBM), 69, 105, 108
   eldercare and, 29
   as innovator, 82–84
   manager guidelines, 190–191
   medical leave, 141
   referral services, 133
   spouse employment assistance, 40
   training programs on work/family issues, 16
International Foundation of Employee Benefit Plans, 73
International transfers, 39
Israel, 161–162

J

Jamison, Linda, 130
Japan
   child benefits, 162
   labor shortage in, 57–58
Job development programs, 136
Job-sharing, 33–35
   Chubb & Sons, Inc., 65
   as option, 140
Johnson, Arlene, 113, 118, 119, 176
Johnson & Johnson
   corporate credo, 186
   education, 16
   as innovator, 98–101
   "Live for Life" program, 56
   management training, 191
   planning policies, 116, 117
   profitability, 104

Johnson & Son, Inc., S. C., 56
   Johnson Wax Development Corp., 181
Johnsonville Foods, 69, 70

K

Kamerman and Kahn, 160
Kansas, 164
Kanter, Donald, 196
Kanter, Rosabeth Moss, 110, 145
Kellogg Co., 56
Kelly Services, Inc., 181
Kennedy, Robert D., 11
Kibbutz, 161–162
Kinder, Lydenberg, Domini & Co., 56
KIRO, Inc., 57
Koren, P. E., 60
Kuhlman, Leslie, 136

L

Labor, U.S. Department of, 105, 129, 179
Labor unions, 30
"L.A. Law," 51
Larsen, Ralph, 101
"Latchkey" children, 27
Law firms
   female employees, 47–48
Leadership, redefinition of, 190–192
Leaves of absence, 33
Leaving the Office Behind (Barbara Mackoff), 194
Leibold, Karen, 58
Leo Burnett (firm), 133
Levine, James A., 177
Levi Strauss Associates, Inc., 35, 57, 80–82, 113
   telecommuting, 38
Levy, Frank, 179
Life Cycles (Savings and Loan Data Corporation), 136
Life-cycle stages and company programs (chart), 122–123
Life skill education, 133–136
Lindner, Don, 59
"Live for Live" program, 56
Lobbying, 169
Loblaws, 56
Local government, 165–167
Lockheed Corporation, 72
Los Angeles, 167
Loyalty, employee, 186

M

Mackoff, Barbara, 194
Magid, Renee, 182
Management
   women in, 47, 49
Manager, role of, 130–131
Marieskind, Helen, 175
Marriott Corporation, 30–31
Maternity benefits

Carver Corporation, 89
   foreign countries, 160–162
   Stride-Rite Corporation, 102
McCord, Robert, 155
McCroskey, Jacquelyn, 107
McGovern, R. Gordon, 21
McNulty, Pat, 69
Media
   women's role in workplace and, 50–51
Medical leave, 140–141, 146
Megatrends 2000 (John Naisbitt and Patricia Aburdene), 8, 191
Merck & Co., Inc., 66, 106
   family education programs, 134
   as innovator, 76–78
   profitability, 105
Meredith Corporation, 193
Meschi, Rosemarie, 90–91, 119–120
Metal Forming and Coining, 68
METRO (Seattle), 114
Michigan, 164
Microsoft Corporation, 104, 186–187
   as innovator, 86–88
   part-time work, 36
Milwaukee, 167
Minimum wage, 23
Minorities, 189–190
   in labor force, 3
   Merck & Company program on attitudes toward, 77
   obsolete corporate responses to, 11
   women, 51–53
Mirvis, Philip H., 196
Mission statements, 11
"Mommy track," 48–49, 184–185
Mothers' Rooms, 95
Motorola, Inc., 130
Myths about alternative work schedules, 143–144

N

Naisbitt, John, 8, 179, 191
National Broadcasting Co. (NBC)—*See NBC*
National Convenience Stores, 121
National Council of Jewish Women, 65
National Council on Aging, 28
National Employer-Supported Child Care Project, 108, 132
National Report on Work and Family (Bureau of National Affairs), 178
National Westminster Bank USA, 90

Natural Institute of Environmental Health Science, 127
NBC (National Broadcasting Co.), 72
Near-site child-care, 126–127
Neuville Industries, 61
New Jersey, 163, 174
New Realities, The (Peter Drucker), 1–2
Newsweek (magazine), 43
New values, 183–188
New Ways To Work, 33
New York City, 165
New York State, 174
New York Times, The, 83, 179
Night shifts
    overnight dependent care and, 28
9 to 5, 114
Norris, William, 57
Norway, 158–159, 160
NUMMI (Toyota-GM joint venture), 69–70
Nursing mothers' rooms, 176
Nyloncraft, Inc., 62

O

Obsolete responses to work/family revolution, 10–13
Olsten Corporation, 139
On-site child-care, 88–89, 126–127
On-the-job training, 66–68
Oregon, 164
Organization Man, The (William H. Whyte), 5–6, 14
Ostling, Paul, 91
Overnight dependent care, 28, 127
Overnight Dependent Care (Hewitt Associates), 94–95

P

Pacific Bell, 106
Parental leave
    foreign countries, 160
Parental/medical leave, 140–141, 146
Parenting programs, 134–136
Parent Network, The (Honeywell), 134–135
Paris, Claudine, 68
Partnering, 192–193
Part-time plus work, 36
Part-time work, 33, 35–36, 140
Pascal, Glen, 37
Passion for Excellence, A (Tom Peters and Nancy Austin), 68
Paternity leave, 31
Pay equity, 46–47
Payless Cashways, Inc., 181
Penney Co. Inc., J. C., 57
Pepsi-Cola Co., 84
Personal influences, 112–115

Personal leave, 83
Personnel (magazine), 34
Peters, Tom, 68
Phased retirement, 142–143
Phillips, J. Douglas, 55, 66, 78
Physio Control Corporation, 57
Pitney Bowes Inc., 182
Pleck, Joseph, 178
Political action committees, 156
Portland (Oregon), 107–108, 166
Prenatal care, 30–31
Preschool child care, 23–27
Presser, Harriett, 28
Preventative education, 97–98
Procter & Gamble Co., 31, 69, 104–105
Productivity
    false equation of work hours and, 12
    family/work issues and, 59–60
    foreign competition and, 2
    increased worker participation and, 68–71
Profitability
    quality of life and, 54–55
    work/family benefits and, 104–105
Protestant work ethic, 119
Prumatico, John, 86–88
Purdue University, 2

Q

Questionnaire, employee, 152–153

R

Real Estate Board of New York, 165
Recruiting costs, 108–109
Referral services, 131–133
    eldercare, 29
Reinventing the Corporation, 179
Relocation assistance, 39, 138–139
Resource and referral systems, 131–133
Resources for Parents at Work (Philadelphia), 134
Retirement, phased, 142–143
Retraining costs, 96, 108–109
Revolution in work and family, 1–16
    companies' interests, 9–10
    definition of success, 7–9
    foreign countries' solutions, 13–14
    interdependence, 14–16
    new realities, 1–4
    new values, 4–7
    obsolete company responses, 10–13
Rhode Island, 174

Right action, 193–194
Robert Half International, 37
Rodgers, Charles, 12
Rodgers, Fran S., 12
Roper Poll, 8, 56
Rose, Karol, 78, 118, 119
Rosow, Jerome, 59
Rutgers University, 63

S

St. Francis's Extended Health Care, 103, 187
St. Luke's Rush Presbyterian Medical Center, 128
St. Paul (Minnesota), 167
San Francisco, 165, 166
SAS Institute, 65–66
Savings and Loan Data Corporation, 135–136
Scandinavia, 159
School-age after-school programs, 128
School districts, 175
Schroeder, Pat, 155
Schwartz, David C., 63
Scordato, Christine, 143
Seal, Stephen, 133–134
Seattle, 165–166
Seattle Times, 16, 88, 113
    child care, 117, 138
Security Pacific Bank, 133, 186
    as innovator, 84–86
    part-time work, 36
Self-sufficiency
    living wage and legacy of, 23
Senior Services Act, 164
Service Employees International Union, 112
Shanker, Steven, 63–64
Shenandoah Life Insurance Co., 69
Shift work
    overnight dependent care and, 28
Sick child care, 28
Sick dependent care, 94–95, 127
Single mothers, 43–44
Single parents, 26
Skadden, Arps, Slate, Meagher and Flom, 90, 106
Skinnic, Frank, 104
Small Business Administration, U.S., 43, 71
Small businesses
    family issues and, 71–73
    women-owned, 49–50
Social responsibility
    corporate image and, 55–57
    Security Pacific Bank, 84–86
Soft Sheen, 27
Solutions for the New Workforce, 112

Spain, 160
Special problem help, 38–40
Spouse re-employment assistance, 39–40
Stanley, David, 181
State governments, 162–164
State of Small Business, The, 71
Stayer, Ralph, 69
Steelcase, Inc., 31, 35, 116
Steps to obtaining solution to work/family needs (outline), 124–125
Stinson, Burke, 16
Stress
  from outside the job, 10
  productivity and, 59–60
  work-family balance and, 22
Stride-Rite Children's Centers, 116
Stride-Rite Corporation, 58, 101–103
Strohmer, Arthur, 14, 134
Styles, Jill, 140
Subsidies, 137
Success
  new definition of, 7–9, 191
Summer day camps, 129
Supermarkets General Holdings Corp., 56
Supervisors
  sensitivity of, 130, 131
Surveys
  childcare, 149–150
  development of, 117–118
Sweden, 130, 159

T

Tandem Computers Inc., 67–68
Task forces, 116–117
Tate, Dianna, 105
Tax credits
  child care, 168
  dependent-care, 171
Tax-exempt care incentives, 137–138
Telecommuting, 38
  California, 164
  Levi Strauss, 80
Teleflex, 67
Television
  lack of positive role models for women on, 50–51
3M Corporation, 27, 97–98, 132
  flextime, 140
Time (magazine), 35, 104
Time, Inc.—See Time Warner, Inc.
Time Warner, Inc., 35, 78–80, 90, 118–119, 132
Torgersen, Trand, 158
Tot Memos (newsletter), 136
Towers Perrin, 9
Toyota Motor Sales, U.S.A., Inc., 69
Trainer, Steven, 166

Training programs, 136
Treybig, James G., 67–68
Trumka, Richard, 30
Turnover, 96, 106

U

Union Bank (Monterey Park, California), 63–64
Unisys Corporation, 132
United Hospitals, 142
United Nations Conference on Children, 20
Universal Studios, 72
U.S. government, 31
U.S. Sprint, 58
U.S. West Communications, 35, 47, 113, 182
USA Today, 61

V

Value-added profit and loss statements, 55
Values, new, 4–7
Vaughn, Judy, 100
VEBA—See Voluntary Employee's Beneficiary Association
Vermont, 163
Virginia Slims Opinion Poll, 45–46, 47
Voluntary Employee's Beneficiary Association (VEBA), 167
Volunteerism, 157–158
Voucher programs for child care, 72
V-time, 33

W

Wage, living, 23
Wake Medical Center Kidwinks, 127
Wall Street Journal, 44
Wang Laboratories, 27, 116
Warm-lines, 128–129
Washington, D.C., 167
Washington Magazine, 103
Washington Post, 113
Washington state, 31, 163
Wasserman, Janis, 73
Weekend day camps, 129
Welfare, 160
Wellness activities, 129
Weyerhaeuser Company, 129
When Giants Learn to Dance... (Rosabeth Moss Kanter), 110, 145
White, E(lwyn) B(rooks), 188
Whyte, William H., 5, 14
Williams, Cecilia, 130
Wiser Ways program, 39
Wohl, Faith, 182–183
Women
  alternate management by, 191–192

balance and, 184
child care and, 26
as executives, disproportionate burden of, 44
future outlook, 178–183
housework and, 45–46
increased representation in labor force, 3, 42–44
influencing of corporate policy by, 112–113
at Levi Strauss, 81
media and, 50–51
Merck & Company program on attitudes toward, 77
and minorities, 51–53
money issues and, 46–50
obsolete corporate responses to, 11
sexism in business world and, 177–178, 180–181
split between work and family and, 20
at Time Warner, 78
Wood, Hal, 71
Workaholism, 183
Work and Family Initiative (Johnson & Johnson), 99
Work and Family Newsletter, The, 79–80
Worker participation
  productivity and increased, 68–71
Work/family benefits
  future trends of, 73–74
  statistics on, 64
Work/Family Directions, 12, 120, 133, 190
Work/family programs
  advantages of companies with, 109–110
  costs of, 12
  firms without, 110–111
Workforce 2000: Work and Workers for the 21st Century (report), 9–10
Working and Caring (T. Berry Brazleton), 178
Work/Life Program (IBM), 83
Workplace Flexibility Program (U.S. Sprint), 58
Worksheets, 148
Work-team concept, 69–70
Wright Runstad Development Company, 166
Wyatt Co., 18–19

X

Xerox Corporation, 189

Y

Yale University, 174
Yankelovich Clancy Schulman, 8, 142–143
Youngblood, S. A., 61–62